Schomburg Studies on the Black Experience

Schomburg Studies on the Black Experience

Howard Dodson, *Managing Editor*
Colin Palmer, *Series Editor*

Ideology, Identity, and Assumptions
Cultural Life
Origins
The Black Condition
Theory, Methodology, and Pedagogy
Struggle for Social Justice

SSBE   Schomburg Studies on the Black Experience

The Black Condition

Edited by Howard Dodson *and* Colin Palmer

 The New York Public Library

 SCHOMBURG CENTER FOR RESEARCH IN BLACK CULTURE

 Michigan State University Press • *East Lansing*

♾ The paper used in this publication meets the minimum requirements of ANSI/NISO Z39.48-1992 (R 1997) (Permanence of Paper).

 Michigan State University Press
East Lansing, Michigan 48823-5245

Printed and bound in the United States of America.

15   14   13   12   11   10   09   1   2   3   4   5   6   7   8   9   10

LIBRARY OF CONGRESS CATALOGING-IN-PUBLICATION DATA
The Black condition / edited by Howard Dodson and Colin Palmer.
p. cm. — (Schomburg studies on the Black experience)
Includes bibliographical references.
ISBN 978-0-87013-838-6 (pbk. : alk. paper)
1. African Americans—Social conditions. 2. African Americans—Economic conditions. 3. African Americans—Politics and government. 4. United States—Armed Forces—African Americans—History. 5. African Americans—Education—History. 6. African Americans—Religion—History. I. Dodson, Howard. II. Palmer, Colin A., 1942–
E184.7.B523 2008
305.896'073—dc22
2008017052

Cover and book design by Sharp Des!gns, Inc., Lansing, MI

ℊ green press INITIATIVE   Michigan State University Press is a member of the Green Press Initiative and is committed to developing and encouraging ecologically responsible publishing practices. For more information about the Green Press Initiative and the use of recycled paper in book publishing, please visit *www.greenpressinitiative.org*.

Visit Michigan State University Press on the World Wide Web at *www.msupress.msu.edu*

Contents

Series Introduction

Howard Dodson

The Schomburg Center for Research in Black Culture, the ProQuest Company, and Michigan State University Press are pleased to present this unique research, study, and teaching resource. In the more than thirty-five years since the field of black studies established its presence in American higher education, the volume of research, writing, and publications on the global black experience has increased exponentially. Scholars in African American and African Diasporan studies have contributed in significant ways to the development of this new knowledge. So have scholars in mainstream disciplines in the United States and Europe, as well as scholars and intellectuals in Africa and throughout the Americas. When added to the extraordinary volume of research resources on the black experience that existed before the coming of Black Studies, the challenge of selecting appropriate materials for research, for study, and for teaching has become extremely difficult. Schomburg Studies on the Black Experience is a resource designed to assist users in making such choices.

This project had its origins some fifteen years ago. In the course of a conversation with a publisher about what kinds of reference works would be of greatest use to students and scholars in the developing field of African American Studies, I proposed that we jointly publish a judiciously curated collection of 25 to 30 volumes on major themes in African American Studies. At the time, I envisioned a process by which leading authorities on major themes in the field would write critical reviews of the scholarship, as well as select articles and book chapters that were essential to grounding oneself on the subject matter. I also envisioned the author/editor of each thematic volume projecting an agenda for future research on the topic.

The late Dr. Ruth Simms Hamilton and her African Diasporan Studies Program at Michigan State University collaborated with the Schomburg Center in identifying themes, selecting contributing editors, and commissioning volumes. Well into this ambitious project, the publisher became overextended and was obliged to cancel it. When the staff at ProQuest came to the Schomburg Center looking for an intellectual framework in which to develop an on-line resource on African American Studies, I proposed to revisit the project conceived more than a decade earlier. The resulting website is an on-line realization of my initial vision, which has now come full circle and is finally being published in book form.

Both the electronic and the printed editions of Schomburg Studies on the Black Experience contain a critical review essay for each theme, recommendations for essential readings, and research questions for the future. Extensive bibliographies, lists of primary research materials, timelines, and other resources are also included. Included in the online edition are many full-text recommended readings, as well as a multimedia library.

An ideal resource for faculty curriculum preparation and research, the online version of the Schomburg Studies on the Black Experience offers a dynamic online teaching and learning environment. Easily searchable across all of the diverse content, the electronic version allows users to select and store their search results, full-text key resources, bibliographic records, and multimedia records in their personal MyArchive section of the database, for retrieval at any time. Users may also add their annotations and create a reading list in their MyArchive space. Over 2,000 images and 200 video clips add a rich dimension to each topic. More information about the database may be found at *http://ssbe.chadwyck.com.*

Schomburg Studies on the Black Experience offers users a way to understand the evolution of scholarship on the selected themes and to access the essential literature that supports it. Schomburg Studies affirms both the quantity and the quality of the intellectual underpinnings of Black Studies.

Substantive academic programs are measured by the quality of intellectual/scholarly content that undergirds them. Of course, administrative structures are necessary and trained faculty are essential. But without a solid, well-researched, authenticated body of knowledge about their subject matter, academic programs are doomed to fail.

....

The field of African American or Black Studies emerged out of the political and cultural renaissance among African Americans that exploded on the American national scene in the wake of the assassination of Dr. Martin Luther King, Jr., in April 1968. Stokely Carmichael and Willie Ricks of the Student Nonviolent Coordinating Committee had announced the emergence of this new black consciousness movement in 1966 when they had asserted the need for Black Power at the Meredith March Against Fear in Mississippi. King's death transformed their plea into a demand. Eventually, every sector of American society was faced with the challenge of accommodating an assertive, newly conscious, critically thinking African American presence in all spheres of human endeavor. The urban rebellions that started in the mid 1960s and intensified after King's death were the catalyst for the emergence of Black Studies in the American academy.

The political context out of which Black Studies came into existence led many of its critics to question the intellectual viability of the field. What the critics implied by raising this question was that there was not sufficient content—intellectual/scholarly resources—to support sustained study of the history and cultural legacy of people of African descent. What they obviously did not know was that the Schomburg Center for Research in Black Culture and the Moorland/Spingarn Research Center were repositories of thousands of books and millions of pages of documents on the black experience worldwide. Central to the development of the Schomburg and Moorland/Spingarn collections was a nascent body of scholarship by African American and African descended scholars. That material, dating back to the nineteenth century, provides the foundations of the black intellectual tradition. Most of the work by these intellectuals took place outside of the academy.

One of the pioneering organized efforts to promote scholarship on the black experience among African Americans was the American Negro Academy (ANA), founded in 1897 by Episcopalian minister and intellectual Rev. Alexander Crummell. The ANA was "an organization of Colored authors, scholars and artists" that included among its objectives: "to promote the publication of literary and scholarly works"; "to aid, by publications, vindication of the race from vicious assaults in all the lines of learning and truth"; and "to publish, if possible, at least once a year an 'Annual' of original articles upon various Literary, Historical and Philosophical topics, of a racial nature, by selected members, and by these and diverse other means, to raise the standard of intellectual endeavor among American Negroes."[1] The Academy eventually counted among its members eminent African American intellectual luminaries such as Carter G. Woodson, W. E. B. Du Bois, and Arturo Alfonso Schomburg, all of whom would become major catalysts in the development of a black (American) intellectual tradition.

Schomburg, the renowned bibliophile and self-taught historian, had teamed up with New York–based journalist and sponsor of his membership in the Academy John E. Bruce, to found the Negro Society for Historical Research in 1911. The Society became a global network of black nationalists, largely lay historians, and counted among its membership Edward Wilmot Blyden of Sierra Leone, J. E. Casely Hayford of the Gold Coast (Ghana), General Evaristo Estenoz of Cuba, and journalist Pedro C. Timothee of San Juan, Puerto Rico.[2] With Bruce as president and Schomburg as secretary, the Society collected and loaned books, sponsored lectures, and published occasional papers on black-related themes. Schomburg's larger contribution to promoting scholarship on the global black experience, however, was as a bibliophile. His personal collection of more than 10,000 items became the foundation on which today's Schomburg Center rests. Over the years, the Schomburg Center has become the most comprehensive public research library in the world devoted exclusively to documenting and interpreting the black experience worldwide.

Both Du Bois and Woodson were Harvard University trained historians. Together, they pioneered the development of twentieth-century scholarship on the black experience. Following his graduation from Harvard in 1895 with a PhD, Du Bois organized and developed a major program of research on the black condition at Atlanta University. His Atlanta University Conferences, which started in 1895 and continued through 1910, summarized research and public policy regarding the black condition, the proceedings of which were published. In addition, over the course of his 95 years, he founded and edited the NAACP's *Crisis*, founded and edited Atlanta University's scholarly journal *Phylon*, and published some of the classic works in African American and African Diasporan scholarship.

Woodson earned his PhD from Harvard in 1912. Three years later he organized the Association for the Study of Negro Life and History, and a year later (1916) he began to publish the *Journal of Negro History*, the first significant scholarly journal devoted to the study of black life. Woodson published the quarterly journal until his death in 1950 without ever missing an issue. *The Journal of Negro History* provided scholars (black and white) a vehicle through which to publish research findings on the black experience. Woodson's Associated Publishers offered scholars a vehicle through which to publish book-length monographs. As founder of Negro History Week (now Black History Month), Woodson promoted the study of the black experience in schools, churches and other public settings and inspired new generations to pursue scholarly careers devoted to research and study of the black experience. His pioneering contributions earned him the title of "father of black history."

By the 1960s, the tradition of black intellectuals—lay and academic— working to rescue and reconstruct the true history and cultural legacy of people of African descent had been well established. Except in a few histori- cally black colleges and universities, however, teaching based on this knowl- edge had not been institutionalized. Even in the historically black colleges and universities, the course offerings were random—more a reflection of individual teachers' interests than part of a formal African American Studies curriculum. The Black Studies Movement, a by-product of the Black Power

Movement of the late 1960s, brought the black intellectual tradition into the academy.

Black students were recruited to enroll in mainstream universities in the wake of King's assassination and the attendant urban uprisings. What students found on these campuses was not very inviting—no black faculty members, no black administrators, few if any courses on the black experience, and research by mainstream scholars that affirmed and reinforced negative characterizations of people of African descent. Conspicuously absent was any acknowledgement of the existence of a black intellectual tradition.

Shortly after King's assassination, Columbia University in conjunction with WCBS-TV launched a project to produce 108 half-hour programs on African American history. Billed as an eighteen-week college-level course, *Black Heritage: A History of Afro-Americans* was the largest single undertaking by a commercial television station to present the history of African Americans to a broad, general public. Vincent Harding, chairman of the History and Sociology Departments at Spelman College in Atlanta, Georgia, served as chair of the project's advisory board, and John Henrik Clarke as the project consultant. These two scholars—Harding, a Columbia PhD in history who was teaching at an historically black college, and Clarke, a widely respected lay historian—assembled a faculty of some thirty scholars, artists, and intellectuals to deliver the content of this televised course. Lecturers included leading scholars from historically black colleges, lay historians, activists/intellectuals from the civil rights movement, artists and art critics within and outside of the mainstream academy, and a few black and white scholars from mainstream institutions who specialized in black history. Significantly, the quality of the lectures demonstrated to the viewing public as well as to the academy that there was, indeed, sufficient intellectual content to offer substantive courses, programs, and departments in African American Studies.

On college and university campuses across the country, black students demanded change in their respective academic environments—changes in the ratio of black students to white students; changes in the number of black faculty and administrators employed on the campuses; changes in the college and university curriculums to more adequately reflect the presence and roles of people of African descent in world affairs; and, yes, the establishment of

Black Studies programs and departments to better organize and coordinate research and teaching on the black experience.

College and university administrators responded in uneven ways. San Francisco State College in California yielded to organized student pressures, demonstrations, and a strike by establishing a Black Studies program in 1968. Yale University, through black student prodding and leadership, organized a national symposium on Black Studies, Black Studies in the University, in 1968. Riding on the momentum of the symposium, a student-faculty committee put together a proposal to establish an Afro-American Studies Program at Yale. On December 12, 1968, the Yale College faculty approved the first degree-granting Afro-American Studies program at a major university in the United States. In time, more than three hundred colleges and universities established Black Studies programs or departments. The major challenge facing most of them was not the intellectual foundations on which such programs and departments would rest, but who would teach courses in African American Studies. Whereas San Francisco State students had demanded all black faculty members, Yale, from the inception of the Black Studies program idea, had included white scholars who specialized in African American–related themes in their faculty ranks. In the furious competition for qualified faculty members that ensued, new opportunities opened on mainstream university campuses for African American, Caribbean, and African scholars.

Recruiters for Black Studies programs at mainstream universities first turned to historically black colleges. Hundreds of black college faculty members were enticed to take positions in Black Studies programs and departments. Advanced African American graduate students were also targeted. African and Caribbean scholars who specialized in African, African American, or Caribbean subjects were also recruited as universities and Black Studies program directors tried to strengthen the intellectual credibility of their faculties.

At the same time, colleges and universities collaborated with foundations to offer graduate study opportunities for individuals interested in African American and African Diasporan themes. Given the fact that there were no graduate study programs in African American Studies, students enrolled in traditional disciplines with major or minor emphasis in African American and

African Diasporan related themes. The Ford Foundation and the Andrew W. Mellon Foundation were among those most active in promoting graduate study in the field.

Black student activism led black scholars and intellectuals to launch their own organizing efforts. Sometimes, groups of black scholars within mainstream professional and academic organizations formed themselves into black caucuses within the organization to increase black membership and promote advancement opportunities in the discipline. They also used these formations to create opportunities for members to present papers on African American themes. The Caucus of Black Economists (1969) and the Caucus of Black Sociologists (1969) were among those that chose to work within their respective mainstream professional organizations. Others chose to form their own independent professional organizations. The National Association of Black Psychologists (1968), the National Conference of Black Political Scientists (1969), and the African Heritage Studies Association (1967) are among the associations of scholars that chose to take the independent route.

Research centers and institutes were also established to organize and coordinate the research activities of scholars and intellectuals related to the field. Many of those who participated in the CBS Black Heritage Series became affiliated with the Institute of the Black World, founded by Vincent Harding in 1969 as the research arm of the Martin Luther King, Jr. Center in Atlanta, Georgia. The Institute and Harding broke with the King Center a year later and established an independent think tank of black intellectuals that included on its agenda promoting the development of black studies and scholarship on the black experience.

The Black Economic Research Center was also founded in 1969. Black economist Robert Brown spearheaded the founding of the Center as well as the Center's scholarly journal, *The Review of Black Political Economy*. The Center also sponsored and supported research on the black economic condition, including a major study and initiative to prevent the loss of black-owned land in the American South. *The Review of Black Political Economy*, a quarterly, provided a forum in which black economists and others could carry on sustained, critical dialogues on themes affecting the economic well-being of blacks. The Black World Foundation, a non-profit organization, was founded in the San Francisco Bay area in 1969 by Nathan Hare and Robert Chrisman to "provide analysis, research and symposium on all the basic issues that concern Black America." The Foundation published a monthly journal, *The Black Scholar*, which became one of the major organs for black intellectuals seeking to present research and analysis on themes affecting black people worldwide. A year later, Molefi Asante (aka Arthur L. Smith) founded the *Journal of Black Studies*, sponsored by the UCLA Center for the Study of Afro-American History and Culture (1970). Observing that "sustained intellectual development in this area [Afro-American Studies] . . . cannot be based upon awakening rhetoric," Smith/Asante contended that the purpose of the journal was to "nurture the expanding community of scholars whose interests are in adding to the factual, analytical and evaluative bases upon which Black Studies must be established." Johnson Publication's *Negro Digest/Black World*, under the editorship of Hoyt Fuller, served a similar function, as did the longstanding movement journal *Freedomways*, based in New York. At the same time, most of the major scholarly journals of mainstream professional disciplinary associations made space for more frequent articles and occasional special issues on black-related themes.

Publishers, acknowledging the emergence of this new field of study in the academy, rushed to supply content to support these new academic programs. Publishing houses "discovered" places like the Schomburg Center and the Moorland-Spingarn Research Center, where they could go to package major reprint series in the field. Significant works by black scholars that had received little or no attention by the academy when they were originally published were reprinted along with historic texts that had long since been out of print. *The Dictionary Catalogs* of the Schomburg Center and the Moorland-Spingarn Collections were published and distributed to college and university librarians across the country to serve as guides for building research collections in the field. Microfilm and fiche publishers also created reprint collections. African American and African intellectuals established their own publishing houses to give voice to authors to whom mainstream publishers had turned a deaf ear. In addition to Johnson Publications, Haki Madhubuti (Don L. Lee) and Dudley Randall, among others, established their own presses to publish and disseminate works by black writers.

In the three decades since those formative years, Black Studies programs and departments have proliferated throughout the country. Most are based in part on the Yale University model in which faculty members hold joint appointments in a traditional disciplinary department and the African American Studies program. But there are also departments that award degrees in African American Studies, whose faculty members are only accountable to their department. Finally, in recent years, masters- and doctoral-degree programs in African American Studies have begun to make their presence felt in American universities.

Graduate study in the field was nurtured throughout the 1970s and 1980s through graduate fellowships in African American and African Diasporan Studies funded by the Ford, Mellon, and other foundations. While this support tapered off in the 1990s, the overall decline in humanities PhDs has sparked new interest in the foundation community in supporting graduate level education and faculty development efforts. The National Endowment for the Humanities, through its summer seminars and fellowships programs, has also been supporting the development of scholars and scholarship in the field. Finally, each of the traditional academic disciplines, especially in the humanities and social sciences, has been obliged to explore more fully than ever before, the African American (as well as the Hispanic, Asian, and Native American) experience in their research, publications, and pedagogy.

As a consequence, the last three decades have witnessed the publication of more research and scholarship on the global black experience than all the previous decades/centuries combined. The existence of such an expansive intellectual basis for the development of black studies is what makes a project like Schomburg Studies on the Black Experience necessary. We thank Colin Palmer, managing editor, and all of the contributing editors for making Schomburg Studies possible. And we thank the thousands of scholars and intellectuals who have taken the African American and African Diasporan experience seriously and have contributed to the development of the intellectual foundations of the field. Thanks to their work, the intellectual validity of Black Studies is no longer a question.

. . . .

NOTES

1. William M. Banks, *Black Intellectuals: Race and Responsibility in American Life* (New York: Norton, 1996), 58.
2. Elinor Des Verney Sinnette, *Arthur Alfonso Schomburg, Black Bibliophile and Collector: A Biography* (New York: New York Public Library, Distributed by Wayne State University Press 1989), 42–43.

Economic Inequality and the African Diaspora

William A. Darity Jr.

Abstract

This essay opens by examining a fundamental divide in perspectives. The division arises between scholars seeking to explain why peoples who possess visible markers signaling African descent generally experience lower earnings, income, and wealth regardless of their location in the Diaspora. One side, the cultural determinists, contends that the observed disparities are due primarily to group-based collective dysfunctionality on the part of blacks; the other side, the stratification economists, argues that the observed disparities are due primarily to the interaction of racism and structural obstacles. The author concludes that the stratification economists have the better of the argument.

Subsequently the essay examines the literature on ethnic/racial diversity or ethnic/racial conflict and its respective effect on economic growth. Next, attention is given to the extensive literature that seeks to measure and estimate the magnitude of labor-market discrimination against blacks across the Diaspora both indirectly, by using regression analyses, and directly, by using audit and correspondence tests. Finally, the paper surveys the literature that addresses the transmission of advantage and disadvantage across generations by race and ethnicity, including the intergenerational transfer of wealth, and critically takes up various remedies that have been implemented or proposed to address racial economic inequality.

Introduction: Divided Visions and the Black Diaspora

The primary lever of diasporization of the peoples of the African continent in the modern era was the Atlantic slave trade and the construction of plantation economies in the Americas. The long-term effect has been the production of populations of persons with visible apparent markers of their African ancestry who have experienced denigration and dispossession across three continents. The practices of colonization and colonialism on the African continent itself crystallized racial/ethnic hierarchies in a wide array of countries, sorting people between dominant and subaltern groups. On all three continents, whiteness has become the established marker of cognitive, social, and material superiority, while blackness bears the burden of racialized inequality.

Correspondingly, a theoretical apparatus has evolved to explain the comparatively depressed status of black people, regardless of their location, that supports the precepts of white supremacy. In its early formulations, the emphasis was placed on black constitutional and intellectual deficiencies that were alleged to be genetic in origin. Today, while the genetic arguments still are resuscitated with alarming frequency, greater emphasis is placed on assertions of black cultural dysfunctionality and black embrace of self-defeating behaviors as the root of observed racial disparities.[1] Whether these negative cultural/behavioral practices are attributed to past black subjugation or long-standing African norms, this popular theoretical apparatus de facto makes blacks largely responsible for their own relegation to the bottom of the social ladder by their own failure to pursue actions that will generate high achievement.

This perspective is hardly limited to white academics and pundits. Black scholars such as Thomas Sowell, Glenn Loury, Walter Williams, and Roland Fryer all share variants of this point of view.[2] The black entertainer Bill Cosby has trumpeted this sentiment nationwide. Nor is this a pattern confined to the United States. For example, Britain's Trevor Phillips, ironically while serving as director of that nation's Commission for Racial Equality, has expressed a similar perspective.[3] Sowell, in a decidedly perverse twist on the argument, most recently has claimed that black dysfunctionality is a product of sustained interaction with the retrograde culture of southern whites, which he dubs "redneck" culture.

Sowell's most recent position is reminiscent of Herrnstein and Murray's 1994 defense of their genetic explanation for racial disparity. When confronted with compelling evidence that there was no significant correlation between the degree of "white ancestry" and IQ scores in a sample of American blacks, Herrnstein and Murray utilized sheer sleight of hand with the following observation: "If the whites who contributed this ancestry were a random sample of all whites, then this would be strong evidence of no genetic influence on black-white differences." They concluded with deceptive quietude, "There is no evidence one way or another about the nature of the white ancestors."[4] The implication is, of course, that white ancestors of American blacks were an inferior breed of whites, thereby producing a dysgenic effect when intermixed with the African gene pool. It must have been those "redneck" whites once again who were the source of the problem.

The tradition of black scholars seizing on models of collective dysfunction as the explanation for disproportionate black poverty is hardly new. Even W. E. B. Du Bois railed long and hard in *The Philadelphia Negro* about the moral and cultural backwardness of many members of the city's black population, especially those newly arrived from the South.[5] But it is also fairly clear that Du Bois's emphasis on these themes was not solely motivated by his elitism, but by his desire to meet the expectations and confirm the beliefs of powerful white patrons who were financing his study.[6] Still, even under these constraints, Du Bois managed to provide such a clear and detailed presentation of the scope and magnitude of labor-market discrimination in Philadelphia—both in terms of outright exclusion of blacks from jobs that they were fully qualified to hold, and by gross underpayment for comparable work—that a careful reader could discern that these inequities could explain the generally unequal status of blacks and whites in the city.[7] Thus, Du Bois actually offered two conflicting visions of the determinants of racial inequality in *The Philadelphia Negro*.

Stratification Economics

The emerging field of stratification economics follows the lead of Du Bois's second argument that focuses on resource deprivation due to racial discrimination.[8] It takes a structuralist view of the processes generating racial inequality. It does not presume that any socially marked group has a monopoly on exceptional behavior or on dysfunctional or self-defeating behavior, but rather that within any social group there will be some who rise to extraordinary heights against great odds and others who will undermine their own lives—and they will be present in all groups in similar proportions. In stratification economics, the salient differences across groups are two major factors: their material inheritance of advantage and disadvantage, and the structure of opportunity facing them as members of a socially marked group. In the case of black people throughout the Diaspora, both the historical conditions that shape their material inheritance and the current structure of opportunity that confronts them have been drenched in racism.[9] It is these competing perspectives that inform the body of research represented in the articles included in this volume and that shape the study of racial disparity. The juxtaposition is between the systemic emphasis of stratification theory and the collective deficiency emphasis of cultural determinism. On empirical grounds alone, stratification economics has the upper hand, but cultural determinism speaks from the high castle of the media moguls and the conventions of "common sense." Counterevidence, no matter how strong, does not seem to dislodge cultural determinism from its position of authority.

Stratification economics does not deny that a subaltern population may have deficiencies in comparison with the dominant group, but it finds the origins of these deficiencies in consciously adopted policies and practices undertaken by the dominant group. It utilizes the John Stuart Mill–Arthur Lewis concept of the "noncompeting" group—the group rendered unable to get into the game by dint of the efforts of another group to deny them access to the credentials that would enable them to be contestants.[10] Thus, their deficient status—their lack of "human capital"—is socially constructed, just as the boundary between them and their rival group is socially constructed.

C. M. Battey / Hulton Archive / Getty Images

W. E. B. Du Bois (*c.*1918) was the first African American to receive a PhD from Harvard University. A key figure in the formation of the Civil Rights Movement and one of the foremost intellectuals of his time, Du Bois was a proponent of pluralist integration: that is, the commitment to achieving a social order that is integrated socially, politically, and economically, though made up of a plurality of racial and ethnic groups who maintain their distinctivenesses to the extent that doing so does not threaten the integration of the social whole. His influential *The Souls of Black Folk* (1903), the third of his seventeen books, offered "many things which if read with patience may show the strange meaning of being black here at the dawning of the Twentieth Century." He was one of the founders of the Niagara Movement and of the National Association for the Advancement of Colored People, for which he edited the journal *Crisis* from 1910 to 1934. A tireless advocate for higher education, he believed that the "talented tenth," the top 10 percent of the black community, would lead the way toward a self-sufficient black society. A member of the communist party during the 1940s, Du Bois traveled throughout the world pursuing his social programs. He won the Lenin Peace Prize in 1959. Dr. Du Bois died on August 27, 1963, at the age of 95 in Accra, Ghana, where he lived in self-imposed exile. His death was announced the next day by NAACP president Roy Wilkins at the March on Washington.

Economist William Arthur Lewis (photographed here in October 1979), born in St. Lucia in the British West Indies, earned his doctorate in the United Kingdom at the University of London and taught at the University of Manchester for over twenty years. In 1963, he was knighted by Queen Elizabeth II and became the first black tenured professor at Princeton University. In 1979, Lewis and Theodore W. Schultz were jointly awarded the Nobel Prize in Economics "for their pioneering research into economic development research with particular consideration of the problems of developing countries."

Furthermore, as some members of the out-group manage to acquire credentials that make them legitimate contestants for preferred positions, mechanisms of direct exclusion or reward differentiation come to operate more forcefully. In short, stratification economics maintains that not only is discrimination persistent—because it serves the interests of the dominant social group—but it is endogenous in the intensity of its application. It may be applied more forcefully when the credentials bar no longer can be used to prevent entry by members of the out-group. Thus, discrimination is "functional" in the sense that it has a purpose. It is used most intensively when other merit-based barriers have been breached.[11]

Exclusion to protect occupational turf for one's own group may not be primarily the prerogative of employers. Employees can consolidate around race/ethnicity to form their own color- or caste-coded cartel to preserve a set of jobs for their "own kind." This can occur in more formal ways via the screening practices of trade or craft unions, or in a less formal way via job networking systems that rule in the "old boys" and "old girls" and rule out the new boys and new girls.

Warren Whatley's essay in this collection examines the history of blacks in American labor markets from the 1860s through the 1930s, their exclusion from numerous labor unions, and their strikebreaking activities as a means of circumventing the color bar.[12] Whatley's study makes it clear that black workers were far from unwitting tools of white capitalists, who were seeking to destroy the union movement, nor were black workers readily categorized as "scab" laborers, since black workers were not intrinsically hostile toward the union movement. Indeed, in the immediate postbellum period, formerly enslaved blacks embraced practices and ideas that were the most militantly prolabor of any ethnic group in the nation.[13]

Whatley's article identifies job competition in a system of occupational stratification as the climate producing conditions where white workers utilized discriminatory practices within the union movement as a mechanism for reserving places for themselves. It extends the innovative discussion of black strikebreaking and the racial divide in the labor movement inaugurated in Spero and Harris's important work, published during the Great Depression, *The Black Worker*.[14] This discussion has had a much richer subsequent life in sociology than in economics.

One of the most provocative studies to explore racial turf wars in the job market is sociologist Oliver Cox's exegesis on the "divide-and-rule" hypothesis in his brilliant critique of Gunnar Myrdal's 1944 *American Dilemma*.[15] While profound and aggressively presented, Cox's *Caste, Class and Race* legitimately can be charged with presenting an excessively hegemonic vision of capitalists as a class manipulating the racial divide in the workplace to weaken the labor movement in toto—in contrast to Whatley, who assigns greater agency to both white and black workers in the arenas of strikes and strikebreaking.[16] Sociologist Edna Bonacich's interpretation of race, strikes, and strikebreaking through the lens of her "split labor market" hypothesis is more muted in assigning responsibility for the color bar in the labor market, acknowledging both the capitalists' preference for a divided labor movement and white workers' desire to keep the jobs to themselves.[17]

Black Ghetto Economic Development

Bennett Harrison's review-article, originally published more than thirty years ago, provides a perspective on racial economic inequality in the United States that has all but evaporated from the vision of economists at the start of the twenty-first century.[18] Harrison examined the argument that the problem of elevated rates of low income, joblessness, and ill health among black Americans, disproportionately living in racially homogeneous urban neighborhoods beset by concentrated poverty, should be viewed as analogous to the problem of economic development in Third World countries. An obvious parallel in the African Diaspora would be Afro-Brazilians in the favelas of that nation's cities. Thus, black ghetto economics would follow the same range of strategies advanced to uplift the developing countries.

Of course, the range of strategies consistent with modeling black economic advance as an economic-development problem could be procapitalist or anticapitalist. In the former case, building the ghetto might involve provision of incentives for corporations to locate and invest and to hire black workers in low-income black communities via tax credits and other subsidies. Even black cultural nationalists could subscribe to the procapitalist position, but they would want the incentives for private-sector activity to promote the development of black-owned businesses, rather than induce expanded "foreign" entrepreneurship in the ghetto.

The latter perspective is compatible with a purely nationalistic variant of dependency theory that emphasizes reliance on domestic capital, rather than on capital from abroad, to achieve economic growth and higher standards of living. The advocates of this position are not hostile to capitalism itself, but are primarily concerned with the marked underrepresentation of black Americans in the ranks of the nation's capitalists. Their companion assumption is that a dramatic increase in the numbers of black-owned enterprises will necessarily lead to improved economic conditions in black communities. From this vantage point, a special concern is whether spending circulates in a self-contained fashion within black communities, thereby generating the attendant multiplier effects on black incomes, instead of leaking outside to white America.[19]

An alternative radical strand of thought in the economic-development context sees the status of black Americans — and blacks throughout the Americas — best understood as a colonial problem, their depressed status created by the extension of a world system of capitalism. Therefore, blacks across the Americas constitute "internal colonies," and authentic economic development would require "decolonization" — a successful liberation struggle — and the emergence of a society predicated on communal or socialist principles. From this perspective, the goal is not to get inside of IBM or General Motors, nor to create a black-controlled version of IBM or General Motors, but to reorganize society around goals other than the pursuit of profit. For example, William Tabb concluded his discussion of the black ghetto as an internal colony with an observation that indicates that the only avenue to black economic development is social revolution:

> The dismantling of the colonial barriers against blacks carries with it a challenge to the dominant position of the profit motive in guiding production decisions. The black colony is forced to demand just such changes. If the wealth of America is to be shared on a more "equitable" basis, new rationales for distribution have to be developed. Unlike those in overseas colonies who can win their freedom and go their own way, blacks must remake the total economic and social system in America if they wish to change their situation.[20]

This path to economic development, no doubt, presents a significant challenge. The inattention given by economists today to the radical dependency view of the requirements for substantive black economic advance may simply be due to the daunting nature of the change required. Of course, the impression, fostered by the breakup of the Soviet Union, that socialism is not a viable option also may have contributed to the abandonment of this perspective. But even the procapitalist variant of the dependency theory gets little voice in contemporary discussions of racial inequality. This may be due to the consensus among policymakers in Washington that the best way to achieve economic development everywhere is via liberalization and privatization—a strategy without concern for such niceties as the specific nationality or ethnicity of the capitalists themselves, or of the impact of their business activities on the poor.

Intergroup Inequality and General Inequality

More recently, the economic-development literature has intersected with the literature on racial inequality in the context of Romie Tribble Jr.'s treatment of the venerable Kuznets hypothesis.[21] The Kuznets hypothesis has been widely interpreted as the claim that in the early stages of economic growth, rising per capita income is associated with a worsening of the income distribution until a threshold level of income per head is reached; thereafter, further increases in per capita income tend to be associated with greater equality in the size distribution of income, resulting in an inverted U-shaped distribution. The conundrum for the standard formulation of the Kuznets hypothesis has been the observation of a significant deterioration in income distribution in the richest countries in the world—countries well beyond the turning point—during the 1980s and 1990s.

Tribble proposes that the U.S. data on per capita income and income distribution better fits a sideways S shape. He says that there is a second threshold level of income per head that marks the beginning of a renewed negative association between higher levels of per capita income and the degree of income equality in a society. Tribble argues that the relationship between income and equality after the second turning point may be attributable to the shift in economic structure from the relative importance of manufacturing to the relative importance of professional services and information technology. He also says that underlying variations in class and race-linked patterns of inequality have been ignored in earlier studies of the Kuznets hypothesis, and brings these considerations to the fore at the close of his essay.

Indeed, Tribble's argument opens the door for consideration of the interesting question of the direction of causality between general inequality across a society and intergroup disparity within the same society. Does the overall pattern of income distribution drive income disparities among various ethnic/racial subgroups in a society, or do subgroup inequalities shape the overall degree of inequality in the society? Furthermore, subgroup inequalities have two dimensions: first, the gap in mean incomes across the groups, and second, the dispersion in incomes among members of each of the groups.

It can be shown that the nice decompositional properties of Henry Theil's index of inequality make it possible, at least conceptually, to sort between the relative impact of between-group income disparity and within-group income disparity.[22] Whether one reads the Theil index from left to right or from right to left indicates which causal interpretation is being imposed upon the data. There are some societies where the direction of causation must run in some significant way from long-established inequalities across groups onto the overall level of inequality. For example, embedded caste stratification in India must affect the general degree of inequality in India. Similarly, in the context of the African Diaspora, overall income inequality in South Africa must be driven to a significant degree by the extent of racial inequality, the product of more than a century of colonialism and apartheid. The essays by researchers contributing to the volume *No Longer Invisible: Afro-Latin Americans Today* suggest that long-standing color-stratification patterns in numerous countries in the Americas—including Colombia, Cuba, the Dominican Republic, Puerto Rico, Mexico, Nicaragua, Panama, Costa Rica, Honduras, Venezuela, Peru, Ecuador, Bolivia, and Uruguay—must have an impact on the general degree of inequality in each.[23]

The Functionality Hypothesis

By making use of comparative cross-national findings on intergroup disparity, a theory of endogenous discrimination can be advanced.[24] Discrimination in the sense of direct exclusion or underpayment of members of an out-group who are fully qualified for the positions for which they are denied access or full compensation deepens as more members of the out-group become eligible for the positions. As members of the out-group become better educated and more skilled, it becomes increasingly difficult for the in-group to preserve turf by claiming there are no out-group members who are "qualified" for the preferred slots. The in-group then resorts to pure discrimination, because they no longer can use merit standards—whether legitimately or artificially put in place—as seemingly legitimate grounds for preserving the desired slots for their own.

Evidence of this phenomenon includes the dramatic rise in discriminatory losses in occupation status experienced by black Americans between 1880 and 1920. This was the period of the consolidation of the Jim Crow system throughout the U.S. South and the practices of virulent racism in the U.S. North, including the institutionalization of residential segregation in northern cities. It was also the period of a spectacular increase in literacy and schooling among black Americans.[25]

A study using Brazilian data also provides further support for the functionality hypothesis.[26] The authors of this study find evidence that measured discriminatory losses in earnings actually rise for Afro-Brazilians as their educational attainment rises. While more highly educated Afro-Brazilians do, indeed, tend to earn more than their less educated peers, they also suffer slightly greater relative losses in earnings when compared against similarly educated Brazilian whites. Tomaskovic-Devey, Thomas, and Johnson demonstrate a parallel result with U.S. data: as educational attainment increases for black Americans, relative discriminatory losses also increase.[27] Educational attainment is not insulation from discrimination; if anything, it appears to be a magnet for attracting discriminatory treatment.

Peggy Lovell, in another Brazilian study, provides a different type of evidence consistent with the functionality hypothesis.[28] She finds that the lowest levels of measurable market-based discrimination were suffered by Afro-Brazilians in regions where educational gaps between them and the white Brazilians are the widest. Hence, there could be lower levels of measurable discrimination because such tactics are less necessary in those regions for whites to protect turf.

However, as Darity acknowledges in his essay, the South African case poses an anomaly for the functionality hypothesis.[29] Under apartheid, South African blacks were subjected to conditions where the system of "Bantu education" systematically deprived them of both years of schooling and quality schooling. Mean schooling levels were so low among black South Africans that only a very small proportion of them could have been serious contestants for jobs requiring basic literacy and numeracy. But all researchers have found high levels of discrimination in earnings against blacks during the same time span.[30] A severe double whammy operated against blacks under apartheid: deprivation of the opportunity to acquire formal human capital, and subjugation to virulent labor-market discrimination. The functionality hypothesis would suggest that the latter should not have been as severe, given the devastating impact of the former.

Ethnic Diversity, Ethnic Conflict, and Economic Growth

There is also a growing literature on the relationship between ethnic diversity, ethnic conflict, and economic growth that brings intergroup disparity back into the arena of economic development. Easterly and Levine's highly influential contribution to this discussion was prompted by their desire to explain the comparatively poor growth performance of so many nations on the African continent over the course of the past thirty years.[31] They argue that arbitrarily drawn boundaries separating African nations—drawn to serve the interests of the colonial powers in the late nineteenth century—brought ethnic groups together, in a single national unit, who shared little in common and who might have had a prior history of conflict.

Easterly and Levine's focus is on the effects of ethnic variation on the growth process. They theorize that the efficiency and the productivity-enhancing impact of the public sector is reduced by the higher level of rent-seeking activities associated with a society riven by a greater variety of ethnic cleavages.[32] By using a Herfindahl index, which measures the concentration of elements within an environment, they compute an Ethno-Linguistic Fractionalization (ELF) measure that captures the probability that any two randomly selected citizens in a country belong to groups speaking different languages. The ELF is their measure of the degree of ethnic variation in a country. But it is not necessarily ethnic variation in and of itself that has a particularly negative effect on economic growth; ethnic conflict leading to sustained episodes of violence potentially have much greater significance.

Léonce Ndikumana emphasizes that the critical distinction is between ethnic groups and ethnic antagonism.[33] It is the latter rather than the former that can lead to economically destructive conditions associated with civil war or other forms of internal armed conflict. The mere presence of multiple ethnic groups does not inevitably lead to high degrees of ethnic antagonism; for Ndikumana, ethnic antagonism is "an acquired phenomenon, arising from biased distribution of economic resources and political power."[34] Ndikumana also has documented the relationship between genocidal violence in Burundi in 1994 and the collapse of the nation's economy, leading to sharply negative rates of economic growth during the period of the genocide and its immediate aftermath.[35] Ironically, in the context of the Easterly and Levine analysis, Burundi, which scores a low of 1 out of a possible 100 on the Ethno-Linguistic index, is not an ethnically diverse society based upon the ELF, because Hutus and Tutsis speak the single language of the nation's colonial heritage, French.[36] Similarly, Haiti, which scores a 4 out of a possible 100, is a society with a recent history of high levels of social violence and poor economic performance, but negligible ethnic variation on the basis of the ELF. Again, it is a society where virtually everyone speaks French.

Pranab K. Bardhan has identified two major sources of ethnic conflict — colonial divide-and-rule policies (which, in the case of Belgian practices, definitely played a key role in the development of ethnic antagonism between Hutus and Tutsis in both Burundi and Rwanda), and the relationship between natives and immigrants.[37] But he also concludes that there is no clear relationship between ethnic conflict, economic conflict, and economic development, while cataloging a variety of ways in which intergroup frictions can arise. It should be noted that while immigration frequently leads to conflict between natives and newcomers, periods of rapid immigration also typically are associated with phases of positive economic growth in the receiving country. In the case of the United States, the recent growth in a

Spanish-speaking population would make the society appear to be more ethnically fractionalized, using the ELF, but that increase in fractionalization has not been associated with a fall in per capita income levels.

At least two researchers—political scientist Daniel Posner and economist Tade Okediji—have provided critiques of the ELF as a measure and have proposed alternative measures of ethnic diversity. Posner's key point is the absence of a one-to-one relationship between the number of ethnic groups and the number of political competitors. In many cases ethnicity—which may be captured by linguistic distinctiveness—is not salient for political activity. Instead, he advances a new measure constructed for forty-two African countries, the Politically Relevant Ethnic Groups (PERG) measure.[38] Okediji proposes a measure that takes into account additional dimensions of ethnic differentiation. In addition to linguistic variation, Okediji incorporates religious and racial differentiation in designing what he terms the Social Diversity Index (SDI).[39]

Not surprisingly, persistent violence, whatever the cause, appears to be a major inhibitor of economic growth. One cause could be ethnic conflict, and Easterly and Levine do consider an alternative measure that comes closer to capturing the degree of ethnic antagonism in a society.[40] This is an ethnic-conflict index developed by Ted Gurr at the Minorities at Risk Project at the University of Maryland at College Park.[41] In this alternative index, a "minority at risk" is a communal ethnic group that either has been subjected to political and/or economic discrimination, or has been acting politically on its own behalf as a group. Under the Gurr index, the entire populations of Burundi, Chad, and South Africa are at risk. African particularism is the clear message here, since Gurr concludes that African nations taken collectively have the largest proportion of their populations composed of "minorities at risk" in his global sample.

The substantive counterpoint is present in Robert Bates's work. Bates demonstrates that the presence of "minorities at risk" and its correlate, high levels of interethnic tension in Africa or elsewhere, is not generally associated with the economically destructive effects produced by political violence. Bates proposes that the level of political violence represented by riots, demonstrations, revolts, and assassinations is actually lower than one might predict throughout Africa, given the large presence of minorities at risk.[42]

Bates contends that political violence blocks economic growth, not ethnic diversity in and of itself. He even argues that ethnic groups can have a positive impact on economic growth by establishing "credible contracts between generations" that promote human-capital formation.[43] Suffice it to say, Africa has no monopoly on the "tribalisms" that lead to internecine violence resulting in economic losses:

> Communal divisions leading to inter-ethnic strife in Eastern Europe, especially the former Yugoslavia, Indonesia in 1997 and 1998, and Cambodia under the Khmer Rouge, have all contributed to economic decline. Other non-African nations where ethnic divisions have played a key role in armed strife in recent years include Turkey, the United Kingdom, Iraq, Iran, Israel, Lebanon, Colombia, Guatemala, Bangladesh, India, Laos, Myanmar, Pakistan, the Philippines, Sri Lanka, and Tajikstan. . . . [44]

One of the important dimensions of Gurr's Minorities at Risk measure is whether a particular ethnic group is confronted with economic discrimination. For economists, this is rarely an uncontested condition and requires systematic investigation. Conventional economic theory denies the possibility of persistent discrimination. The presumption of orthodox economics is that employers who prefer profits to prejudice will drive those out of the market who have the reverse preference. In the process, they will hire competent out-group workers at levels that will bring their wages to par with comparably competent in-group workers. Thus, most economists actually are surprised if they discover evidence of differential pay or employment among ascriptively differentiated workers that cannot be explained by differences in human-capital characteristics—for example, educational attainment, training, experience, motivation, or cognitive ability.

Indirect Tests for Racial Discrimination

The standard procedure to test for the presence of labor-market discrimination is to control for all possible differences in human-capital characteristics across groups and then determine whether there is still a gap in compensation. This procedure, generally known among economists as a Blinder-Oaxaca decomposition and generally known among sociologists as a Blau-Duncan decomposition, seeks to determine whether there is an economic penalty exacted in labor markets purely for one's ethnic/racial affiliation.[45] For years, researchers consistently found evidence of a significant gap in earnings between black and white men in the United States that could not be explained away by the measures of human capital they had included as controls in their regressions.

Then, in a paper published in 1990, June O'Neill reported evidence that ran counter to a long pattern of research findings.[46] O'Neill recognized that the 1980 routine of the National Longitudinal Survey of Youth (NLSY) included the results of the Armed Forces Qualification Test (AFQT) for each of the respondents to this randomized, nationwide survey—scores which she interpreted as indicators of either academic achievement (and school quality) or cognitive skills; Herrnstein and Murray actually treated the AFQT as a test of intelligence throughout *The Bell Curve*.[47] By including these scores in her regression analysis, O'Neill eliminated virtually the entire earnings differential between blacks and whites for both men and women. Her results were replicated by Ronald Ferguson and in a more comprehensive study by Derek Neal and William Johnson.[48] Thus, a new consensus began to emerge that was more consistent with the perspective of the "collective dysfunctionality" school of thought, whether or not that was the intent of the researchers who had produced these findings. The new consensus had it that labor-market discrimination was of minor importance in explaining black-white labor-market disparities; far more important were factors dubbed "premarket" that led African Americans to present themselves to employers as, on average, inferior job candidates to most non-black workers. Since he is not specific about the evidence he uses to reach this conclusion, one can speculate that it was the combined force of the O'Neill (1990), Ferguson (1995), and Neal and Johnson (1996) studies that led Glenn Loury to state a decade later in his *Anatomy of Racial Inequality* that

> for both empirical and philosophical reasons I conclude that a continued
> focus on the classic racial discrimination problem is now misplaced. Anti-

black reward bias has declined sharply in the United States over the past half-century.[49]

Almost immediately, William Rodgers and William Spriggs posed a response, reporting their findings[50]

> that AFQT scores [predict] wages less well for African-Americans than whites; and there are significant differences in the ability of common [predictors] to estimate African-American and white AFQT scores. Further, Rodgers and Spriggs show that when the math and verbal components of the AFQT are used to predict wages, instead of the composite score, the coefficients on the verbal components are positive and significant for African-Americans while the coefficient on the math component is basically zero. The relationships for whites are exactly the opposite. To the extent that there actually is an interracial skills gap, interracial differences in AFQT scores severely overestimate this gap. [Rodgers and Spriggs conclude that because] there are substantive interracial differences in how family (and other so-called premarket) environments are captured by the AFQT, racial differences in AFQT scores are greater than racial differences in skills rewarded in the labor market.[51]

The Rodgers-Spriggs verbal-math racial paradox, also studied in a working paper by Janet Currie and Duncan Thomas, has not been explored in subsequent research, but merits greater attention.[52] It is noteworthy that the O'Neill, Ferguson, and Neal and Johnson result has not been replicated in other data sets that provide measures that control for cognitive skills. For example, the Panel Study of Income Dynamics is another longitudinal data set that includes scores on an IQ test for all respondents. When those test scores are included in wage regressions, there is actually evidence of an increase in discrimination over the interval 1973–1991, despite evidence of an increase in returns to the cognitive-skill measure.[53] Furthermore, what proved to be startling to many economists was the additional finding in further research that there is evidence of greater effort or motivation among blacks in a wide range of circumstances, but particularly in the pursuit of education.[54] Arthur Goldsmith, Jonathan Veum, and William Darity show that when a wage equation is augmented not only with AFQT scores but also with measures of motivation, a form of psychological capital, that evidence of significant discriminatory differentials reemerge in the statistical analysis.[55] Major Coleman, after including direct controls for employers' evaluations of workers after the employers have observed their performance, still finds evidence of significant discriminatory differentials; in short, after adjusting for the employers' own assessments of worker quality, Coleman still finds a significant earnings gap between black and white workers.[56] The upshot is that the empirical case is substantial that the "classic racial discrimination problem" is still a reality for black Americans.[57]

Mason has also examined the impact of firm-level patterns of job segregation on racial wage differentials and contends that those patterns of job segregation are attributable in large part to within-firm discriminatory practices.[58] Barry Hirsch and David McPherson contend, in contrast, that firm-level patterns of job assignment can be explained primarily by racial skill differentials.[59] Thus, Mason's work sides with those who argue that internal job segregation also is substantially influenced by unequal treatment of black and white workers, while Hirsch and McPherson stand on the opposite side, arguing again that internal job segregation is systematically linked to human capital differences across the groups—and hence, if there is discrimination, it occurs in pre-market or extra-market processes of human capital acquisition.

The presence of anti-black discrimination in the United States has been documented in many contexts extending beyond the labor market. John Yinger's remarkable body of work utilizing both statistical methods and audit studies—to be discussed in greater detail below—has demonstrated the perniciousness of anti-black discrimination in a wide range of consumer markets, particularly in the market for housing.[60] Helen Ladd has provided a critical review of the literature on evidence of discrimination in mortgage lending, including her own research in the area, and concludes that the weight of the evidence indicates that discrimination has been practiced routinely by mortgage lenders.[61] Gary Dymski's study establishes the persistence of anti-black discrimination generally across credit markets.[62]

The criminal-justice system also is the site of drastically unequal treatment by race. Samuel Myers Jr., a specialist on the economics of race and crime, has established that a significant component of racial sentencing disparities must be attributable to unequal treatment, while Charles Betsey has documented the scope of the economic distributional effects from blacks to whites of the discriminatory sentencing differentials.[63] In a working paper, Billy Close and Patrick Mason have documented the gross inequities associated with racial-profiling practices of state police in Florida.[64]

Discriminators seem to respond to the physical characteristics of their targets of discrimination. Social psychologists Eberhardt, Goff, Purdie-Vaughns, and Davies have shown that the more a person matches stereotypical norms of what a black person is believed to look like, the greater the inclination of others to assume the person is a criminal.[65] More damning still, in an even newer study, Eberhardt, Davies, Purdie-Vaughns, and Johnson found that defendants with a more stereotypically black appearance are far more likely to be sentenced to death in capital cases when the victim is perceived as white.[66] Goldsmith, Hamilton, and Mason, utilizing the phenotypical data from the Multi City Study of Urban Inequality, have shown that darker skin-toned and medium skin-toned black males incur significantly greater discriminatory wage losses than light complexioned black males.[67] They conclude that since the vast majority of employers are white, these discriminatory effects are exercised across racial "lines." A similar study conducted by Espino and Franz with a sample of Latino workers demonstrates that darker (or "blacker looking") Latino males suffer significantly greater discriminatory losses in occupational status than lighter-skinned Latino men.[68]

Those enamored with the African American collective-dysfunctionality hypothesis are inclined to downplay the significance of discrimination in shaping racial inequality in the United States by invoking the successes of West Indian immigrants. The customary version of the argument has it that West Indians are phenotypically indistinguishable from African Americans and have proven to be a black success story, so discrimination cannot explain lags in African American economic performance.[69] Suzanne Model's excellent analysis of the West Indian immigrant provides a valuable antidote to this overly simplistic analysis of race, immigration, and economics in America.[70]

A strong prior in conventional economics is the belief that competition will eliminate discriminatory behavior, since discrimination seems to serve a preference that is inconsistent with profit maximization. After all, the most efficient course of action putatively would be always to hire the most qualified employee, regardless of race, creed, or color. Rivalrous competition should winnow out the discriminators, since they are not using the most profitable hiring practices. According to this line of reasoning, sectors of the economy where there are higher levels of competition should be the sectors with the least evidence of discrimination in employment outcomes; sectors in which firms exercise more monopoly power would be the ones that are most likely to demonstrate higher levels of discrimination. This inference simply is not borne out by a series of empirical studies that regularly find no consistent relationship between the measured degree of competition and estimates of the magnitude of discrimination in the sector.[71]

Direct Tests for Racial Discrimination

The method of detection of discrimination utilized in virtually all of the empirical studies discussed above is some variant of the Blinder-Oaxaca or Blau-Duncan statistical technique. An alternative procedure is to utilize field experiments that

> involve introducing bogus participants to the market place; for instance, pairs of black and white applicants for housing, or pairs of male and female applicants for employment. The intention is to test whether real estate agents and/or employers exercise a consistent preference for a particular race or sex.[72]

In contrast with the indirect character of the statistical methods for attempting to identify the presence of discrimination, these field experiments, also known as audit studies, provide a direct method for identifying the presence of discrimination. Peter Riach and Judith Rich critically analyzed a variety of these studies in a major survey article published in the *Economic*

Journal.[73] Field experiments to detect racial, sexual, age, and disability discrimination have been conducted in Belgium, Germany, Britain, the Neth-
erlands, Australia, Austria, Spain, Canada, and the United States.

Audit studies using trained actors with artificially designed resumes (to
insure that the applicants have equivalent qualifications, or that the target-
group member has superior qualifications) applying for employment generally have found strong evidence of discrimination against blacks in the U.S.
labor market.[74] Indeed, the audit studies have found substantial evidence of
discrimination against black women as well as black men, a labor-market
finding confirmed considerably less often by the statistical method of investigation.[75] This would appear, on the face of it, to be the smoking gun for
establishing that the "classic racial discrimination problem" is still with us in
the twenty-first century.

However, two major types of reservations have been raised about the
field experiments with trained actors. One set of reservations does not really
undermine the findings; it is the complaint that the deceptive nature of the
experiments violates the conditions of informed consent as a standard for
ethical experimentation. For instance, field experiments of this type were not
conducted in Sweden, because the Social Research Council there deemed
the method to be "unethical."[76] As Riach and Rich observe:

> Clearly deception is involved in field experiments of discrimination, as real
> estate agents are approached by individuals who do not genuinely wish to
> buy or rent. Likewise employers are approached by job applicants who do
> not genuinely want employment. Those subject to the research are deceived
> and have not had the opportunity to provide their consent.[77]

They conclude, on ethical grounds, that the agents who function as the
testers always should be fully informed about the intent and nature of the
study, but there is no ethical reason to inform the real estate agents or employers whose behavior is being evaluated.[78]

> The justification we offer for the deception of subjects in field experiments
> in labour, housing and product markets is that a lack of veracity is endemic

in these markets; that great harm is done to the social fabric by discriminatory practices in such markets; that minimal inconvenience is imposed on the entrepreneurs in the experiment; and that the technique provides evidence with a degree of accuracy and transparency which is not available from any other procedure.[79]

But fully informing the agents in field experiments opens the door for the second major complaint, advanced by James Heckman and Peter Siegelman in their assessment of the methodology of the Urban Institute's labor-market audit study.[80] Heckman and Siegelman argued that testers, knowledgeable about the objectives of the investigation, may have behaved, unconsciously, in such a way that they induced the subjects to act in ways that produced the discrimination finding. This would have been a bias in the results, created by what has been termed an "experimenter effect." Riach and Rich propose an alternative to deception of agents inspired by a study by Ian Ayres:[81]

Experimenter effects are a cause for concern, but there is an alternative to deception in this case, which is to employ professional actors and have them engage in role-playing, observed by independent academics/professionals to confirm equivalent behaviour, before they enter the field. At the very least, this approach should be used in parallel with a study involving deception of agents to establish the extent, or otherwise, of "experimenter effects," and whether there can be any justification for such deception in the future. This is exactly what Ayres did in his study of racial and sexual discrimination in car negotiations. In his initial tests the agents were aware that discrimination was being tested, but most significantly his "subsequent 'double blind' testing, conducted so that neither the sellers nor the buyers/testers knew that the study tested for race or gender discrimination, yielded similar results. . . ."[82]

Thus, the Ayres study affords at least one empirical instance where an "experimenter effect" does not appear to have had an impact on the findings. Riach and Rich conclude that, at least in this context, experimenter effects are more hypothetical than substantive.[83]

An alternative type of field experiment that forgoes use of actual testers necessarily bypasses the problem posed by an experimenter effect altogether. These are correspondence tests, where letters are sent to employers with faux resumes enclosed by the experimenter. The "sender's" name or address (or both) are designed to signal race/ethnicity and/or gender. The investigator then can gauge whether the pattern of which "sender" receives a call-back for an interview indicates that there is a systematic pattern of discrimination against a particular racial/ethnic or gender group. These are precisely the types of studies that characterized the first wave of field experiments testing for discrimination originally conducted in Britain in the 1960s.[84]

The American-based correspondence test that has received the widest attention is the one conducted by Bertrand and Mullainathan, where they sent five thousand letters of inquiry to employers in two cities who had advertised positions. The race of the "applicants" was supposed to be signaled by their names. Artificial résumés were enclosed to ensure that black and white "applicants" had equivalent credentials. In the initial phase of their study, names that were white-sounding received call-backs for interviews at twice the rate of black-sounding names. In the next phase of the study, Bertrand and Mullainathan mailed a new set of letters with enhanced résumés. The call-back rate rose for the white "applicants" but remained unchanged for the black "applicants," evidence strikingly at odds with the statistical version of the economic theory of discrimination. The Bertrand and Mullainathan study points toward the operation of raw racism, with employers seeming to conjure up visual images of acceptable and unacceptable employees, independent of the individuals' purported qualifications.[85]

Nevertheless, Coate and Loury have pushed the limits of the statistical model of discrimination to produce a vicious-circle effect and a damning self-fulfilling prophecy that excludes black workers from equal pay.[86] Derek Neal (forthcoming) has summarized the Coate and Loury model as follows:

Coate and Loury described a model of statistical discrimination in which blacks do not invest because they expect employers to be less likely to reward them for investing [in themselves]. Employers do not see investment levels but rather a noisy signal of worker skill. Because employers believe that black workers are less likely to invest, they screen black workers more stringently, thus lowering the returns to black skill investments, as black workers anticipated. Further, the rational reluctance of black youth to invest confirms the beliefs of employers concerning black investment behaviour.

But, Neal points out that "the model is squarely at odds with a key feature of data on skills and labour market outcomes . . . [the fact that] gradients between earnings and wages on the one hand and measures of achievement and attainment on the other are almost always as steep among blacks as among whites, and often steeper"; that is, the relative gains for additional schooling among blacks are greater than the relative gains from additional schooling among whites. However, it should be recalled that when blacks and whites at comparable educational levels are compared, blacks at higher educational levels earn relatively less than whites at similar educational levels than blacks at lower educational levels.[87]

Research on the degree of discrimination experienced by persons of apparent African descent across the Diaspora utilizes a variety of procedures for detecting discrimination—ranging from statistical tests with relatively large data sets, to ethnographic studies. Statistical studies include the work of Nelson do Valle Silva, Telles, Telles and Lim, and Peggy Lovell on Brazil; Coppin and Olsen on Trinidad and Tobago; Shields and Wailoo on Britain; Ndikumana on Burundi; Reza Nakhaie, Morton Stelcner and Nota Kyriazis, and Stelcner on Canada; Kollehlon on Liberia prior to its civil war; Knight and McGrath, Treiman, McKeever, and Fodor, Sherer, and Allanson, Atkins, and Hinks on South Africa; Alejandro de la Fuente's study of Cuba; Halpern and Twine's research on Ecuador; and Roger Lancaster's examination of race in Nicaragua all rely primarily on ethnographic data.[88] All of these investigations point toward significant discriminatory penalties for persons socially identified as black throughout the Americas and in South Africa, or significant cleavages grossly disadvantaging some ethnically marked group (or groups) in the other African countries studied.

Conclusion: Remedies for Racial Inequality

In the United States, remedies for intergroup disparity have largely been placed under the rubric of affirmative-action programs. Similar antidiscrimination measures to induce inclusion of underrepresented groups have been adopted widely on an international scale. India's national system of reservations in the civil service, in parliament, for university admissions, and for university faculty positions has been in existence since the late 1940s with the first post-independence constitution, though in 2006 students protested a proposal to increase the quota for lower-caste admissions to medical school from 27 percent to 49.5 percent. Malaysia's affirmative-action program was inaugurated in 1970 with the establishment of the New Economic Policy. Northern Ireland has had a system of balanced employment for Catholics and Protestants for several years. Brazil initiated an affirmative-action program for higher-education admissions two years ago.

Generally, though, the most careful studies assessing the impact of affirmative action have been performed in the United States. Cecilia Conrad's clever examination of the costs of affirmative action in the United States demonstrates that there have been no net positive or negative aggregate productivity effects from changes in the racial or gender demography of the American workforce, and that there have been low adverse efficiency effects on management from implementation of the policy.[89] Holzer and Neumark and Coleman demonstrate that the best available evidence does not support the proposition that black workers hired under affirmative-action initiatives have been any less productive than their non-black counterparts hired by dint of white privilege or other conditions.[90] In an intriguing study, legal scholar Tanya Hernandez looks at Cuba's experience with aggressive race-blind, class-conscious social policies since the revolution and shows that such policies have not resulted in closure of the economic gap between Afro-Cubans and (phenotypically) white Cubans.[91] She concludes that group-based affirmative action is essential to address disparities between a subaltern and a dominant social group.

Affirmative action can be effective as an instrument for addressing contemporary discriminatory practices. Indeed, Heckman and Payner have shown, using the specific case of the State of South Carolina, that federal antidiscrimination policies writ large had a dramatic positive effect on the economic status of African Americans.[92] Indeed, the largest decline in measured wage or occupational discrimination against blacks in the United States took place roughly between 1965 and 1975, the decade following the passage of the major federal civil rights legislation of the 1960s.[93] However, thereafter the level of measured discrimination in wages or occupational status stabilized at lower but still significant levels. This suggests that antidiscrimination policies either reached a zone of diminishing returns or suffered from inadequate enforcement.

What affirmative action cannot address effectively is the legacy of transmission of disadvantage across generations, particularly in the transmission of wealth. Sacerdote's study comparing educational attainment among descendants of free blacks and enslaved blacks in the United States suggests that the adverse intergenerational effects of slavery had dissolved by 1920, or within two generations after slavery.[94] But he does not address the effects of differential access to property and wealth associated with slave and nonslave status. He also makes the assumption that all blacks in the South prior to the Civil War were slaves. In contrast, Darity, Dietrich, and Guilkey find enduring and substantial adverse effects on occupational status of blacks in 1980 and 1990 from the discriminatory treatment endured by their ethnic ancestors in the interval 1880–1910, the period of consolidation of Jim Crow practices in the U.S. South.[95]

Today, the most pronounced racialized economic legacy transmitted across generations probably is wealth. Chiteji and Stafford show, by using a variety of data sets, how extreme the racial differentials are in terms of net worth—far more extreme than differentials in earnings, wages, or income.[96] The most recent data available from the Survey of Income and Program Participation (SIPP) for 2002 indicates that the median net worth of black households was a mere $5,988, or about 6 percent of white households' median net worth of $88,651.[97] This was an absolute gap of $83,000. Black households would have to save 300 percent of their median annual income to close the gap in a single year—an obvious impossibility. Thirty-two percent of black households had zero or negative net worth in 2002, in contrast with 13 percent of white households.[98]

The primary sources of wealth today are inheritances and in vivo transfers.[99] Historical black deprivations of wealth, dating from slavery times and the Reconstruction failure to execute the delivery of "forty acres and a mule" to the ex-slaves, have been visited systematically upon subsequent generations. The consequences are immense and include the relatively low level of business formation among African Americans.[100] At the heart of the cases made by Robert Browne and Darity and Frank, in papers published thirty years apart in the *American Economic Review*, is the recommendation for a full-scale program of a racial redistribution of wealth, a program best placed under the rubric of reparations—which may be applicable to other societies of the African Diaspora, though at this point, detailed data on wealth differences by race is available only in the United States.[101]

. . . .

NOTES

1. See, for example, Herrnstein and Murray, *The Bell Curve.*
2. See, for example, Sowell, *Black Rednecks and White Liberals;* Loury, *The Anatomy of Racial Inequality;* Austen-Smith and Fryer, "An Economic Analysis of 'Acting White'"; Williams, *Do the RIGHT Thing: The People's Economist Speaks.*
3. "Britain, Too, Has a Clarence Thomas," 2004.
4. Scarr et al., "Absence of a Relationship between Degree of White Ancestry and Intellectual Skills within a Black Population"; Herrnstein and Murray, *The Bell Curve,* 729 n. 130.
5. Du Bois, *The Philadelphia Negro.*
6. Lewis, *W. E. B. Du Bois,* 179–210.
7. Du Bois, *The Philadelphia Negro,* 322–54.
8. Darity, "Stratification Economics."
9. See Darity and Myers, *Persistent Disparity;* Mason, "Understanding Recent Empirical Evidence on Race and Labor Market Outcomes in the USA"; and Darity, "Intergroup Disparity: Why Culture Is Irrelevant."
10. Lewis, *Racial Conflict and Economic Development.*
11. Darity, "The Functionality of Market-Based Discrimination."
12. Whatley, "African-American Strikebreaking."
13. See Du Bois, *Black Reconstruction;* Rose, *Rehearsal for Reconstruction;* Foner, *Nothing But Freedom;* and Saville, *The Work of Reconstruction.*
14. Spero and Harris, *The Black Worker.*

15. Myrdal, *An American Dilemma.*

16. Cox, *Caste, Class and Race.*

17. Bonacich, "A Theory of Ethnic Antagonism," and "Advanced Capitalism and Black-White Relations in the United States."

18. Harrison, "Ghetto Economic Development."

19. See, for example, Davis, *The Economics of Black Community Development.*

20. Tabb, *The Political Economy of the Black Ghetto,* 33.

21. Tribble, "A Restatement of the S-Curve Hypothesis."

22. Darity and Deshpande, "Tracing the Divide."

23. Minority Rights Group, *No Longer Invisible.* See also Patrinos, "The Costs of Discrimination in Latin America."

24. Darity, "The Functionality of Market-Based Discrimination."

25. Darity, Dietrich, and Guilkey, "Racial and Ethnic Economic Inequality in the United States."

26. Arias, Yamada, and Tejerian, "Education, Family Background and Racial Earnings Inequality in Brazil."

27. Tomaskovic-Devey et al., "Race and the Accumulation of Human Capital across the Career."

28. Lovell, "The Geography of Economic Development and Racial Discrimination in Brazil."

29. Darity, "The Functionality of Market-Based Discrimination."

30. See Treiman, McKeever, and Fodor, "Racial Differences in Occupational Status and Income in South Africa"; Sherer, "Intergroup Economic Inequality in South Africa"; and Allanson, Atkins, and Hinks, "No End to the Racial Wage Hierarchy in South Africa?"

31. Easterly and Levine, "Africa's Growth Tragedy."

32. Krueger, "The Political Economy of the Rent-Seeking Society."

33. Ndikumana, "Distributional Conflict and Peace Building in Burundi."

34. Ibid., 3.

35. Ndikumana, "Institutional Failure and Ethnic Conflict in Burundi."

36. Easterly and Levine, "Africa's Growth Tragedy."

37. Bardhan, "Method in the Madness?"

38. Posner, "Measuring Ethnic Fractionalization in Africa."

39. Okediji, "The Dynamics of Ethnic Fragmentation."

40. Easterly and Levine, "Africa's Growth Tragedy."

41. Gurr, *Minorities at Risk.*

42. Bates, "Ethnicity and Development in Africa," 133.

43. Ibid., 131.

44. Darity, "Racial/Ethnic Disparity and Economic Development," 133.

45. See National Research Council, "Statistical Analysis of Observational Data," for a description and discussion of strengths and weaknesses.

46. O'Neill, "The Role of Human Capital in Earnings Differences between Black and White Men."

47. Herrnstein and Murray, *The Bell Curve*.
48. Ferguson, "Shifting Challenges"; Neal and Johnson, "The Role of Premarket Factors in Black-White Wage Differences."
49. Loury, *The Anatomy of Racial Inequality*, 95.
50. Rodgers and Spriggs, "What Does AFQT Really Measure."
51. Mason, "Understanding Recent Empirical Evidence on Race and Labor Market Outcomes in the USA," 323.
52. Currie and Thomas, "Race, Children's Cognitive Achievement, and 'The Bell Curve.'"
53. Mason, "Race, Culture, and Skill."
54. Ibid.
55. Goldsmith et al., "Motivation and Labor Market Outcomes."
56. Coleman, "Job Skill and Black Male Wage Discrimination."
57. See the detailed literature reviews in Darity and Mason, "Evidence on Discrimination in Employment," and in Mason, "Understanding Recent Empirical Evidence on Race and Labor Market Outcomes in the USA."
58. Mason, "Race, Competition, and Differential Wages," and "Male Interracial Wage Differentials."
59. Hirsch and McPherson, "Wages, Sorting of Skill, and the Racial Composition of Jobs."
60. Yinger, "Access Denied, Access Constrained," and "Evidence on Discrimination in Consumer Markets."
61. Ladd, "Evidence on Discrimination in Mortgage Lending."
62. Dymski, "Is Discrimination Disappearing?"
63. Myers, "Statistical Tests of Discrimination in Punishment"; Betsey, "Income and Wealth Transfer Effects of Discrimination in Sentencing."
64. Close and Mason, "Beyond the Traffic Stop: Intersections of Race, Ethnicity, Gender, and the Decision to Search."
65. Eberhardt et al., "Seeing Black: Race, Crime, and Visual Processing."
66. Eberhardt et al., "Looking Deathworthy."
67. Goldsmith et al., "Shades of Discrimination."
68. Espino and Franz, "Latino Phenotypic Discrimination Revisited."
69. See Sowell, "Three Black Histories."
70. Model, "Caribbean Immigrants." See also Suzuki, "Success Story?" and "Selective Immigration and Ethnic Economic Achievement"; James, "Explaining Afro-Caribbean Social Mobility in the United States"; Darity, "Stratification Economics."
71. Haessel and Palmer, "Market Power and Employment Discrimination"; Agesa and Hoover, "Market Structure and Racial Earnings"; Agesa and Hamilton, "Competition and Wage Discrimination"; Coleman, "Racial Discrimination in the Workplace."
72. Riach and Rich, "Deceptive Field Experiments of Discrimination," 457–70.
73. Riach and Rich, "Field Experiments of Discrimination in the Market Place."
74. See Fix, Galster, and Struyk, "An Overview of Auditing for Discrimination"; Riach and Rich, "Field Experiments of Discrimination in the Market Place"; Darity and Mason, "Evidence on Discrimination in Employment."

75. Marlene Kim and Mary C. King do find ongoing statistical evidence of discrimination in employment against black women, and Kim discusses the weaknesses in other studies that typically fail to find such a result. Kim, "Has the Race Penalty for Black Women Disappeared?"; King, "Human Capital and Black Women's Occupational Mobility."
76. Riach and Rich, "Deceptive Field Experiments of Discrimination," 457.
77. Ibid., 458–59.
78. Ibid., 464–66.
79. Ibid., 463.
80. Heckman and Siegelman, "Determining the Impact of Federal Anti-Discrimination Policy on the Economic Status of Blacks."
81. Riach and Rich, "Deceptive Field Experiments of Discrimination," 464–65.
82. Ayres, "Fair Driving."
83. Riach and Rich, "Deceptive Field Experiments of Discrimination."
84. Daniel, *Racial Discrimination in England*; Jowell and Prescott-Clarke, "Racial Discrimination and White-Collar Workers in Britain."
85. Bertrand and Mullainathan, "Are Emily and Greg More Employable Than Lakisha and Jamal?"
86. Coate and Loury, "Will Affirmative Action Policies Eliminate Negative Stereotypes?"
87. Again, see Tomaskovic-Devey et al., "Race and the Accumulation of Human Capital across the Career."
88. Silva, "Updating the Cost of Not Being White in Brazil"; Telles, "Racial Inequality among the Brazilian Population"; Telles and Lim, "Does It Matter Who Answers the Race Question?"; Lovell, "The Geography of Economic Development and Racial Discrimination in Brazil"; Lovell, "Race, Gender, and Regional Inequalities in Brazil"; Coppin and Olsen, "Earnings and Ethnicity in Trinidad and Tobago"; Shields and Wailoo, "Exploring the Determinants of Unhappiness for Ethnic Minority Men in Britain"; Ndikumana, "Institutional Failure and Ethnic Conflict in Burundi"; Nakhaie, "Class, Gender and Ethnic Income Inequalities in 1973 and 1984"; Stelcner and Kyriazis, "An Empirical Analysis of Earnings among Ethnic Groups in Canada"; Stelcner, "Earnings Differentials among Ethnic Groups in Canada"; Kollehlon, "Occupational Status Attainment in Liberia"; Knight and McGrath, "An Analysis of Racial Wage Discrimination in South Africa"; Treiman et al., "Racial Differences in Occupational Status and Income in South Africa, 1980 and 1991"; Sherer, "Intergroup Economic Inequality in South Africa"; Allanson et al., "No End to the Racial Wage Hierarchy in South Africa?"; de la Fuente, "Recreating Racism"; Halpern and Twine, "Antiracist Activism in Ecuador"; Lancaster, "Skin Color, Race and Racism in Nicaragua."
89. Conrad, "The Economic Cost of Affirmative Action."
90. Holzer and Neumark, "Assessing Affirmative Action"; Coleman, "Job Skill and Black Male Wage Discrimination."
91. Hernandez, "An Exploration of the Efficacy of Class-Based Approaches to Racial Justice."

92. Heckman and Payner, "Determining the Impact of Federal Anti-Discrimination Policy on the Economic Status of Blacks."
93. See Darity, Dietrich, and Guilkey, "Persistent Advantage or Disadvantage?"
94. Sacerdote, "Slavery and the Intergenerational Transmission of Human Capital."
95. Darity, Dietrich, and Guilkey, "Persistent Advantage or Disadvantage?"
96. Chiteji and Stafford, "Portfolio Choices of Parents and Their Children as Young Adults."
97. Kochhar, "The Wealth of Hispanic Households."
98. Ibid.
99. See Blau and Graham, "Black-White Differences in Wealth and Asset Accumulation"; Darity and Nicholson, "Racial Wealth Inequality and the Black Family."
100. See Butler and Herring, "Ethnicity and Entrepreneurship in America."
101. Browne, "The Economic Basis for Reparations to Black Americans"; Darity and Frank, "The Economics of Reparations."

BIBLIOGRAPHY

Agesa, Jacqueline, Richard U. Agesa, and Gary A. Hoover. "Market Structure and Racial Earnings: Evidence from Job Changes." *American Economic Review* 91 (May 2001): 169–73.

Agesa, Jacqueline, and Darrick Hamilton. "Competition and Wage Discrimination: The Effects of Interindustry Competition and Import Penetration." *Social Science Quarterly* 85 (March 2004): 121–35.

Allanson, Paul, Jonathan P. Atkins, and Timothy Hinks. "No End to the Racial Wage Hierarchy in South Africa?" *Review of Development Economics* 6 (October 2002): 442–59.

America, Richard F. "Reparations and Public Policy." *Review of Black Political Economy* 26 (Winter 1999): 77–83.

Arias, Omar, Gustavo Yamada, and Luis Tejerina. "Education, Family Background and Racial Earnings Inequality in Brazil." *International Journal of Manpower* 25, no. 3–4 (2004): 355–73.

Austen-Smith, David, and Roland Fryer. "An Economic Analysis of 'Acting White.'" *Quarterly Journal of Economics* 120 (May 2005): 551–83.

Ayres, Ian. "Fair Driving: Gender and Race Discrimination in Retail Car Negotiations." *Harvard Law Review* 104 (February 1991): 817–72.

Bardhan, Pranab. "Method in the Madness? A Political Economy Analysis of the Ethnic Conflicts in Less Developed Countries." *World Development* 25 (September 1997): 1381–98.

Bates, Robert. "Ethnicity and Development in Africa: A Reappraisal." *American Economic Review* 90 (May 2000): 131–34.

Bertrand, Marianne, and Sendhil Mullainathan. "Are Emily and Greg More Employable Than Lakisha and Jamal? A Field Experiment on Labor Market Discrimination." *American Economic Review* 94 (September 2004): 991–1013.

Betsey, Charles L. "Income and Wealth Transfer Effects of Discrimination in Sentencing." *Review of Black Political Economy* 32 (Winter–Spring 2005): 111–20.

Blau, Francine D., and John Graham. "Black-White Differences in Wealth and Asset Accumulation." *Quarterly Journal of Economics* 105 (May 1990): 321–39.

Bonacich, Edna. "Advanced Capitalism and Black-White Relations in the United States: A Split Labor Market Interpretation." *American Sociological Review* 41 (February 1976): 34–51.

Bonacich, Edna. "A Theory of Ethnic Antagonism: The Split Labor Market." *American Sociological Review* 37 (October 1972): 547–59.

"Britain, Too, Has a Clarence Thomas." *Journal of Blacks in Higher Education* 45 (Autumn 2004): 51.

Brown, Michael K. "Is Race Experienced As Class?" *Labor History* 41 (November 2000): 513–16.

Browne, Robert. "The Economic Basis for Reparations to Black Americans." *American Economic Review* 62 (May 1972): 39–46.

Butler, John Sibley, and Cedric Herring. "Ethnicity and Entrepreneurship in America: Toward an Explanation of Racial and Ethnic Group Variations in Self-Employment." *Sociological Perspectives* 34 (Spring 1991): 79–94.

Carnoy, Martin. "Education and Racial Inequality: The Human Capital Explanation Revisited." *Economics of Education Review* 15 (June 1996): 259–72.

Chiteji, Ngina, and Darrick Hamilton. "Family Connections and the Black-White Wealth Gap among the Middle Class." *Review of Black Political Economy* 30 (Summer 2002): 9–28.

Chiteji, Ngina S., and Frank P. Stafford. "Portfolio Choices of Parents and Their Children as Young Adults: Asset Accumulation by African American Families." *American Economic Review* 89 (May 1999): 377–80.

Close, Billy, and Patrick Mason. "Beyond the Traffic Stop: Intersections of Race, Ethnicity, Gender, and the Decision to Search." Florida Department of Transportation, 2003.

Coate, Stephen, and Glenn C. Loury. "Will Affirmative Action Policies Eliminate Negative Stereotypes?" *American Economic Review* 83 (December 1993): 1220–40.

Coleman, Major G. "Job Skill and Black Male Wage Discrimination." *Social Science Quarterly* 84 (December 2003): 892–906.

Coleman, Major G. "Racial Discrimination in the Workplace: Does Market Structure Make a Difference?" *Industrial Relations* 43 (July 2004): 660–89.

Conrad, Cecilia. "The Economic Cost of Affirmative Action: A Review of the Evidence." In *Economic Perspectives on Affirmative Action*, ed. Margaret C. Simms, 33–47. Washington, D.C.: Joint Center for Political and Economic Studies, 1995.

Conrad, Cecilia A., and Rhonda V. Sharpe. "The Impact of the California Civil Rights Initiative (CCRI) on University and Professional School Admissions and the Implications for the California Economy." *Review of Black Political Economy* 25 (Summer 1996): 30–60.

Coppin, Addington, and R. N. Olsen. "Earnings and Ethnicity in Trinidad and Tobago." *Journal of Development Studies* 34 (February 1998): 116–34.

Cox, Oliver C. *Caste, Class and Race: A Study in Social Dynamics.* New York: Doubleday, 1948.

Daniel, William W. *Racial Discrimination in England: Based on the P. E. P. Report.* Harmondsworth, U.K.: Penguin, 1968.

Darity, William, Jr. "The Functionality of Market-Based Discrimination." *International Journal of Social Economics* 28, no. 10–12 (2001): 980–86.

Darity, William, Jr. "Intergroup Disparity: Why Culture Is Irrelevant." *Review of Black Political Economy* 29 (Spring 2002): 77–90.

Darity, William, Jr. "Racial/Ethnic Disparity and Economic Development." In *A Post-Keynesian Perspective on Twenty-First Century Economic Problems*, ed. Paul Davidson, 126–36. Northampton, U.K.: Edward Elgar, 2002.

Darity, William, Jr. "Stratification Economics: The Role of Intergroup Inequality." *Journal of Economics and Finance* 29 (Summer 2005): 144–53.

Darity, William, Jr., and Ashwini Deshpande. "Tracing the Divide: Intergroup Disparity across Countries." *Eastern Economic Journal* 26 (2000): 75–86.

Darity, William A., Jr., Jason Dietrich, and David Guilkey. "Persistent Advantage or Disadvantage? Evidence in Support of the Intergenerational Drag Hypothesis." *American Journal of Economics and Sociology* 60 (April 2001): 435–70.

Darity, William, Jr., Jason Dietrich, and David Guilkey. "Racial and Ethnic Economic Inequality in the United States: A Secular Perspective." *American Economic Review* 87 (May 1997): 301–5.

Darity, William, Jr., and Dania Frank. "The Economics of Reparations." *American Economic Review* 93 (May 2003): 326–29.

Darity, William A., Jr., Darrick Hamilton, and Jason Dietrich. "Passing on Blackness: Latinos, Race, and Earnings in the USA." *Applied Economics Letters* 9 (October 2002): 847–53.

Darity, William, Jr., and Patrick L. Mason. "Evidence on Discrimination in Employment: Codes of Color, Codes of Gender." *Journal of Economic Perspectives* 12 (Spring 1998): 63–90.

Darity, William, Jr., and Samuel L. Myers, Jr. *Persistent Disparity: Race and Economic Inequality in the United States since 1945.* Cheltenham, U.K.: Edward Elgar, 1998.

Darity, William Jr., and Melba Nicholson. "Racial Wealth Inequality and the Black Family." In *African American Family Life: Ecological and Cultural Diversity*, ed. Vonnie McLoyd, Nancy Hill, and Kenneth Dodge, 78–85. New York: Guilford Press, 2005.

Davis, Frank Green. *The Economics of Black Community Development: An Analysis and Program for Autonomous Growth and Development.* Chicago: Markham, 1972.

Du Bois, W. E. B. *Black Reconstruction: An Essay toward a History of the Part Which Black Folk Played in the Attempt to Reconstruct Democracy in America, 1860–1880.* New York: Harcourt, Brace, 1935.

Du Bois, W. E. B. *The Philadelphia Negro: A Social Study.* Philadelphia: University of Pennsylvania Press, 1899.

Dymski, Gary. "Illegal-Seizure and Market-Disadvantage Approaches to Restitution: A Comparison of the Japanese American and African American Cases." *Review of Black Political Economy* 27 (Winter 2000): 47–78.

Dymski, Gary. "Is Discrimination Disappearing? Racial Discrimination in Access to Credit, 1992–1998." *International Journal of Social Economics* 28, no. 10–12 (2001): 1025–45.

Easterly, William, and Ross Levine. "Africa's Growth Tragedy: Policies and Ethnic Divisions." *Quarterly Journal of Economics* 112 (November 1997): 1202–49.

Eberhardt, Jennifer L., Paul G. Davies, Valerie J. Purdie-Vaughns, and Sherri Lynn Johnson. "Looking Deathworthy: Perceived Stereotypicality of Black Defendants Predicts Capital-Sentencing Outcomes." *Psychological Science* 17 (May 2006): 383–86.

Eberhardt, Jennifer L., P. A. Goff, Valerie J. Purdie-Vaughns, and Paul G. Davies. "Seeing Black: Race, Crime, and Visual Processing." *Journal of Personality and Social Psychology* 87 (December 2004): 876–93.

Espino, Rodolfo, and Michael M. Franz. "Latino Phenotypic Discrimination Revisited: The Impact of Skin Color on Occupational Status." *Social Science Quarterly* 83 (June 2002): 612–23.

Ferguson, Ronald P. "Shifting Challenges: Fifty Years of Economic Change toward Black-White Earnings Equality." *Daedalus* 124 (Winter 1995): 37–76.

Fix, Michael, George Galster, and Raymond Struyk, eds. "An Overview of Auditing for Discrimination." In their *Clear and Convincing Evidence: Measurement of Discrimination in America*, 1–67. Washington, D.C.: Urban Institute Press, 1993.

Foner, Eric. *Nothing But Freedom: Emancipation and Its Legacy.* Baton Rouge: Louisiana State University Press, 1983.

de la Fuente, Alejandro. "Recreating Racism: Race and Discrimination in Cuba's 'Special Period.'" *Cuba Briefing Papers Series* (18 July 1998): 1–12.

Gibson, Karen J., William A. Darity Jr., and Samuel L. Myers Jr. "Revisiting Occupational Crowding in the United States: A Preliminary Study." *Feminist Economics* 4 (November 1998): 73–95.

Goldsmith, Arthur H., Darrick Hamilton, and William Darity Jr. "Shades of Discrimination: Skin Tone and Wages." *American Economic Review* 96 (May 2006): 242–45.

Goldsmith, Arthur H., Jonathan Veum, and William Darity Jr. "Motivation and Labor Market Outcomes." *Research in Labor Economics* 19 (2000): 109–46.

Gurr, Ted. *Minorities at Risk: A Global View of Ethnopolitical Conflicts.* Washington, D.C.: United States Institute of Peace Press, 1993.

Haessel, Walter, and John Palmer. "Market Power and Employment Discrimination." *Journal of Human Resources* 13 (Fall 1978): 545–60.

Halpern, Adam, and France Winddance Twine. "Antiracist Activism in Ecuador: Black-Indian Community Alliances." *Race and Class* 42 (October–December 2000): 19–31.

Harrison, Bennett. "Ghetto Economic Development: A Survey." *Journal of Economic Literature* 12 (March 1974): 1–37.

Heckman, James, and B. Payner. "Determining the Impact of Federal Anti-Discrimination Policy on the Economic Status of Blacks: A Study of South Carolina." *American Economic Review* 79 (March 1989): 138–77.

Heckman, James J., and Peter Siegelman. "The Urban Institute Audit Studies: Their Methods and Findings." In *Clear and Convincing Evidence: Measurement and Discrimination in*

America, ed. Michael Fix, George Galster, and Raymond Struyk, 187–258. Washington, D.C.: Urban Institute Press, 1993.

Hernandez, Tanya K. "An Exploration of the Efficacy of Class-Based Approaches to Racial Justice: The Cuban Context." *U. C. Davis Law Review* 33 (Summer 2000): 1135–71.

Herrnstein, Richard J., and Charles Murray. *The Bell Curve: Intelligence and Class Structure in American Life*. New York: Free Press, 1994.

Hirsch, Barry T., and David McPherson. "Wages, Sorting of Skill, and the Racial Composition of Jobs." *Journal of Labor Economics* 22 (January 2004): 189–210.

Holzer, Harry J., and Jens Ludwig. "Measuring Discrimination in Education: Are Methodologies from Labor and Markets Useful?" *Teachers College Record* 105 (August 2003): 1147–78.

Holzer, Harry, and David Neumark. "Assessing Affirmative Action." *Journal of Economic Literature* 38 (September 2000): 483–568.

James, Winston. "Explaining Afro-Caribbean Social Mobility in the United States: Beyond the Sowell Thesis." *Comparative Studies in Society and History* 44 (April 2002): 218–62.

Jowell, Roger, and Patricia Prescott-Clarke. "Racial Discrimination and White-Collar Workers in Britain." *Race* 11 (April 1970): 397–417.

Kim, Marlene. "Has the Race Penalty for Black Women Disappeared?" *Feminist Economics* 8 (July 2002): 115–24.

King, Mary C. "Human Capital and Black Women's Occupational Mobility." *Industrial Relations* 34 (April 1995): 282–98.

Knight, J. B., and M. D. McGrath. "An Analysis of Racial Wage Discrimination in South Africa." *Oxford Bulletin of Economics and Statistics* 39 (November 1977): 245–71.

Kochhar, Rakesh. "The Wealth of Hispanic Households: 1996 to 2002." *Pew Hispanic Center Report* (16 October 2004).

Kollehlon, Konia T. "Occupational Status Attainment in Liberia: The Roles of Achievement and Ascription." *Social Science Research* 18 (June 1989): 151–73.

Krueger, Anne O. "The Political Economy of the Rent-Seeking Society." *American Economic Review* 64 (June 1974): 291–303.

Ladd, Helen F. "Evidence on Discrimination in Mortgage Lending." *Journal of Economic Perspectives* 12 (Spring 1998): 41–62.

Lancaster, Roger. "Skin Color, Race and Racism in Nicaragua." *Ethnology* 30 (October 1991): 339–53.

Lewis, W. Arthur. *Racial Conflict and Economic Development*. Cambridge, Mass.: Harvard University Press, 1985.

Lewis, David Levering. *W. E. B. Du Bois: Biography of a Race, 1868–1919*. New York: Holt, 1993.

Loury, Glenn. *The Anatomy of Racial Inequality*. Cambridge, Mass.: Harvard University Press, 2002.

Lovell, Peggy A. "The Geography of Economic Development and Racial Discrimination in Brazil." *Development and Change* 24 (January 1993): 83–106.

Lovell, Peggy A. "Race, Gender, and Regional Inequalities in Brazil." *Review of Social Economy* 43 (September 2000): 277–93.

Mason, Patrick L. "Male Interracial Wage Differentials: Competing Explanations." *Cambridge Journal of Economics* 23 (May 1999): 261–99.

Mason, Patrick L. "Race, Competition, and Differential Wages." *Cambridge Journal of Economics* 19 (August 1995): 545–68.

Mason, Patrick L. "Race, Culture, and Skill: Interracial Wage Differences among African-Americans, Latinos, and Whites." *Review of Black Political Economy* 25 (Winter 1997): 5–40.

Mason, Patrick L. "Understanding Recent Empirical Evidence on Race and Labor Market Outcomes in the USA." *Review of Social Economy* 58 (September 2000): 319–38.

Minority Rights Group, ed. *No Longer Invisible: Afro-Latin Americans Today.* London: Minority Rights Group Publications, 1995.

Model, Suzanne. "Caribbean Immigrants: A Black Success Story?" *International Migration Review* 25 (Summer 1991): 248–76.

Myers, Samuel L. "Statistical Tests of Discrimination in Punishment." *Journal of Quantitative Criminology* 1 (June 1985): 191–218.

Myrdal, Gunnar. *An American Dilemma: The Negro Problem and Modern Democracy.* New York: Harper, 1944.

Nakhaie, M. Reza. "Class, Gender and Ethnic Income Inequalities in 1973 and 1984: Findings from the Canadian National Surveys." *Review of Radical Political Economics* 26 (March 1994): 26–55.

National Research Council. "Statistical Analysis of Observational Data." In *Measuring Racial Discrimination*, 118–61. Washington, D.C.: National Academies, 2004.

Ndikumana, Léonce. "Distributional Conflict and Peace Building in Burundi." *The Round Table* 94 (September 2005): 413–27.

Ndikumana, Léonce. "Institutional Failure and Ethnic Conflict in Burundi." *African Studies Review* 41, no. 1 (1998): 29–47.

Ndikumana, Léonce. "Towards a Solution to Violence in Burundi: A Case for Political and Economic Liberalisation." *Journal of Modern African Studies* 38 (September 2000): 431–59.

Neal, Derek A., and William R. Johnson. "The Role of Premarket Factors in Black-White Wage Differences." *Journal of Political Economy* 104 (October 1996): 869–95.

Okediji, Tade O. "The Dynamics of Ethnic Fragmentation: A Proposal for an Expanded Measurement Index." *American Journal of Economics and Sociology* 64 (April 2005): 637–62.

O'Neill, June. "The Role of Human Capital in Earnings Differences between Black and White Men." *Journal of Economic Perspectives* 4 (Fall 1990): 25–45.

Patrinos, Harry Anthony. "The Costs of Discrimination in Latin America." *Human Capital Development and Operations Working Papers, World Bank.* http://www.worldbank.org/html/extdr/hnp/hddflash/workp/wp_00045.html (accessed 27 July, 2006).

Posner, Daniel N. "Measuring Ethnic Fractionalization in Africa." *American Journal of Political Science* 48 (October 2004): 849–63.

Riach, Peter, and Judith Rich. "Deceptive Field Experiments of Discrimination: Are They Ethical?" *Kyklos* 57, no. 3 (2004): 457–70.

Riach, Peter A., and Judith Rich. "Field Experiments of Discrimination in the Market Place." *Economic Journal* 112 (November 2002): 480–518.

Riach, Peter A., and Judith Rich. "Testing for Racial Discrimination in the Labour Market." *Cambridge Journal of Economics* 15 (September 1991): 239–56.

Rodgers, William M., III, and William E. Spriggs. "What Does AFQT Really Measure: Race, Wages, Schooling, and the AFQT Score." *Review of Black Political Economy* 24 (Spring 1996): 13–46.

Rose, Willie Lee. *Rehearsal for Reconstruction: The Port Royal Experiment.* Indianapolis: Bobbs-Merrill, 1964.

Sacerdote, Bruce. "Slavery and the Intergenerational Transmission of Human Capital." *Review of Economics and Statistics* 87 (May 2005): 217–34.

Saville, Julie. *The Work of Reconstruction: From Slave to Wage Laborer in South Carolina, 1860–1870.* Cambridge: Cambridge University Press, 1994.

Scarr, Sandra, Andrew J. Pakstis, Solomon H. Katz, and William B. Barker. "Absence of a Relationship between Degree of White Ancestry and Intellectual Skills within a Black Population." *Human Genetics* 39 (November 1977): 69–86.

Sherer, George. "Intergroup Economic Inequality in South Africa: The Post-Apartheid Era." *American Economic Review* 90 (May 2000): 317–21.

Shields, Michael A., and Allan Wailoo. "Exploring the Determinants of Unhappiness for Ethnic Minority Men in Britain." *Scottish Journal of Political Economy* 49 (September 2002): 445–66.

Silva, Nelson do Valle. "Updating the Cost of Not Being White in Brazil." In *Race, Class and Power in Brazil,* ed. Pierre-Michel Fontaine, 43–55. Los Angeles: Center for Afro-American Studies, University of California Press, 1985.

Sowell, Thomas. *Black Rednecks and White Liberals.* San Francisco: Encounter Books, 2005.

Sowell, Thomas, ed. "Three Black Histories." In *Essays and Data on American Ethnic Groups,* 7–64. Washington, D.C.: Urban Institute Press, 1978.

Spero, Sterling Denhard, and Abram Lincoln Harris. *The Black Worker: The Negro and the Labor Movement.* New York: Columbia University Press, 1931.

Stelcner, Morton. "Earnings Differentials among Ethnic Groups in Canada: A Review of the Research." *Review of Social Economy* 58 (September 2000): 295–317.

Stelcner, Morton, and Nota Kyriazis. "An Empirical Analysis of Earnings among Ethnic Groups in Canada." *International Journal of Contemporary Sociology* 32, no. 1 (1995): 41–79.

Suzuki, Masao. "Selective Immigration and Ethnic Economic Achievement: Japanese Americans before World War II." *Explorations in Economic History* 39, no. 3 (2002): 254–81.

Suzuki, Masao. "Success Story? Japanese Immigrant Achievement and Return Migration, 1920–1930." *Journal of Economic History* 55, no. 4 (1995): 889–901.

Tabb, William K. *The Political Economy of the Black Ghetto.* New York: Norton, 1970.

Telles, Edward E. "Racial Inequality among the Brazilian Population." *Ethnic and Racial Studies* 25 (May 2002): 415–41.

Telles, Edward E., and Nelson Lim. "Does It Matter Who Answers the Race Question? Racial Classification and Income Inequality in Brazil." *Demography* 35 (November 1998): 465–74.

Tomaskovic-Devey, Don, Melvin Thomas, and Kecia Johnson. "Race and the Accumulation of Human Capital across the Career: A Theoretical Model and Fixed Effects Application." *American Journal of Sociology* 11 (July 2005): 58–89.

Treiman, Donald, Matthew McKeever, and Eva Fodor. "Racial Differences in Occupational Status and Income in South Africa, 1980 and 1991." *Demography* 33 (February1996): 111–32.

Tribble, Romie, Jr. "A Restatement of the S-Curve Hypothesis." *Review of Development Economics* 3 (June 1999): 207–14.

Whatley, Warren. "African-American Strikebreaking from the Civil War to the New Deal." *Social Science History* 17 (Winter 1993): 525–58.

Williams, Walter. *Do the RIGHT Thing: The People's Economist Speaks.* Palo Alto, Calif.: Hoover Institution Press, 1995.

Yinger, John. "Access Denied, Access Constrained: Results and Implications of the 1989 Housing Discrimination Study." In *Clear and Convincing Evidence: Measurement of Discrimination in America*, ed. Michael Fix and Raymond J. Struyk. Washington, D.C.: Urban Institute Press, 1993.

Yinger, John. "Evidence on Discrimination in Consumer Markets." *Journal of Economic Perspectives* 12 (Spring 1998): 23–40.

CHRONOLOGY

1419   Portuguese explorers reach Porto Santo, one of the Madeira Islands, beginning contact with West African coastal communities.

1479   Spain becomes engaged in the slave trade of Africans.

1492   Columbus's first voyage of "discovery" opens Europe to the prospects of colonization of the Americas.

1492   Expulsion of the Sephardic Jews from Spain at the apex of the Inquisition prompts a substantial migration on their part to the Americas, where they play an important role in the development of the slave plantation system there.

1500   Kingdoms of Kongo and Benin are at the pinnacles of their power and development.

1502–18   Spanish-born Africans are transported to the Americas as slaves to work in mines.

1527   Married black slaves in Mexico are permitted to purchase their freedom for twenty pieces of gold.

1543   Bartolomé de Las Casas, in seeking to relieve the indigenous peoples of Spain's colonies from oppressive labor, recommends their replacement with Africans imported from Spain.

1562   British involvement in the slave trade of Africans begins.

1570   Portuguese establish a colony in Angola.

1619   Slave trade extends to the importation of Africans to North America.

1641   Massachusetts becomes the first British colony to legalize slavery.

1642   French involvement in the slave trade of Africans begins.

1647   Swedish involvement in the slave trade of Africans begins.

1650   Success of Brazil's sugar refineries, reliant on enslaved African labor, owned and operated by Sephardic Jews in the provinces of Pernambuco and Bahia.

1697   Danish involvement in the slave trade of Africans begins.

1739   Spain grants a thirty-year *asiento* to Britain to import slaves into Spanish colonies.

1760–1800 Height of the Triangular Trade, centered on the slavery trade between Europe, Africa, and the Americas.

1772   Granville Sharp convinces the British judiciary to declare that slavery cannot be practiced in England.

1784   Denmark prohibits participation of its nationals in the slave trade.

1787   Abolition society formed in England, led by Thomas Clarkson, Granville Sharp, and Josiah Wedgwood.

1804   Former French slave colony of Saint Domingue achieves independence as the nation of Haiti after a successful revolution conducted primarily by enslaved blacks.

1807   Britain prohibits the participation of its nationals in the slave trade.

1808   United States prohibits the importation of new slaves. The law does not prohibit the internal slave trade.

1810   Mexican Declaration of Independence includes the abolition of slavery in Mexico.

1833   British emancipation of slaves in the West Indies colonies, with a five-year apprenticeship proviso.

1838   Comprehensive emancipation of slaves in the British West Indies colonies.

1850   Fugitive Slave Act enacted by the U.S. Congress.

1857   U.S. Supreme Court declares *Dred Scott v. Sanford* decision, holding that slaves are not eligible for citizenship and that slavery is permitted in all U.S. territories.

1859   John Brown leads a raid on Harpers Ferry, Virginia, with the intent of sparking a revolt of enslaved blacks throughout the United States.

1861   Secession of the Southern states leads to the onset of the Civil War in the United States.

1863   President Lincoln issues the Emancipation Proclamation during the U.S. Civil War.

1865   President Andrew Johnson, successor to Lincoln after the latter's assassination, abrogates the promise of forty acres and a mule to the ex-slaves.

1865–70 Passage and ratification of the Reconstruction amendments to the U.S. Constitution, 13th, 14th, and 15th amendments.

1868–70 Reconstruction-era legislatures in the former states of the Confederacy, heavily influenced by newly enfranchised black voters, provide universal public schooling, universal male suffrage, and home rule, and abolish the whipping post, branding irons, and stocks as state-sanctioned forms of punishment.

1878	President Rutherford B. Hayes withdraws U.S. troops from the South, thereby formally ending Reconstruction and inaugurating nearly a century of black disenfranchisement throughout the region.
1880	Spain abolishes the practice of slavery in Cuba.
1888	The gradual abolition of slavery is inaugurated in Brazil.
1890–1915	Consolidation of legal segregation and anti-black violence in the U.S. South.
1896	*Plessy v. Ferguson* decision by the U.S. Supreme Court establishes the doctrine of "separate but equal."
1898	White riot in Wilmington, N.C.—the culmination of a white terror campaign to eliminate black political participation in the state—signals the end of Fusion government in North Carolina and throughout the South.
1899	W. E. B. Du Bois publishes *The Philadelphia Negro* (Du Bois, 1899).
1899–1902	The Boer War in South Africa.
1944	Eric Williams publishes *Capitalism and Slavery.*
1944	Gunnar Myrdal publishes *An American Dilemma* (Myrdal, 1944).
1948	Oliver Cox publishes *Caste, Class and Race.*
1948	Official inauguration of apartheid in the Republic of South Africa.
1954	*Brown v. Board of Education* decision, U.S. Supreme Court, overturns the *Plessy v. Ferguson* precedent.
1964	Passage of the Civil Rights Act of 1964, U.S. Congress.
1978	Bakke decision declared by U.S. Supreme Court, ruling that rigid use of racial quotas in higher-education admissions policies is unconstitutional.
1988	Passage of American Civil Liberties Act that provided reparations for Japanese Americans incarcerated during World War II.
1994	Formal end of apartheid in the Republic of South Africa.
2003	Grutter and Gratz decisions declared by the U.S. Supreme Court, approving race-sensitive criteria for college admissions.

GLOSSARY

Affirmative Action. An antidiscrimination measure that attempts by the use of either quotas or preferential criteria, or a combination of both, to include members of groups in positions from which they have been subjected to exclusion or significant underrepresentation.

Apartheid. The system of legally enforced racial separation practiced officially in the Republic of South Africa from 1948 until 1994. It was a system that effectively established conditions of white privilege.

Armed Forces Qualification Test (AFQT). The AFQT primary aptitude test used by the U.S. armed forces to determine eligibility for military service. For purposes of establishing national norms for the test, it was administered to respondents to the National Longitudinal Survey of Youth (NLSY) in 1980. Subsequently, numerous researchers have interpreted the scores appended to the 1980 NLSY as measures of certain human-capital attributes, for example, cognitive skills, IQ, and educational quality, previously treated as unobservables in other large, random national data sets. Inclusion of the AFQT scores—instead of educational attainment, and without measures of psychological capital—as variables influencing wages or earnings in regression analyses significantly reduces evidence of discrimination in employment in U.S. labor markets.

Audit Studies. Audit studies involve the use of trained paired testers in the field who are utilized for the purpose of detecting direct evidence of discrimination on the part of employers, real estate agents, or other persons engaged in market activities where they have discretion over whom to hire, serve, or privilege.

Blinder-Oaxaca Decomposition. A statistical procedure introduced into economics by Alan Blinder and Ronald Oaxaca for the purpose of detecting discrimination in labor markets. It seeks to sort between the portion of the gap in wages or earnings between groups that is due to differences in average levels of human capital and differential treatment of comparable levels of human capital (the latter is interpreted as evidence of discrimination). The procedure actually was developed earlier, in a slightly different form, by sociologists Peter Blau and Otis Dudley Duncan.

Collective Dysfunctionality. The hypothesis that a group that displays inferior social outcomes falls into such a pattern because of cultural and/or genetic deficiency.

Discrimination, Economic. A condition where individuals from a particular social group, delineated by race, ethnicity, phenotype, or gender, with similar levels of productivity as members of another group are assigned lower rewards because their ascriptive characteristics are denigrated. Rewards are assigned prejudicially when economic discrimination is operative.

Discrimination, Statistical. A condition that arises when individuals from a particular group are assigned rewards based upon the employer's or selector's beliefs about the productivity attributes of the group to which the individual is perceived to belong. For example, suppose an employer believes that members of group A are drawn from a frequency distribution with a lower mean productivity and a higher variance in productivity than members of group B. If employers are risk-averse and uncertain about the exact productivity of candidates from group A and group B, employers may infer that their odds are better of getting a higher quality worker from group B. They then become less likely to hire workers from group A, or more likely to pay workers from group B a higher wage. They need not have any aversion toward persons from group A. They are simply making economic use of the information they have at hand. As their information about any individual worker improves, enabling them to better predict their performance regardless of the group from which they are drawn, economic theorists would predict that statistical discrimination would decline.

Field Experiments. *See* Audit Studies.

Genocide. The act of attempting to exterminate a people.

Human Capital. The acquired and developed set of attributes an individual possesses that are viewed as being associated with his or her productivity in the workplace. These typically include educational attainment (including years of schooling and quality of schooling), previous work experience, motivation, and tenure at a specific job.

Intergenerational Transmission. The movement of tangible and intangible practices and resources from ancestors to descendants.

Internal Colony. A citizen population subjugated within their own country in a fashion that parallels the subjugation visited upon a people whose country is occupied by invaders from abroad.

Inverted U-Curve. *See* Kuznets Hypothesis.

Jim Crow System. The system of legally enforced racial segregation established in the United States of America, more pronouncedly in the Southern states, that existed largely from 1876 through the mid-1960s. It was a system that effectively established conditions of white privilege throughout the United States.

Kuznets Hypothesis. A hypothesis attributed to Simon Kuznets that as a country experiences economic growth it will first experience a rise in income inequality, and then after a threshold level of per capita income is reached, it will experience a decline in income inequality. Kuznets advanced the hypothesis in a far more qualified and tempered manner than many of his intellectual disciples.

Premarket Factors. The circumstances that shaped a person's human-capital characteristics that are presented to potential employers when the person enters the market for employment. Those circumstances ostensibly occur outside of, or prior to, entry into the labor market.

Productivity. Productivity refers to the level at which an individual or team of workers fulfills a task or performs a job. Employment that involves the production of physical output may be susceptible to direct measurement of an individual's or a team's performance. Frequently, an individual's potential in terms of productivity is estimated or measured by the set of human-capital characteristics the person possesses.

Psychological Capital. The array of mental-health and mental-strength attributes an individual has acquired or developed that can contribute to workplace productivity. Psychological capital can include motivation and positive self-esteem.

Reparations. Steps taken to compensate an individual, a group, or a people for having been subjected to a grievous injustice.

Stratification Economics. A newly emerging branch of economics, arising in direct counterpoint to the collective-dysfunctionality perspective, that advances analyses of intergroup inequalities, focusing on structural sources of disparities and power differentials.

American Political Systems and the Response of the Black Community

Ronald Walters

Abstract

Black politics is a set of behaviors that has been developed by black leaders and the constituency they represent to fight against racial oppression. Historically, it has been the primary activity through which the interests of the black community have been accommodated. Analyses and descriptions of this historical process have been concerned with the distinctive sectional quality of politics in the South, given the legacy of slavery, but they have also been concerned with factors that have shaped political systems of the entire nation in each era. As such, I use the conceptual devices of these political systems as a foil against which to exhibit the related leadership, issues, and strategies as well as the responses they elicited.

To be sure, the political relationship between blacks and whites is regarded here as a dynamic "conflict system" that has been conducted under rules that arise within the general framework of a governance that has historically described itself as a democracy. Thus, a major problem of analysis has been to understand how the objectives and actions of African Americans have affected the various political systems under which they have lived.

During British colonialism, the new United States of America, the Civil War, Reconstruction, the rise of the white South and the Great Depression, the post–World War II era, and the rise of neoconservatism, the status of blacks has modulated, causing a responsive agenda that has led blacks to take either an offensive attitude toward expanded opportunities, or a defensive set of tactics and strategies to maintain their forward progress in others. Running through most of the scholarship on this subject—whether the concern is with voting rights, political mobilization, changes in public policy representation, or the policies themselves—is pessimism about the ability of black politics to mobilize the power to prevail. Nevertheless, a primary feature of black politics is consistency in the attempts to utilize and perfect various political tactics to create the power necessary to transform the subordinate position of the black community in the social order.

Introduction

Scholars attempting to conceptualize the use of power by blacks in the political system have examined the issue from various perspectives, including the social context of political mobilization, the effectiveness of various tactics of mobilization, and the history of attempts to negate the exclusion of blacks from fair access to the social institutions. The acquisition of political rights was important to blacks not only as a badge of citizenship, but as a necessary tool in the competition to acquire the requisite social benefits political empowerment brings.

In this context, it has been axiomatic for some scholars, represented by Hanes Walton, to perceive black politics as having been shaped by black exclusion from the larger society.[1] But while this view emphasizes the subordinate status of blacks in the political process, it devalues the emergence of a coherent culture that was and is the basis of black political ideology and mobilization. While racism and exclusion help to define black politics, the existence of a significant black culture in America means that there would have been a political manifestation in any case, as happened with other groups. Professor Mack Jones is an example of those who regard black politics as requiring a different frame of reference to express the unique condition in which black people have existed in America, which informs their politics.[2] Jones's view is consistent with Walton's, both asserting that in the larger political system dominated by whites, blacks constitute a subordinate group that is characterized by various challenges to alleviate the oppressive circumstances created by that status—producing, in effect, a "conflict system."[3]

This conflict has had an inevitable sectional quality. While the North provided relatively more elastic avenues for a better way of life, the South was the main battlefield in the efforts of blacks to free themselves from slavery and entrenched patterns of postslavery racism. After slavery, the national struggle has been characterized by the attempt of blacks to counter various forms of racism that have impeded their efforts to achieve equality with whites in every vital category of life in every section of the country. The attempt of blacks to utilize a politics of conflict to improve their status has produced a legacy of citizenship rights and principles that have enriched the practice of democracy for all people in American society. The conflict system assumes that black political behavior is based on a model of conflict that constitutes a historical dialectic of efforts by whites to limit the opportunities of blacks and control their social function, inviting challenges by blacks to expand the freedoms they might enjoy. Therefore, insofar as the paradigm that was constructed as the national blueprint for the governance of the nation offers the promise of freedom to all, the deviations in the structure and function of that governance and the challenge by blacks have, historically, created formidable political issues. These issues, such as abolishing slavery, Reconstruction, post-Reconstruction subordination, the Civil Rights Movement, and others may be viewed as political subsystems to the main politics of the day, but with a racial impact that either constitutes new barriers to the fulfillment of democratic inclusion or facilitates the quest for true democracy.

A political system is the way in which authority is exercised by the state and responded to by society. Within the social system, however, there are various groups, and as Charles Merriam once said, "In examining the roots of government, it is essential to explore the nature of the association or groups with which government is concerned."[4] "To this extent," he continues, "as government is consistently concerned with equilibrium, it manages the affairs of various groups in accordance with their challenges and needs and, once the need or advantage of governance is generally recognized whether through consent, duress, prestige, or other elements of cohesion, the governmental power comes into being [in order to address it]." That equilibrium is expressed as "common interests," and group dynamics are driven by government to achieve that goal.

David Easton also followed this argument in his trilogy on the political system in which he declared that the study of political life can be described as a set of social interactions, essentially between government using its authority and individuals and groups.[5] While there are many such groups and categories of groups—that is, religious, economic, and so on—this essay will concentrate on the processes involved in the response of government to the racial category in its group relations.

The nature of these various subsystems, or political systems, began before the Declaration of Independence became a living fact, when slavery, in the context of British colonialism, characterized the first political system as the dominant form of control for blacks in America. Although slavery was introduced in the American colonies as an economic model for the use of African labor, in its comprehensive terms it defined the entire set of relationships between the African peoples and their white colonial masters. After the British colonial system fell, the newly formed United States of America created a political system that codified the basic relationship of an enhanced central government to its states. This system lasted until the Civil War, when, with the South defeated, Northern political interests shaped the public policies and power relationships of the political system. Thereafter, the gradual return of the South to functional regional authority by the deference of Northern politicians created a substantial change in American political culture at both the state and national levels that legitimized the ruthless resubordination of blacks. Two major challenges affected this system: the Depression of the 1930s and World War II, both of which led to a substantial expansion of government services in the lives of citizens. These factors helped provide the foundation for the Civil Rights Movement; ironically a conservative movement emerged in reaction that became the dominant force in American politics and government into the twenty-first century.

Each of these political eras affected the status of blacks somewhat differently, causing a responsive agenda that either led blacks to take an aggressive attitude toward the expanded opportunities that existed in one era, or a defensive set of tactics and strategies to maintain their progress in others. While it is clear that both offensive and defensive movements were permanent features of black politics, still, the critical changes in the political system created a difference in emphasis as well.

This analysis, therefore, will present a narrative of critical historical events that affected the political status of black people in America as the backdrop against which to recognize important problems and aspects of that behavior, as well as vital debates about their meaning.

Colonialism

British colonialism was the political system within which slavery grew and became legitimate in America. For nearly forty years after the landing of British settlers in Jamestown, Virginia, in 1619, the legal status of Africans gradually changed from indentured servants with certain terms of service, to servants in a perpetual state of servitude.[6] The first African held for life was John Punch of Virginia. For his attempt to flee his condition, the court decided in 1640 that he was to "serve his said master or his assigns for the time of his natural life here or elsewhere."[7] In 1641, Massachusetts passed the first laws defining Africans as slaves. By 1661, Virginia passed a law defining Africans as being in a status of "durante vita," or slaves for life.[8] British colonialism was the cauldron within which slavery was legitimized and by which it was regulated, because of the vast wealth the American colonies generated for Britain's national welfare and global designs.

When the settlers in the American colonies broke with the British and became rulers of the new nation by virtue of the revolution in 1776, most of the African population was enslaved. The first census of the United States of America in 1790 found over 750,000 Africans altogether—about 60,000 of that number constituting a free population, mostly in the North.[9] Each of the states regulated the conduct of slavery, and each slave state had a body of laws known as the slave codes, which set forth in some detail the relations between master and slave, confirmed the slave's status as a person without rights, and defined the conditions under which manumission might occur.

The existence of slavery also affected the rights of the so-called black freedmen. The opposition to their intermediate status between slavery and freedom was the stimulus for the initial politics of civil rights, as individual blacks used the courts to claim their freedom and demand their civil rights. In the nineteenth century, there were several well-known cases involving blacks in New England whose status as slaves was extended past the promised term, causing some to file lawsuits for their freedom that they eventually won.[10] The courts were also used in early attempts to obtain the right to vote. Many free blacks in New England voted, but others were prohibited by custom and tradition rather than law, marking the ambiguous status of blacks as citizens. Moreover, the tensions created by the effort of blacks to obtain a position in the workplace alienated many whites, making gainful employment with which to support a family difficult.[11]

Nevertheless, by 1787 blacks were bold enough to demand equal access to education. One of their first petitions to the Massachusetts legislature held that despite their fidelity in paying an equal share of taxes for the burdens of the colony, "we are of the opinion that we do not have the right to enjoy privileges of free men." They asked that provisions be made by the colony to have their children educated.[12] Thus, they utilized the argument of no taxation without representation, which was an underlying cause of the American Revolution.

By degrees, blacks understood that organizations formed to secure their rights would be more effective than individual petitions. Perhaps taking advantage of the spirit of revolutionary change, a series of mutual-aid societies were founded in New York, Boston, and Newport. In New York they also formed the African Free School. Other organizations, such as the Prince Hall Masonic lodges, were established as early as 1784. The Free African Society, founded in Philadelphia on April 12, 1787, by two well-known free blacks, Absolom Jones and Richard Allen, was the forerunner of the first African American church in the city in 1794.[13]

The New Nation

The promulgation of a constitution by the thirteen colonies of the United States was at first a failure, because the Continental Congress (1781) had created a central governmental structure as a "confederacy" with a loose association among the states. This was done in part to pacify the slaveholding states of the country, and had given them cause to justify their support of the Union—a concern reflected, to a lesser extent, in the Constitution that became permanent in 1789. Thus, the era contained a second political system, one that legitimized the practice of slavery; while abolishing the slave trade in 1808, it resolved the thorny problems of the basis of Southern representation and taxation by declaring that slaves constituted three-fifths of a person for the allocation of seats in Congress. But it did not resolve the question of the status of the citizenship of the freed African American population, which by 1850 had grown to well over 300,000. That was resolved in 1857 by the decision of the Supreme Court in the Dred Scott case, which placed blacks totally outside constitutional protection, defining blacks as individuals incapable of becoming citizens. Chief Justice Roger Taney, speaking for the majority of the Court, said: "We think they [people of African descent] are not included . . . under the word 'citizens' in the constitution, and can therefore claim none of the rights and privileges which that instrument provides for and secures to citizens of the United States."[14] In any case, blacks continued to mobilize to end slavery, oppose extradition, and attain American citizenship, largely through the efforts of the National Convention of Colored Men, and the leadership of men such as Frederick Douglass, who held that this decision was promulgated by the "slave-holding" wing of the Supreme Court.[15]

In 1829 David Walker wrote his famous "Appeal to the Colored Citizens of the World," arguing fiercely against slavery, saying that if freedom were not voluntarily given to blacks, they should take it.[16] That sentiment motivated Nat Turner, a minister in Virginia, and on August 21, 1831, in Southampton, Virginia, he struck for freedom in a violent rebellion that was the climax of three years of militant actions against slavery all over the region. In this era, these actions were augmented by those of others—not only Frederick Douglass, but important women such as Sojourner Truth and Harriet Tubman, the venerable "Moses" of her people, who literally brought many blacks out of slavery to freedom in the North and into Canada. Frederick Douglass, a former slave, agitated for an end to slavery—as the publisher of a black newspaper, *The North Star*, and as a spellbinding orator associated with William Lloyd Garrison, who founded the American Anti-Slavery Society. Douglass became the foremost black leader of the nineteenth century.

But as suggested above, there was also the emergence of a significant black organization, the National Convention of Colored Men, which was the pioneer of the Negro Convention Movement beginning in 1830. Like the Colored Association of Boston, Massachusetts, the agenda of this national organization was dedicated to opposing slavery and winning civil and human rights for black people. As a black abolitionist organization, it adopted the Garrisonian platform of "moral suasion," though in their Buffalo Convention of 1843, Henry Highland Garnet, a young militant, placed a resolution on the floor that called for the violent overthrow of slavery. His motion was defeated by just one vote.[17]

The fight to abolish American slavery was for many a losing cause, and like Garnet, many believed that it called for a radical solution—perhaps emigration to some more compatible region of the world. Some perceived accurately that even the American Colonization Society, while otherwise opposed to slavery, had not adopted a positive position supporting American citizenship of former slaves, arguing that blacks and whites could not coexist in society on equal terms. Perhaps because that thought was fueled by some cultural sympathy with the English belief of African inferiority, it was vehemently opposed by black leaders. Nevertheless, Rev. Garnet and a prominent supporter of African emigration, Martin Delany, made a trip to Africa in 1859 to seek out a suitable place for blacks to emigrate from the United States. And although they found the coast of West Africa (Liberia, Sierra Leone) to be somewhat suitable, their proposal was never considered seriously, perhaps because of the coming of the Civil War. The National Convention of Colored Men and others continued to oppose emigration as a solution to slavery, instead urging free blacks to invest their future in America.

Black leaders took hope from the places in the North where blacks could participate in politics. While the right to vote was accorded blacks episodically

Harriet Tubman (far left, photographed in 1900), an ex-slave who escaped from her masters, became a guide for the Underground Railroad, the movement that helped slaves escape to Canada or to the Northern states. Known as the "Black Moses," she was renowned for her bravery and cunning, and was never caught, despite a $40,000 bounty for her capture.

in many states, in the New England states of Maine, Massachusetts, Vermont, and Rhode Island, blacks voted without restrictions. But even in the North, where Republican-controlled state legislatures supported the franchise for blacks, Democrats largely opposed it. Moreover, Professor Walton shows that as the racial conflict resulted in a Civil War, black voting declined from a high of twelve territories (that later would become states) in 1700 to less than half that number of states by 1864.[18] In the South, however, the Democratic Party was the party of slavery, and it dominated the region and largely excluded blacks from political participation—although a few blacks who could meet the property and other qualifications were allowed to vote, so long as the number did not threaten white control. White control would be broken only briefly by the Civil War.

One of the early debates by black leaders was whether or not they should support the Liberty Party, founded in 1840, which carried an antislavery plank in its platform, or the Republican Party, founded in 1854, which had not yet proposed to eliminate slavery. The Liberty Party cultivated many of the leading black abolitionists of that day—for example, supporting John Mercer Langston, an Oberlin graduate, in his election to the position of town clerk in Brownhelm, Ohio, in 1855, becoming apparently the first black person elected to public office. He helped move the Republican Party in Ohio toward a strong antislavery position. Other blacks supported prominent Republicans, including presidential candidate Abraham Lincoln, whose winning effort elevated him to the White House on the eve of the Civil War.

Post Civil War

The end of the Civil War ushered in a new political era. Because the North had won the war, it was far more congenial to African freedom from slavery, and to participation in the life of the nation as citizens. Thus, at the end of the war, the control of Congress by a radical Republican faction made possible the enactment of a new constitutional framework of citizenship, bounded by the 13th Amendment, which stated that "Neither slavery nor involuntary servitude, except as a punishment for crime whereof the party shall have been duly convicted, shall exist within the United States, or any place subject to their jurisdiction." The 14th Amendment followed, guaranteeing citizens of the United States equal protection and due process of law, and the 15th Amendment forbade any state to deny citizens the right to vote due to their race or color and previous condition of servitude. The effect of these laws was to accord blacks a relatively temporary license to participate in the body politic as equals with whites. Beginning in 1870, with the adoption of the 15th Amendment, blacks contributed substantial margins of victory to Republican candidates for president and local offices.

The politics of Reconstruction, which were meant to bring blacks into the Union as full citizens, conflicted with another political objective, which was to repair the national rupture between North and South caused by the Civil War. Black rights became expendable, and the promises of the post–Civil

War amendments were violated by politicians in both sections of the country in order to achieve national unity.

This era wrote a powerful paean to the fact that race could be a more dominant factor in America than the pursuit of the democracy that brought the divorce from Britain, or that American democracy could be deployed within the dominant group to the exclusion of all others. Thus, the struggle for power by blacks has been marked by the effort to widen the circle of rights and opportunities to expand the meaning of democracy for blacks and others who experience some form of oppression.

As Frederick Douglass was a tireless advocate for the abolition of slavery prior to the Civil War, he became equally effective in his demand for the franchise afterward as an instrument of personal citizenship and group empowerment. His alliance with Republican president Abraham Lincoln gave him a standing in that party as the leader of blacks in a coalition that was a critical element in electing Republican presidents, members of Congress, and many state and local officials in the period between 1868 and 1872. One could make the case that with the political participation of blacks based on their new legal status as citizens, the post–Civil War political era was, indeed, one not envisioned by the original founding fathers.

This new political era appeared to offer an abundance of opportunities for blacks to participate as full citizens, especially since the power of the white South, which had been their main oppressor, was in the hands of pro-Union victors. The Civil Rights Act of 1875 was passed, giving blacks access to public accommodations, foreshadowing the 1964 Civil Rights Act. White Southerners considered it a "force act" and began an aggressive guerrilla movement to oppose it and to regain power in the region through violent, extralegal groups—one of which, the Ku Klux Klan, originally emerged in winter 1865–1866.

Nevertheless, the 15th Amendment had opened the way for blacks to vote for black candidates, who were elected to office in a variety of positions across the South. In consecutive elections from 1864 to 1876, blacks contributed a significant number of votes to the Republican Party victories, as over 700,000 became registered by 1867.[19] But that level of participation was not to be sustained, as the Republican margin of victory in the 1872 presidential election was 763,474 votes, while their margin in the 1880 presidential election was only 1,898. Republicans won the presidential election of 1876 by only 9,500 votes, and Democrats won the election of 1880.[20] This signaled to many Republican politicians the necessity to court Southern Democrats, a step which meant that they had to sacrifice the principle of Reconstruction and the citizenship rights of blacks.

As a result, the participation of blacks as voters and officeholders began to be challenged after the infamous "Hayes Bargain," when the presidential election in 1876 between Democrat Samuel Tilden and Republican Rutherford B. Hayes deadlocked in the electoral college and the two parties had to negotiate the problem. The result gave the victory to Hayes, who promised to remove Union troops from the South—an act which exposed blacks to the fury of renewed white supremacy.

The Civil Rights Act of 1875 was declared unconstitutional by the Supreme Court in the 1883 civil rights cases by a logic that construed the 14th Amendment as applying only to the federal citizenship of blacks, leaving the states free to treat them as they might, so long as they appeared not to contravene federal privileges and immunities. This legal path of black citizenship rights spiraled downward, ending with the Supreme Court decision in the *Plessy v. Ferguson* case of 1896.[21] This decision established the "separate but equal" doctrine, which held that the separate access of the races to public accommodations could be justified as long as they were provided on an equal basis. For much of the twentieth century, it was the legal capstone of racial exclusion. Blacks were intended to be made totally subordinate to whites once again, through the intimidating effect of lynching and the reestablishment of white political power, regardless of the numerical strength of the black population. To ensure this outcome, whites amended the state constitutions to create laws that denied blacks access to the polls, and thus the opportunity for elective office. Between 1870 and 1900, twenty-two blacks had served in the Congress of the United States.

Two blacks served in the U.S. Senate—Hiram Rhodes Revels and Blanche K. Bruce, both from Mississippi—and twenty in the House. Of these twenty-two black members of Congress, sixteen were elected in the period 1870 to 1975, but only six from 1883 to 1897, suggesting that the decline fostered by the latter part of the Reconstruction had set in, and by 1901 they were all gone. This situation was replicated at state and local levels as well.

Thus began the period of what Professor Rayford Logan called "the Nadir" in his *The Negro in American Life and Thought: The Nadir, 1877–1901* (1954).[22] Blacks began the twentieth century in a state of only nominal freedom. They were victims of cultural attitudes, prevalent most notably in the South, imposing racial stereotypes that questioned their humanity, physical subordination to a system of labor often worse than slavery, and political exclusion.

The "New Negro" and the Protest Era

The new century produced a social group called the "New Negro," a term coined by Dr. Alain LeRoy Locke, a professor of philosophy at Howard University, in an essay by that name in a special issue of *Survey Graphic* devoted to the Harlem Renaissance, which he guest-edited.[23] He observed a significant cadre of pugnacious college-educated blacks who were determined to throw off the racial stereotype of slavery's past and establish a new identity based on their professional achievements in such fields as law, business, education, and the arts. Attendant to the growth of this group was the parallel development of civil rights organizations. The turn of the twentieth century had spawned several such organizations, especially in the North, to oppose not only racial subordination, but also the complementary program that Booker T. Washington and his powerful white allies in business and education had devised for blacks.

Although Washington may have had good reasons for advocating industrial education to promote the economic progress of African Americans and submission to white rule by blacks in the South of that day, the Northern militant anti-Bookerites were determined to promote higher education and political participation on equal terms with whites — determined that Washington's formula would not become the national model for black advancement. Building on the early National Negro Conventions, the movement continued with the 1906 Niagara Convention, which contributed to the birth of the

National Association for the Advancement of Colored People (NAACP) in 1909 and the formation of the National Urban League (NUL) in 1910, among other organizations.

A most auspicious development was that led by Marcus Mosiah Garvey, a Jamaican immigrant whose oratory and organizing skill attracted blacks to support one of the largest black nationalist movements in American history. Garvey espoused ideas of autonomous black development, business acumen in support of Booker T. Washington's ideas, a strong connection with Africa (even to the point of return), and the creation of black cultural institutions— such as a religious order, a women's auxiliary, and a newspaper (*The African World*). This movement, begun in 1915 in Jamaica, became popular in the United States in the 1920s, but its focus upon black nationalism became attractive among African-descended peoples around the world.[24]

Meanwhile, Dr. W. E. B. Du Bois and other leaders supported the presidential campaign of conservative Democrat Woodrow Wilson in 1912 because Republicans had turned their backs on blacks. Once elected, Wilson supported racial segregation in the nation's capital, but this treachery did not end the attempt of black leaders to find a solution to racial injustice. The answer came from Franklin D. Roosevelt, elected president in 1932 with a significant black vote in response to his program of lifting the nation out of the doldrums of the economic depression by opening employment opportunities in federally subsidized programs. While the shift of the black vote to the Democratic Party in presidential elections began to occur in 1932, by 1936 most wards in large Northern cities where the black population was over 50 percent, such as in Baltimore, Maryland; Detroit, Michigan; Kansas City, Missouri; and Pittsburgh, Pennsylvania, were voting for Roosevelt.[25] So, by 1936, the political transition of blacks to the Democratic Party had been made, and in 1948 the party included a historic plank in its national platform opposing racial segregation. That decisive step split the Democratic Party's Northern and Southern factions that year, and the differences within the party grew as the emerging challenge of the Civil Rights Movement produced a cleavage between those who supported civil rights and those who opposed them.

Dr. Ralph Bunche, a Howard University Professor who served as a research assistant to Dr. Gunnar Myrdal in his famous study *An American*

Dilemma: The Negro Problem and Modern Democracy (1944), was scathing in his assessment of black political leadership in view of the growing political importance of blacks. In his memoranda to Myrdal, he excoriated the political subservience of the black leadership class in the South that, in many places, was the backbone of political machines dominated by whites, as in Memphis, Atlanta, Birmingham, and other cities.[26] Indeed, Robert Smith points to the nascent studies of black political leadership by Matthews and Prothro, Everett Ladd, James Q. Wilson, and especially Harold Gosnell (1935), who refer to black leadership as "functional" or "operational."[27] Beyond that, they developed relatively crude categories, grouping leaders by their stylistic characteristics, such as "militant," "moderate," "race-men," or "accommodationists." Wilson came closest to suggesting that the critical distinction was one based on agenda, whether or not they utilized the "race values" of uplift, pride, solidarity, and service in pursuit of black progress.[28]

Prevailing studies of black leadership also identified the modus operandi of power as the determinant of leadership style and values. An agenda of change, not style, became the most critical aspect defining black leadership, although it was approached historically from many different directions. For example, as black scholars noted in the 1930s, the combination of events abroad, such as the Russian Revolution that initiated a regime dedicated to fostering racial equality as well as raising questions about the values of capitalism, stimulated soul-searching examinations among blacks as to whether their ideological allegiance to either capitalism or socialism would yield the positive change desired in the black condition.[29] This group, strongly influenced by socialism, confronted older black leaders such as W. E. B. Du Bois at the Second Amenia Conference in 1933, sponsored by the NAACP, and in other venues to propose alliance with the American working class through the emerging labor-union movement.[30] The seeds of this internal struggle manifested themselves among the more radical socialists with allegiance to the Communist Party of the United States of America (CPUSA), provoking a debate about whether the critical impediment to black progress, and therefore the most important target, was race or class, racism or the capitalist system. At issue also was the transition of leadership to a new generation that would intensify the use of various tactics and strategies begun in an earlier era, such as electoral politics, agenda building, community organization, demonstrations, and coalition formations. Most important in the post-World War II period, however, was the use of legal strategies to force open the institutions and eliminate social practices that excluded blacks from the mainstream of society.

World War II and New Possibilities

The seedbed for the rise of a new political system after World War II was created by the promotion of concepts and institutions designed to take the motivation out of the settlement of political problems through violence and antihumanistic means, such as the Nazi-Axis campaign used against Europeans. Yet, black Americans wondered aloud whether they should fight in this war at a time when their own life chances were suppressed under the ugly heel of racism and persistent slave-like conditions. Eventually, the decision to support the war was as much about taking advantage of the new industrial opportunities in employment as it was about defeating German racism. A. Philip Randolph, venerable founder of the Brotherhood of Sleeping Car Porters union, seized the opportunity of an America under duress and threatened a protest march on Washington against the Roosevelt administration in 1941 to open up war industries to blacks. However, the march did not occur, because the blacks inside the Roosevelt administration, led by Mary McLeod Bethune, united with those led by Randolph, constituted a formidable force that caused Roosevelt to sign an executive order integrating the war industries. This was also an admission that blacks migrating north in large numbers in order to take advantage of industrial employment had achieved increasing affluence and corresponding social expectations upon which to base their demand for equality in American society.[31]

In 1935, the National Negro Congress, a progressive organization, came into existence as a response to the impact of the Great Depression on the national black community, and Randolph was the first president. Its strategy in the South placed emphasis on stimulating demands for education and other social services in areas of stark poverty and oppression, using interracial

Gordon Parks / Hulton Archive / Getty Images

In 1904 Mary McLeod Bethune (1875–1955) founded the Daytona Normal and Industrial Institute for Negro Girls (now Bethune-Cookman College). She was a leader in the black women's club movement, served as president of the National Association of Colored Women and later founded the National Council of Negro Women. She worked as a delegate and advisor to national conferences on education, child welfare, and home ownership. Between 1936 and 1944 she acted as director of Negro affairs in the National Youth Administration. During World War II Bethune served as consultant to the US secretary of war and was involved in the selection of the first female officer candidates for the American military. As the vice president of the National Association for the Advancement of Colored People (NAACP), Bethune was awarded the Haitian Medal of Honor and Merit, that country's highest award, in addition to receiving the honor of Commander of the Order of the Star of Africa in Liberia.

alliances where possible. But black Southern leaders were resistant to these organizing efforts because of the group's association with the growing Communist movement, opposed by mainline black organizations. Randolph, Dr. Ralph Bunche, and others withdrew their membership under pressure, and the momentum of the organization weakened as the demand for black support for the Second World War intensified.[32]

The war, black migration, the new black intellectuals, and progressive black organizations fostered a more cosmopolitan ethos within the black community that stimulated civic engagement. One indication of the new outlook is that blacks had not only migrated to many Northern cities, but they had begun to vote in large numbers. According to Henry Lee Moon's analysis, blacks, building on Roosevelt's winning coalitions, made the difference in the close presidential election of 1948, won by Democrat Harry S. Truman.[33] They had assumed an unacknowledged balance of power in American elections, not only by flexing their voting muscles gained by migrating into Northern cities, but also by perceiving that rights such as voting were supported by the postwar emphasis on humanistic principles of governance and by America's vaunted role as a leader in the postwar industrial revolution. The end of the war brought a free flow of liberal ideas and institutions to implement them in the hope that by addressing civil and human rights with fair standards of governance, people would be encouraged to find alternatives to violence.

This new environment provided a leaven to the racism in the American political system. The modern Civil Rights Movement seized the opportunity to strengthen black people's demands for freedom and justice by connecting these humanistic principles to those of liberal American democracy enshrined in the American Constitution and in Judeo-Christian religion.[34]

The emergence of a reinvigorated Civil Rights Movement in the post–World War II period also drew upon its past. To be sure, this movement had never really stopped since the founding of the NAACP and other organizations in the early 1900s, but the postwar period provided the impetus for a new attack. In the early 1950s, the board of directors of the NAACP decided that it was time for a "direct attack" on *Plessy v. Ferguson*, the U.S. Supreme Court decision that established the principle of "separate but equal" treatment before the law.[35] Through legal initiatives begun in the 1930s, the NAACP launched a distinctive legal attack on the *Plessy* decision that methodically tested and weakened the flawed logic that held that racially separate public facilities in America could truly perform on a racially equal basis. The major test was the Supreme Court decision in a combination of cases presented as *Brown v. Board of Education of Topeka, Kansas*, in which the Court concluded on May 17, 1954, that "in the field of public education, the doctrine of 'separate but equal' has no place. Separate educational facilities are inherently unequal."[36]

The new responsibility of the nation to move in the direction decided by the Supreme Court to foster equality in education was initiated during the presidency of Republican war hero Dwight D. Eisenhower. Blacks, like most Americans, voted for Eisenhower in the elections of 1952 and 1956, thus returning briefly to their nineteenth-century roots. However, the candidacy of Senator John F. Kennedy of Massachusetts in 1960 attracted blacks back to the Democratic Party, largely because of his expressed sympathy for the emerging Civil Rights Movement and the fact that in the fall of that year, when Dr. Martin Luther King Jr. was incarcerated in Reidsville, Georgia, State Prison for a misdemeanor traffic offense, Kennedy not only called him to ensure fair treatment, but also used his influence to arrange bail. This began a new phase of stability in the relationship between blacks and the Democratic Party, based on the fulfillment to a substantial degree of the principles of equal justice elucidated in Kennedy's address to the nation on June 11, 1963. On that occasion, Kennedy posed the critical issue:

> The heart of the question is whether all Americans are to be afforded equal rights and equal opportunities, whether we are going to treat our fellow Americans as we want to be treated. If an American, because his skin is dark, cannot eat lunch in a restaurant open to the public, if he cannot send his children to the best public schools available, if he cannot vote for the public officials who will represent him, in short, if he cannot enjoy the full and free life which all of us want, then who among us would be content to have the color of his skin changed and stand in his place? Who among us would then be content with the counsels of patience and delay?[37]

Kennedy was not only referring to the counsel of patience urged by Eisenhower in the crisis over school integration in Little Rock, Arkansas, in 1957; he also sensed the determination of blacks to push that issue to its conclusion. But Kennedy also felt, like Dr. King, Gunnar Myrdal, and others, that a moral question was at issue, and therefore he stated his intention to put before the Congress legislation making discrimination in public accommodation illegal.

Kennedy was assassinated in November of that year, but the combination of the rightness of his formulation and the national mood mourning a president created a currency that Lyndon Johnson, his successor was able to utilize.

The Civil Rights Movement

The history of the Civil Rights Movement is often written from the perspective of those in the formal decision-making process, reflecting the extent to which these official managers of the political system were propelled to action by social forces. Likewise, the iconic references to the activity of Dr. Martin Luther King Jr. to describe this period often overshadows widespread involvement of hundreds of thousands of people of all ages and colors who responded to the leadership of blacks to become involved in projects that changed America by making a direct physical and intellectual challenge to the vestiges of racial subordination. Professor Aldon Morris's foundational study *The Origins of the Civil Rights Movement* (1984) helped to create a consensus among scholars that its birth was sustained by the new attitude of blacks who were willing to test the system to achieve freedom, defined as equality with other Americans. It also required the existence of institutions — most especially the black churches, but also black schools, colleges, and other civic organizations that supported the mobilization of blacks — to mount critical campaigns in the cycles of action.[38]

There is no clear agreement among scholars with respect to the exact sequence of events that led to the Civil Rights Movement. Rather, there is rough understanding that a series of events were important. The 1954 *Brown* decision of the Supreme Court legitimized the fact that blacks and their allies were on the right side of history, giving them confidence that change could be made. The killing of young Emmett Till in Money, Mississippi, for addressing a white woman as "baby" on August 28, 1955, fueled national flames of resentment against race prejudice, awakening the determination of blacks to eliminate such violence. The Montgomery bus boycott in 1955 became the test case that marked the determination of blacks to challenge the institutions of racism; it also turned the attention of the nation to the Deep South as the locus of an array of deep-seated anti-black barriers of social control. The victory of blacks over segregated transportation became a story of the courageous people of that city, providing the foundation for the emergence of Dr. Martin Luther King Jr. as a leader with courage and the ability to articulate the pain of oppression that blacks had experienced since slavery. Montgomery stimulated the formation of the Southern Christian Leadership Conference (SCLC) and was accompanied by bus rides to challenge segregation in interstate transportation, by voting-registration campaigns in Albany and Birmingham, by the March on Washington in 1963, and by the crucial voting-rights mobilization in Selma, Alabama, in 1965 that dramatically demonstrated to the nation the massive violence with which voting rights for blacks in the South were suppressed.

A vital spark for these events was the emergence of the student movement—at first by units of the NAACP youth chapters, and later by the Student Nonviolent Coordinating Committee (SNCC), born in 1960 in the wake of the sit-in movement that had begun in the Midwest late in the 1950s and spread southward to Greensboro, North Carolina, and beyond. The SNCC was deployed in some of the most dangerous areas of the South and was the focal point of the "Freedom Summer" of 1964, when many students from around the country gathered to push for an open society in the South.[39] The massive challenge before black leaders was to forge collective black leadership to confront the political system of the postwar-era racism. That emerged in the coordinated action of the "big five" organizations—the NAACP, SCLC, SNCC, NUL, and the Congress of Racial Equality (CORE). Such collective leadership was necessary. Although the rough division of labor often led to clashes of agenda and strategy, it also made possible the management of a large and unwieldy movement through some degree of collaboration.

While historians have largely devalued the role of black female organizations in this pantheon of collective leadership, women were represented in each of the major events by such groups as the National Council of Negro Women, beginning with the mobilization that led to the March on Washington. This legacy, however, goes back to the role of distinguished civil rights activists such as Sojourner Truth, Ida B. Wells-Barnett, Angelina Grimké, Mary McCloud Bethune, and others. The record of black women's contribution to the struggle for civil rights historically is far from complete. It includes heroic projects, such as Wells-Barnett's anti-lynching campaign and the role of the Circle of Peace and Human Relations in sponsoring the Pan African Conference in New York City in 1927. Dr. Bethune's leadership as chairwoman of the so-called Black Cabinet during the Roosevelt administration was astounding for a woman in the black community at any time. Dr. Bethune's successor, Dorothy I. Height, was a participant in the planning of the March on Washington and other related events. Coretta Scott King and Rosa Parks assumed iconic roles as the "mothers" of the Civil Rights Movement in the postmovement era: Parks's initiation of the Montgomery bus boycott, and Coretta Scott King's aid to her husband are legendary aspects of the Civil Rights Movement.[40]

Black women became major figures in the electoral politics movement, beginning with Congresswomen Shirley Chisholm (NY, a founding member), Barbara Jordan (TX), Yvonne Brathwaite Burke (CA), and Cardiss Collins (IL) in the early years of the Congressional Black Caucus, founded in 1970. One of their later colleagues, Katie Hall of Indiana, proposed the legislation establishing the Martin Luther King Jr. holiday. Black women such as C. Delores Tucker, former secretary of state in Pennsylvania, who served as the first black female in the country to hold such an office, have become prominent at state and local levels of government as pioneers. The political role of black women has continued to grow as they have moved from 11 percent of all black elected officials in 1970 to 35 percent by 2000.[41]

The supreme confidence of blacks that sparked and sustained their movements has promoted a spirit of defiance, not only based on the new postwar humanitarian concepts, but growing from the cultural awareness that results from the evaluation of the assault on one's humanity and the determination to correct history. The eloquence of Dr. Martin Luther King Jr., rooted in nonviolence, was matched by that of Malcolm X (who later changed his name to El Hajj Malik El-Shabazz), who demanded that black people forcefully insist on their individual and collective dignity as worthy human beings. This evaluation of the black self gave African Americans a new opportunity to assess their history, identity, and current situation and decide whether they could control their future. He forced many to consider the nobility of their

Nancy R. Schiff / Hulton Archive / Getty Images

After two terms as Texas state senator, the first black woman to serve in that position since Reconstruction, Dr. Barbara Jordan (1936–1996) was elected to the U.S. House of Representatives, where she served three terms, from 1972 to 1978. She was the keynote speaker at the 1976 Democratic Convention. A neurological impairment caused her retirement from elected office in 1979, but she accepted a faculty position at the University of Texas, Austin. She remained active in national politics, delivering her second keynote address to the National Democratic Convention in 1992. President Bill Clinton awarded her the Presidential Medal of Freedom in 1993. She died in 1996, a month before her sixty-first birthday.

long struggle for survival that had earned them the right to demand to be fully American, regardless of the sacrifices.

Without the emergence of a black identity that privileged factors such as black heritage, pride of accomplishment against great odds, and a common destiny, the spirit of black self-determination would not have been possible. Indeed, Peniel Joseph asserts that while there has been an intellectual aversion to analyses of the Black Power Movement, which began in 1966, the ideology of Black Power helped to fuel civil rights mobilizations in important ways.[42] For example, it is highly conceivable that the Black Power Movement was a contributory factor to the greatest proportional turnout of blacks (at 57.7 percent) in presidential history for the 1964 election, one year before the passage of the Voting Rights Act. Nor would it have been possible for the empowerment objectives of the Civil Rights Movement that related to blacks' struggles to achieve political office, social resources, and social justice to have the social consensus that it achieved.[43] As the modern prophet of black nationalism, Malcolm X provided added evidence through his speeches that there was a persistent interplay of dynamics between the Civil Rights and Black Power movements up to the day of his assassination on February 21, 1965, and beyond.[44]

The march to the Edmund Pettus Bridge in Selma, Alabama, by civil rights activists on March 7, 1965, provoked Sheriff Jim Clark to turn the fire hoses into the crowd of marchers, lead his police mounted on horseback into their ranks, and beat them to the ground in a violent expurgation that became known as Bloody Sunday. John Lewis of SNCC and Hosea Williams of SCLC were injured leading the marchers that day, but the march was eventually completed by Dr. King, and it attracted supporters from all over the country, who marched over the Edmund Pettus Bridge on to Montgomery, the capital. The spectacle created by the brutality in Selma and the dramatic march to Montgomery, all shown on national television, helped to create the pressure for change that resulted in the passage of the Voting Rights Act.[45]

Another aspect of the movement was the promise of President Kennedy to promote equality in public accommodations, which was fulfilled after his assassination with the enactment of the Civil Rights Act of July 2, 1964. Title VII of that act declared it illegal to practice racial discrimination in the workplace or in the use of federal funds. Whether this would have happened without the leadership of President Lyndon B. Johnson, who accepted the Kennedy civil rights mandate, is questionable. The pressure of the Civil Rights Movement brought him to confront powerful Southern politicians in key congressional posts on behalf of a wider vision of the application of American democracy.

In this, Johnson was aided by an election landslide in 1964 as 93 percent of blacks who cast ballots voted for him to continue in office. Thus the civil rights community felt that the election created a mandate not only for making public facilities racially accessible, but also for demanding access to the ballot, especially in the South. Nevertheless, the enactment of the Voting Rights Act on August 6, 1965, opened a new chapter in black political empowerment. Increases in voter registration and voting began to occur rapidly, as the following census data indicates.

Percentage of Eligible Blacks Registered to Vote, Deep South States, 1965–1988

STATE	1965	1988	INCREASE
Alabama	19.3	68.4	49.1
Georgia	27.4	56.8	29.4
Louisiana	31.6	77.1	45.5
Mississippi	6.7	74.2	67.5
North Carolina	46.8	58.2	11.4
South Carolina	37.3	56.7	19.4
Virginia	38.3	63.8	25.5
Average Increase			35.4

This chart shows that in most states in the Deep South, black voter registration increased by 35 percent between 1965 and 1988. The continued success of the Voting Rights Act, however, may be seen in the election of 2004, where the difference in registration between blacks and whites was only 1.7 percent in Mississippi and only 6.4 percent in the nation at large. Blacks generally register and vote at a similar rate as whites in the twenty-first century, and in some places blacks exceed whites in the proportion of their respective groups' voting.[46]

The success of the Voting Rights Act was reflected in the wave of black elected officials at all levels of government: nearly 9,500 blacks held office by 2006, whereas the U.S. Civil Rights Commission found that in the late 1960s there were fewer than 400 black elected officials in the United States, only 72 of whom were in the South. The number quickly grew, reaching 388 in the late 1960s, as reported by the Southern Regional Council.[47] However, by 1970, there were 1,469 blacks holding office nationally, including ten who had been elected to the U.S. House of Representatives. This trend reflected a rapid growth of the number of black officials between 1971 and 1976, from 26.6 percent annually to 13.6 percent.[48]

A central issue in the debate about the way in which the Court implemented Section 2 of the Voting Rights Act by legalizing the construction of black-majority districts to carry out the mandate to make the black vote meaningful has been whether it has simultaneously stimulated the growth of Republican majority districts in areas such as the South. Chandler Davidson and Bernard Grofman, noting that the interests of urban blacks and suburban Republicans often overlapped, referred to this problem in the early 1990s in their edited volume: "The movement of the voting rights bar towards the Republicans raises anxieties among white Democrats, the traditional allies of minorities in Congress, and risks a decrease in support for future initiatives on voting rights and other matters. These Democrats are officeholders and value political survival."[49] Blacks wanted political representation at every level of government through the mechanism of black majority districts, which often left few blacks in other districts that were won by Republicans.

David T. Canon, in *Race, Redistricting, and Representation*, subsequently held that this was one of the "unintended consequences" of the way in which the politics of the Voting Rights Act evolved.[50] Likewise, Carol Swain argued that since the Voting Rights Act had this effect, the remedy was for African Americans to permit themselves to be represented by whites to a greater degree, since some whites had proven capable of doing so effectively.[51] This view however, penalizes blacks for desiring the maximum degree of political representation amid substantial evidence that they are able to represent their own constituencies more fully; furthermore, evidence shows that those changed districts are not the result of redistricting alone, but of the massive ideological change that propelled Southern white Democrats into the Republican Party. This process, born of the negative reaction of whites to the new civil rights laws, began in the presidential election of 1968 when George Wallace created the American Independence party and led ten million Southern voters out of the Democratic Party. The immediate result was the election of President

Richard Nixon. His subsequent landslide victory in the 1972 presidential election was aided by the Wallace constituency, as was the election of Ronald Reagan in 1980, which solidified the South as a significant element in the Republican Party coalition. So, the pattern of Southern Democrats switching their party identification to the Republican Party was initiated long before majority-minority districts were firmly in place.

Meanwhile, the growth of black elected officials led to the creation of the Congressional Black Caucus, which represented blacks at the highest level of government in the U.S. House of Representatives. Already exercising leadership of a group of members at that time was Rep. Charles Diggs of Michigan, who had joined the flamboyant Rep. Adam Clayton Powell of New York, who chaired the important House Education and Labor Committee that handled the civil rights legislation. Junior members such as Rep. John Conyers of Michigan and William Clay of Missouri were elected, and their presence added to an important but still unofficial black caucus. At the same time, an African American Republican, Senator Edward Brooke of Massachusetts, served in the U.S. Senate from 1966 to 1979, failing to win reelection in the changing political culture of the late 1970s that promoted more-conservative politicians.

At local levels, 1967 became the "year of the black mayor," with blacks being elected or appointed mayor in major cities — including Walter Washington, who was appointed mayor of Washington, D.C., by President Johnson; Carl Stokes in Cleveland, Ohio; and Richard Hatcher in Gary, Indiana.

This new position of blacks in the American political system, with so many entering political institutions at all levels, led to the call for the historic National Black Political Convention held in Gary, Indiana, in March 1972. Robert Smith compared it to the March on Washington that had signaled the presence of a national movement for civil rights nearly ten years earlier.[52] The convention was called to advocate for a black presidential candidacy and to craft an agenda that represented the issues to be addressed by their new electoral power. The convention adopted a national Black Political Agenda, which reflected the militant tone of the era, declaring that "A major part of the challenge we must accept is that of redefining the functions and operations of all levels of American government, for the existing governing structures—from Washington to the smallest county—are obsolescent."[53] The Gary convention thus signaled the transition of civil rights activity to institutional politics, called for by Bayard Rustin, civil rights strategist and associate of A. Philip Randolph, and Dr. Martin Luther King Jr., who as early as 1964 called for the movement to go "from protest to politics." Rustin called for an emphasis not only on political rights, but on the formation of public policy, the product of institutions that might be influenced by the movement.

The growing strength of the black vote caused Rep. Walter E. Fauntroy of Washington, D.C., to observe that by the early 1970s there was a new "arithmetic of power" that enabled blacks, together with progressive whites, to elect officials in the South. That formula—aided strongly by the Watergate scandal—brought Jimmy Carter into the presidency in 1976, winning 118 electoral votes from Southern states to 12 for Gerald R. Ford, his Republican challenger.[54] Yet, it was observed by Moreland, Steed, and Baker that although blacks in Mississippi have achieved a level of voting often equal to or exceeding that of the white vote, that performance has not yielded the influence to significantly change their socioeconomic status, since "these counties have populations that are largely black, impoverished and uneducated."[55] Voting, then, needed to be tied to more powerful electoral strategies, such as blacks running for president of the United States.

Black Presidential Politics

In 1984, after four years of the Reagan administration, it became clear to African American leaders that his policies had seriously challenged the legacy of the Civil Rights Movement, which had fostered an inclusive, progressive path opening up many avenues in education, employment, voting, and health care through which blacks might pursue the American dream. The perception that aggressive action should be taken resulted in the decision in the spring of 1983 by the Black Leadership Forum, a coalition of twenty-five key national black political and civic organizations, to mount a black presidential candidacy. Very quickly, it became clear that Rev. Jesse Jackson, leader of Operation PUSH (People United to Save Humanity), headquartered in

Born Jesse Louis Burns in Greenville, South Carolina, October 1941, Jackson worked alongside Martin Luther King Jr. in the Southern Christian Leadership Conference (SCLC), and was by his side when he was assassinated. After the death of Malcolm X and King, Jackson began to emerge as one of the key campaigners for civil rights in America in the 1970s. In 1984 he was a candidate for the presidency in the Democratic primaries. In the 1990s Jackson threw his weight behind Bill Clinton's bid for president and became an influential advisor and friend of the Clinton government.

Chicago, Illinois, would be the black candidate for president in the Democratic primary of 1984.

In the postelection period, a spate of works by black scholars analyzing this historic event concluded that although the Jackson campaign was not successful in winning the nomination, the effort was nevertheless successful because the American people were able to receive messages directly from a major black politician about issues central to the black agenda.[56] The Jackson campaign addressed the way in which the primary process violated the spirit of one-person, one-vote by setting a 20 percent threshold of votes won by a candidate to obtain convention delegates. It championed a balanced policy in the Middle East that recognized the right of statehood for Palestinians. It opposed American relations with the white minority regime that practiced apartheid in South Africa. It supported other issues favored by the black community to the point that the campaign received 3.5 million votes, over $2.5 million in campaign contributions, and won seats on the Democratic Party Central Committee. It was also important that Jackson created a new civil rights organization, merging Operation PUSH with the National Rainbow Coalition into the Rainbow/PUSH Coalition, a multiracial organization of activists.

The 1984 campaign laid the groundwork for Jackson's subsequent candidacy in 1988, which attracted an estimated 7 million votes, earned 25 percent of the delegates to the Democratic Convention, and doubled its fundraising, all of which allowed the Rainbow/PUSH Coalition to be considered the presumptive leader of the progressive wing of the Democratic Party.[57] Most of all, the 1988 campaign brought to a prominent level the political theory of leverage, by which a political formation dependent upon a minority of votes can, nonetheless, position itself to make substantial gains in the political process.

Jackson, however, did not run in 1992, leaving the black community to support the candidacy of William Jefferson Clinton, former governor of Arkansas. Robert Smith provides a convincing analysis of the reason Clinton won the presidency, arguing that Clinton presented himself as a nongeneric Democrat in that he "de-marketed" his racial associations and accepted some conservative policy positions. His opponent George H. W. Bush, on the other hand, presented himself to the electorate as a nongeneric Republican, having raised taxes in contradiction to his pledge not to do so. In this context, the black vote was lukewarm toward Clinton at 82 percent support, the lowest of the modern era for a Democratic presidential candidate. In his reelection campaign, Clinton's black support improved markedly and, during his second term, even exceeded past levels because of the threat of his impeachment, his appointment of popular black leaders to posts in his administration, and his continuation of critical policies such as affirmative action and support for African states.[58]

The Jackson presidential campaigns were also the foundation of the candidacies mounted by Rev. Al Sharpton and Senator Carol Moseley-Braun in the 2004 election. These campaigns, however, did not achieve a level of support equal to the 1988 Jackson campaign, partly because of the preoccupation of Democrats with nominating a candidate who could pursue the war on terrorism as a result of the attack on the World Trade Center in New York City on September 11, 2001. Nevertheless, these 2004 candidacies provided a platform that allowed the candidates to speak directly to the American people, conveying, in the case of Senator Braun, where women stood on many issues and, for Rev. Sharpton, the weakness of Republican approaches to poverty, racism, health care, employment, and other issues central to the black agenda. Still, by pursuing these campaigns, they confirmed that given the right set of circumstances, presidential politics is one of the most effective tools in the pursuit of the empowerment of the African American community.

Yet, the strategy inherent in black presidential politics is still misunderstood by many, blacks as well as whites, in terms of the value of its indirect effect on the political system as an instrument of leverage. This is to be expected as long as the dominant mode of black politics remains operationalized in the context of Democratic Party affairs. Although there have been independent third-party presidential candidates, such as Angela Davis (American Communist Party 1980, 1984), Dick Gregory (The New Party, 1968), Eldridge Cleaver (Peace and Freedom Party, 1968), Dr. Lenora Fulani (New Alliance Party, 1988), and others, they have had negligible success.

Scholars of the history of black politics, however, have largely ignored the attempt by black activists to form a black political party in 1980. This event was related to a thread of action linked to the 1972 Black Political Convention in Gary, Indiana, and the promise made to delegates at that time to return home and do the grassroots organizing that would eventually result in the establishment of an independent political party. The party was called for in a New Orleans convention in fall 1980 by leaders of the National Black Political Assembly, including Ron Daniels, Dr. Benjamin Chavis, and others. The founding convention was held in Philadelphia in 1981, and although the effort initially attracted over two thousand delegates, the internal politics of the organization rendered it moribund by 1983.[59]

Nevertheless, the extent to which independent politics matures as a substantial leverage mechanism beyond the major two-party system may depend upon the activism of the post–civil rights generation of black youth, which expresses a far more independent party identification than their elders. But while the low level of the political participation of black youth reflects that of all American youth, the period between 2000 and 2004 witnessed one of the largest increases in youth mobilization and voting since the 26th Amendment to the Constitution, enacted in 1971, reduced the voting age to eighteen. Polling indicates that this increased voting was linked substantially to the disapproval by most youth, especially college-age youth, of the Iraq War and other conservative policies of the Republican administration.[60] In 2004, 44 percent of black youth reported voting, in contrast to 43 percent of white youth and 20 percent of Hispanic youth.[61]

Governance in the "New Nadir"

The conservative era began to form in 1964 with the presidential candidacy of Republican senator Barry Goldwater, a candidacy which was a reaction to the Civil Rights Movement and the expansion of government responsibility for social policy. The movement gathered steam in the late 1970s with the coming of religious politics in the organized guise of the "Moral Majority," and the emergence of powerful interests that funded new conservative think tanks, media outlets, and political candidates, all of which brought Ronald Reagan into the White House in 1980.

In the twenty-four years between 1980 and 2004, conservative Republicans won five of seven presidential elections. Republican control was solidified in the congressional elections of 1994, and in the Supreme Court by 1991 with the addition of Clarence Thomas, a controversial black conservative. A new political system was created that has allowed conservative politicians, judges, and intellectuals to reshape much of the landscape of social justice. Thus, the perception of the substantial changes in the racial equation forged during the period from World War II to 1980 has faded as that era has receded, and as conservative politicians and cultural leaders have mounted a countermovement to roll back gains viewed as racial advantages and preferences.[62]

The result has been referred to as a "second reconstruction," for just as black interests were sacrificed in the nineteenth century for the sake of bringing the white South back into the Union, early in the twenty-first century, the shadow of the plantation has reemerged over the political interests of blacks as the South has made a transition to a one-party region—albeit, this time, to the Republican Party. From that position Southern politicians have become the swing vote, able to influence political change not only by opposing progressive civil rights legislation, but also by injecting a private moral calculus to public issues through church activism. In this way, the region has become the fulcrum of the conservative movement that has blocked the forward thrust of the changes that emerged in the post–World War II era and that provided opportunities for blacks and many other Americans.

For example, the 1964 Civil Rights Act not only empowered blacks; Title VII created a "protected class" defined by race, color, sex, national origin, disability, or age that is entitled to protection from discrimination. More recently, affirmative action, the mechanism that was eventually utilized by government to monitor discrimination and to promote equality, has been weakened by an attack on its role in promoting racial quotas, although quotas are not a part of the legal content or practice of this concept. The failure to enact effective measures to eliminate poverty, indicated by the Harvard Civil Rights Institute as a major source of educational inequality, has prevented rapid change in minority education, and the persistence of regressive funding formulae have institutionalized such inequality, shackling the ability of government to make radical changes in education.[63]

Moreover, higher-education opportunities for blacks have been hindered by the aggressive attack of the conservative movement on college-enrollment policies as they relate to American-born blacks. The Reagan administration has saddled the black middle class with enormous postgraduation debt by switching higher-education finance from grants to loans, an action that has also contributed to the slow comparative economic growth of the black middle class. Moreover, the elimination of affirmative action in California, Texas, Florida, and Michigan has reconfigured opportunity in higher education, so that fewer blacks and Hispanics are enrolled in these states' flagship institutions, causing California State University to restore the policy.[64]

High incarceration rates, due in part to the so-called war on drugs, have accelerated to the point that as of 2007 half of those incarcerated at every level in America are of African American descent. The propensity for politicians to campaign and govern on a "tough-on-crime" agenda led to the Crime Control Enforcement Act of 1994 that featured measures such as "Three Strikes and You're Out" and an expanded felony list for which the federal death penalty could apply.[65] These measures have promoted an increase in incarceration long past the time when crime rates began to fall due to a substantial upsurge in the economy during the second Clinton administration.

The Civil Rights Movement not only led to legislation empowering blacks and other disadvantaged groups, it legitimized a new set of democratic principles that had the capacity to broaden participation by these groups in areas of society formerly denied them. Such principles included eliminating poverty, allowing citizen participation in public policymaking, ensuring equality of women in work and pay, establishing care for the elderly and disabled, enforcing the role of government in the limited expansion of health care as a right and not a privilege, and many others. The political theory of race in America holds that in the historical cycles of the rise and fall of society's concern for equality and the human condition, the behavior of the political system and its institutions—even those that profess to adhere to the most democratic principles—is wholly dependent on the perspective of those who control and direct them at any given moment.

The "New Nadir" has also been characterized by even more forceful attempts to disenfranchise black voters, as the elections of 2000 and 2004 demonstrate. In 2000, for example, studies by the NAACP and the U.S. Civil Rights Commission found abuses that appeared disproportionate in black districts: missing ballot boxes, incorrect information published on the location of polling stations, illegal closure of polling stations, and police intimidation, among others. The Florida secretary of state managed the voter rolls in a manner that excluded thousands of black voters who were identified as having had felony-status criminal records. These practices did not attract the intervention of the Clinton administration's Justice Department, which, under the Voting Rights Act, could have exercised injunctive powers. Moreover, the disputed election was eventually decided by the U.S. Supreme Court, which reversed the Florida Supreme Court decision ordering a partial recount of disputed votes, thus awarding the election to George W. Bush.[66]

There was a similar pattern of attempts to reduce the impact of the black vote in Ohio during the 2004 elections, as reported by Rep. John Conyers, ranking member of the House Judiciary Committee.[67] Many citizens testified that balloting stations were insufficiently deployed in black neighborhoods, while suburban white neighborhoods experienced a surplus of voting facilities. In addition, in both the 2000 and 2004 elections, several anomalies were identified in the performance of electronic voting machines in areas where vote counts were administered by state election officials with strong ties to the political campaign of George Bush. Studies by Berkeley and MIT/Cal Tech found "unexplained discrepancies" in the vote count in many districts, and a disproportionate number of ballots cast in black neighborhoods that were spoiled or eliminated at a rate much greater than those in white neighborhoods.

These problems with voting led to an era of voting reform and legislation, such as the Help America Vote Act, and more intense participation by civic groups in the black community in "election protection" programs. Moreover, the Voting Rights Act was reauthorized by the Congress by strong margins in both houses (33 votes opposed in the House, none in the Senate); nonetheless, the view of the civil rights community is that enforcement is the key to the protection of such a basic right. But while it is possible to argue that enforcement of voting-rights laws (such as the National Voter Registration Act and others) is key to the preservation of the right to vote, this author has argued that the empowerment returns from that vote rest on the extent to which blacks are able to establish a more independent stance in American politics by adopting a mobilizing agenda that privileges the condition and the policy needs of the black community, by institutionalizing (organizing and funding) its politics through a political organization of some type, by assessing the correct environment within which to employ and obtain the maximum results from black presidential politics, and by leveraging the black vote more effectively at every level of government.[68] These issues constitute a substantial political agenda for the future.

Governance

At this writing, there are an estimated 9,500 elected black officials, including thirty-nine blacks serving in the House of Representatives and one in the Senate. The electoral power of blacks, which has resulted in the representation of their interests at every level of government, has been thwarted to a considerable extent by the environment of the "Nadir." This occurs partly because of the hostile ideology and behavior of those in power, and partly because of the location of black political power within the Democratic Party that lost seats at the national level in the mid-1990s, and in many state governments in that decade as well. This means, for example, that although the state of Mississippi contains the largest number of blacks in the state legislature in the country, that legislature is controlled by Republicans, and the same situation obtains in other Southern states. Thus, the political treatment of the issues referred to above is largely representative of the difficulty blacks face in many states. In fact, the illusion of black political power at the local levels where blacks are dominant or are a significant factor in city or county councils, including school boards and other urban and metropolitan bodies, is that a critical share of the resources they require comes from the state and national levels of government that are often hostile to their interests.

This situation brings into bold relief the issue of political incorporation. Rufus P. Browning, Dale Rogers Marshall, and David H. Tabb suggested that black interests will be served effectively to the extent that they become incorporated—that they seek to have their interests made a part of the regular governing agendas of the primary political institutions.[69] Robert Smith, however, has challenged that idea on the strength of the view that politics for minority groups must take advantage of both institutional resources and the extra-institutional resources that are sometimes available as a result of protest and other aspects of civic engagement.

These forms of political mobilization often produce results, when they are utilized effectively, at a much more rapid rate than the often tedious institutional processes.[70] This insight undergirds the rationale for the use of various strategies to effect political changes that both are in concert with traditional political institutions, and challenge from an external location as well. Thus, elected officials, as well as civic elites and civil rights activists, are all-important actors in the search for black political power.

Conclusion

Regardless of the changes in composition and character of American political systems, the politics of the black community will continue to be focused on a set of issues representing both a backward-looking agenda and a forward-looking one as a consequence of the vestiges of its subordinate position in the American social order, largely because of the contradiction between the political and socioeconomic spheres. On the one hand, the trajectory of the Civil Rights Movement created the presumption of a modernizing society, with liberal access to rights and resources becoming a norm. That trajectory changed, however, with the advent of the conservative movement, which has narrowed the scope of rights, in particular, sharpening the opposition to laws allowing rights and resources to be influenced by race. This has been the case with respect to the attention of government to issues of poverty, education, income distribution, and other fields. The narrowing of the scope of public rights has been accompanied by the attempt to redirect the protection of rights into the realm of private schooling and personal responsibility for social resources, economic progress, health care, retirement decisions, and other areas.

On the other hand, blacks have experienced substantial progress, not only in the field of politics, such as voting and registration, but also in secondary-school graduation, an increasing wage rate, home ownership, financial investment, business growth, and an enhanced position in American society. However, the disparity between whites and blacks has in many instances widened: the poverty rate of blacks is three times that of whites; unemployment remains stable at twice that of whites; the wealth gap continues to increase; and the growth of the black middle class remains stagnant. The character of the politics of the black community may depend upon the tension between the demand for increased public responsibility and the call to address racism and social needs in order to close the social and economic gap between blacks and whites in America.

The framework of the struggle for black progress will continue to be founded on the promises inherent in the framework of American democracy. However, the tension in black politics will continue to demand that the concept of democracy be made meaningful by the creation of real opportunity and equality. In that sense, the long struggle of black Americans for equal and meaningful citizenship has not been merely a single group struggle, but in fact has empowered many other groups and enriched the democratic process.

The policy framework of social justice has stimulated civic engagement of other groups; the Voting Rights Act has provided important protections for many groups to exercise their basic rights of citizenship. This is why coalition politics has been a staple of the approach of the black community on issues not only related to civil rights in a narrow sense, but also to principles of human rights.

In that context, political strategies are not an end in themselves, but the process by which the principles of empowerment and the resources necessary to achieve them are provided in both the public and private realms. For a minority group, the efficiency of the use of political strategy must be measured against the opportunities available at any given time. It is one of the ironies of history that a movement designed first to pressure the government to produce policies that would both equalize the citizenship status of blacks and provide the material resources to make that citizenship meaningful within the democratic process has been thwarted by the emergence of a movement with interests counter to that objective. If this movement is not opposed to the interests of blacks and other minorities, then it is designed to slow the pace of change to a rate that is inadequate to address the urgency of the condition of black people.

Nevertheless, one of the lessons of our history is that regardless of whether opportunities exist, persistence and determination in the attempt to become truly free is the surest method to create them and to eventually achieve the forward motion that will produce the desired result. To achieve that objective, it is also vitally necessary that tested and effective strategies of change both be employed where they may be useful, and tailored to a new century and to the new characteristics of the political system. For although there have been many permutations in the American political system, there is also a consistency in its engagement with racial issues and groups.

· ·

NOTES

1. Walton, *Black Politics.*
2. Jones, "A Frame of Reference for Black Politics."
3. Walton, *Black Politics,* 14.
4. Merriam, *Systematic Politics,* 6.
5. Easton, *A Framework for Political Analysis,* 49.
6. Rein, "Mystery of VA's First Slaves Is Unlocked 400 Years Later."
7. Horton and Horton, *The Landmarks of African American History,* 29.
8. Fishel and Quarles, *The Black American,* 20.
9. See "United States—Race and Hispanic Origin: 1790–1990," table 1, Bureau of the Census, U.S. Department of Commerce. Including the states of Connecticut, Maine, Maryland, Massachusetts, New Hampshire, New York, North Carolina, Pennsylvania, Rhode Island, South Carolina, Vermont, and Virginia.
10. Greene, *The Negro in Colonial New England,* 290–98.
11. Ibid., 300–306.
12. Aptheker, *The Nature of Freedom, Democracy, and Revolution,* 19.
13. Franklin and Moss, *From Slavery to Freedom,* 114–15.
14. *Dred Scott v. Sanford,* 1857.
15. Douglass, *Frederick Douglass,* 347.
16. Fishel and Quarles, *The Black American,* 147–52.
17. Papers of the 1843 Buffalo Convention of the National Convention of Colored Men, Special Collections, Buffalo Public Library, Buffalo, N.Y.
18. Walton, *Black Politics,* 22–23.
19. Du Bois, *Black Reconstruction,* 371.
20. *Presidential Elections since 1789,* pp. 104, 106.
21. Bardolph, *The Civil Rights Record.*
22. Revised under the more accurate title *The Betrayal of the Negro from Rutherford B. Hayes to Woodrow Wilson,* 1965.
23. Later that year, Locke edited *The New Negro: An Interpretation,* an augmented version in book form.
24. Garvey, *Philosophy and Opinions of Marcus Garvey;* Martin, *Race First.*
25. Myrdal, *An American Dilemma,* 424, table 1.
26. Bunche, *Political Status of the Negro.*
27. Walters and Smith, *African American Leadership,* 7.
28. Wilson, *Negro Politics,* 195–98.

29. Bethune et al., *What the Negro Wants.*
30. Holloway, *Confronting the Veil.*
31. Bates, *Pullman Porters and the Rise of Protest Politics in Black America.*
32. Ibid.
33. *Balance of Power,* 1948.
34. Cottrol, Diamond, and Ware, *Brown v. Board of Education.*
35. Williams, *The Constraint of Race,* 174–86; Walters, "'The Association Is for the Direct Attack.'"
36. Earl Warren, Chief Justice, Supreme Court of the United States, *Brown v. Board of Education of Topeka, Kansas,* 347 U.S. 483 (1954).
37. John F. Kennedy, June 1963, Public Papers of the Presidents of the United States, National Archives and Records Administration, Washington, D.C. [I think this information is enough here-BFC]
38. Morris, *The Origins of the Civil Rights Movement.*
39. Carson, *In Struggle.*
40. Giddings, *When and Where I Enter.*
41. *Black Elected Officials: A Statistical Summary,* 2000. Available at DataBank, Joint Center for Political and Economic Studies, Washington, D.C., .
42. Joseph, *Waiting 'Til the Midnight Hour.*
43. Carmichael and Hamilton, *Black Power.*
44. See X, Malcolm, *Malcolm X Speaks* (Breitman, ed.); *By Any Means Necessary* (Breitman, ed.); and *The Last Speeches* (Perry, ed.).
45. Garrow, *Protest at Selma.*
46. "Table A-1. Reported Voting and Registration by Race, Hispanic Origin, Sex and Age Groups: November 1964–2004," U.S. Bureau of the Census, Department of Commerce.
47. Voter Education Project, 1969.
48. *Black Elected Officials: A Statistical Summary,* 2000. Available at DataBank, Joint Center for Political and Economic Studies, Washington, D.C.
49. Davidson and Grofman, *Controversies in Minority Voting,* 250.
50. Canon, *Race, Redistricting, and Representation.*
51. Swain, *Black Faces, Black Interests.*
52. Smith, *We Have No Leaders.*
53. "The National Black Political Agenda, 1972."
54. *Presidential Elections since 1789.*
55. Davis, "Blacks' Political Representation in Rural Mississippi," 158.
56. Walters, *Black Presidential Politics in America;* Morris, *The Social and Political Implications of the 1984 Jesse Jackson Presidential Campaign;* Walters and Barker, *Jesse Jackson's 1984 Presidential Campaign.*
57. Bositis, *Blacks and the 1992 Democratic Convention.*
58. Smith, *We Have No Leaders,* 263–71.
59. Walters, *Black Presidential Politics in America.*

60. "Bush Losing Stronghold on College Campuses, Harvard Poll Finds."
61. Reported Voting and Registration by Race and Hispanic Origin, Sex and Age, for the United States, 2005.
62. Dawson, "Black Power in 1996 and the Demonization of African Americans."
63. Orfield and Yun, *Resegregation in American Schools*.
64. Schmidt, "U. of California Ends Affirmative-Action Ban."
65. Hawkins, "Which Way toward Equality."
66. See *Bush v. Gore*, ().
67. "Preserving Democracy: What Went Wrong in Ohio."
68. Walters, *Freedom Is Not Enough*.
69. Browning et al., *Protest Is Not Enough*.
70. Smith, *We Have No Leaders*, 127–37.

BIBLIOGRAPHY

Amaker, Norman C. *Civil Rights and the Reagan Administration*. Washington, D.C.: Urban Institute Press, 1988.

Anderson, Bernard E. *Fairmont Papers: Black Alternatives Conference*. San Francisco: Institute for Contemporary Studies, 1981.

Aptheker, Herbert, ed. *A Documentary History of the Negro People in the United States: From Colonial Times through the Civil War*. Vol. 1. New York: Citadel, 1951.

Aptheker, Herbert. *The Nature of Freedom, Democracy, and Revolution*. New York: International Publishers, 1967.

Baker, Donald P. *Wilder: Hold Fast to Dreams: A Biography of L. Douglas Wilder*. Cabin John, Md.: Seven Locks Press, 1989.

Baraka, Imamu Amiri. "Toward the Creation of Political Institutions for All African Peoples." *Black World* 21 (October 1972): 54–78.

Bardolph, Richard. *The Civil Rights Record: Black Americans and the Law, 1849–1970*. New York: Crowell, 1970.

Barnett, Marguerite Ross, and James A. Hefner, eds. *Public Policy for the Black Community: Strategies and Perspectives*. Port Washington, N.Y.: Alfred, 1976.

Bates, Beth Tompkins. *Pullman Porters and the Rise of Protest Politics in Black America, 1925–1945*. Chapel Hill: University of North Carolina Press, 2001.

Bell, Howard. "National Negro Conventions of the Middle 1840s: Moral Suasion vs. Political Action." *Journal of Negro History* 42 (October 1957): 247–60.

Bethune, Mary McLeod, et al. *What the Negro Wants*. Edited by Rayford W. Logan. 1944; New York: Agathon Press, 1969.

Black Elected Officials. DataBank, Joint Center for Political and Economic Studies, Washington, D.C., 2005, viewed on April 11, 2007, http://www.Jointcenter.org/DB/detail/BEO.htm.

Blauner, Robert. "Internal Colonialism and Ghetto Revolt." *Social Problems* 16 (Spring 1969): 393–408.

Bobo, Lawrence, and Frank Gilliam. "Race, Sociopolitical Participation, and Black Empowerment." *American Political Science Review* 84 (June 1990): 377–93.

Bositis, David. *Blacks and the 1992 Democratic Convention.* Washington, D.C.: Joint Center for Political and Economic Studies, 1992.

Bositis, David. "The Farrakhan Factor: Behind the Increase in Black Male Voting." *Washington Post*, 8 December 1996, C1.

Browning, Rufus P., Dale Rogers Marshall, and David H. Tabb. *Protest Is Not Enough: The Struggle of Blacks and Hispanics for Equality in Urban Politics.* Berkeley: University of California Press, 1984.

Bunche, Ralph. *The Political Status of the Negro in the Age of FDR.* Chicago: University of Chicago Press, 1973.

"Bush Losing Stronghold on College Campuses, Harvard Poll Finds," 2004, viewed on April 11, 2007, http://www.iop.harvard.edu/pdfs/newsroom/survey_april_2004.pdf.

Canon, David T. *Race. Redistricting, and Representation: The Unintended Consequences of Black Majority Districts.* Chicago: University of Chicago Press, 1999.

Carmichael, Stokely, and Charles V. Hamilton. *Black Power: The Politics of Liberation in America.* New York: Random House, 1967.

Carson, Claybourne. *In Struggle: SNCC and the Black Awakening of the 1960s.* Cambridge, Mass.: Harvard University Press, 1981.

Cottrol, Robert J., Raymond T. Diamond, and Leland B. Ware. *Brown v. Board of Education: Caste, Culture, and the Constitution.* Lawrence: University Press of Kansas, 2003.

Dahl, Robert Alan. *Who Governs? Democracy and Power in an American City.* New Haven: Yale University Press, 1961.

Davidson, Chandler, and Bernard Grofman. *Controversies in Minority Voting: The Voting Rights Act in Perspective.* Washington, D.C.: Brookings Institution, 1992.

Davis, Theodore J., Jr. "Blacks' Political Representation in Rural Mississippi." In *Blacks in Southern Politics,* ed. Laurence W. Moreland, Tod A. Baker, and Robert P. Steed. New York: Praeger, 1987.

Dawson, Michael C. *Behind the Mule: Race and Class in African-American Politics.* Princeton, N.J.: Princeton University Press, 1994.

Dawson, Michael. "Black Power in 1996 and the Demonization of African Americans." *Political Science and Politics* (September 1996).

Douglass, Frederick. *Frederick Douglass: Selected Speeches and Writings.* Edited by Philip Sheldon Foner and Yuval Taylor. Chicago: Lawrence Hill, 1999.

Du Bois, W. E. B. *Black Reconstruction.* New York: Harcourt, Brace, 1935.

Du Bois, W. E. B. *Dusk of Dawn: An Essay toward an Autobiography of a Race Concept.* New York: Schocken, 1940.

Du Bois, W. E. B. *The Souls of Black Folk: Essays and Sketches.* Chicago: McClurg, 1903.

Easton, David. *A Framework for Political Analysis.* Englewood Cliffs, N.J.: Prentice-Hall, 1965.

Edsal, Thomas Byrne, and Mary D. Edsal. *Chain Reaction: The Impact of Race, Rights, and Taxes on American Politics.* New York: Norton, 1991.

Fishel, Jeff, Jr., and Benjamin Quarles, eds. *The Black American*. Rev. ed. New York: Morrow, 1970.

Forman, James. *The Making of Black Revolutionaries*. Seattle: University of Washington Press, 1972.

Franklin, John Hope, and Alfred A. Moss Jr. *From Slavery to Freedom: A History of American Negroes*. 5th ed. New York: Knopf, 2000.

Garrow, David J. *Protest at Selma: Martin Luther King, Jr., and the Voting Rights Act of 1965*. New Haven: Yale University Press, 1978.

Garvey, Marcus. *Philosophy and Opinions of Marcus Garvey*. Edited by Amy Jacques Garvey. 1923; New York: Arno, 1968.

Giddings, Paula. *When and Where I Enter: The Impact of Black Women on Race and Sex in America*. New York: Morrow, 1984.

Gilliam, Reginald Earl. *Black Political Development: An Advocacy Analysis*. Port Washington, N.Y.: Kennikat Press, 1975.

Gosnell, Harold Foote. *Negro Politicians: The Rise of Negro Politics in Chicago*. Chicago: University of Chicago Press, 1935.

Greene, Lorenzo Johnston. *The Negro in Colonial New England, 1620–1776*. 1942; New York: Atheneum, 1968.

Hamilton, Charles. "The Politics of Deracialization in the 1990s." *National Political Science Review*, no. 3 (1992): 175–78.

Hawkins, Darnell. "Which Way toward Equality: Dilemmas and Paradoxes in Public Policies Affecting Crime and Punishment." In *African Americans and the Public Agenda*, ed. Cedric Herring. Thousand Oaks, Calif.: Sage Publications, 1997.

Henry, Charles P. *Jesse Jackson: The Search for Common Ground*. Oakland, Calif.: Black Scholar, 1991.

Holden, Matthew, Jr. *The Politics of the Black "Nation."* New York: Chandler, 1973.

Holloway, Jonathan Scott. *Confronting the Veil: Abram Harris Jr., E. Franklin Frazier, and Ralph Bunche, 1919–1941*. Chapel Hill: University of North Carolina Press, 2002.

Horton, James Oliver, and Lois Horton. *The Landmarks of African American History*. New York: Oxford University Press, 2004.

Horton, James Oliver, and Lois Horton. *Slavery and the Making of America*. New York: Oxford University Press, 2004.

James, Joy. "Ella Baker, 'Black Women's Work,' and Activist Intellectuals." *Black Scholar* 24 (Fall 1994): 8–15.

Jennings, James. "The Politics of Black Empowerment in Urban America: Reflections on Race, Class, and Community." In *Dilemmas of Activism*, ed. Joseph M. Kling and Prudence Sarah Posner. Philadelphia: Temple University Press, 1990.

Johnson, Ollie A., and Karin L. Stanford, eds. *Black Political Organizations in the Post–Civil Rights Era*. New Brunswick, N.J.: Rutgers University Press, 2002.

Jones, Mack. "A Frame of Reference for Black Politics." In *Black Political Life in the United States: A Fist as the Pendulum*, ed. Lenneal J. Henderson. San Francisco: Chandler, 1972.

Jones, Mack H. "The Political Thought of New Black Conservatives." In *Readings in American Political Issues*, ed. Franklin D. Jones. Dubuque, Iowa: Kendall Hunt, 1987.

Joseph, Peniel E. *Waiting 'Til the Midnight Hour: A Narrative History of Black Power in America.* New York: Holt, 2006.

Kilson, Martin. "Anatomy of Black Conservatism. *Transition* 59 (1993): 4–19.

Kinder, Donald R., and Lynn M. Sanders. *Divided by Color: Racial Politics and Democratic Ideals.* Chicago: University of Chicago Press, 1996.

King, Martin Luther, Jr. *A Testament of Hope: The Essential Writings of Martin Luther King, Jr.* Edited by James M. Washington. San Francisco: Harper & Row, 1986.

Ladd, Edward. *Negro Political Leadership in the South.* Ithaca, N.Y.: Cornell University Press, 1966.

Lawson, Steven F. *Black Ballots: Voting Rights in the South, 1944–1969.* New York: Columbia University Press, 1976.

Lewis, David Levering. *W. E. B. Du Bois: Biography of a Race, 1868–1919.* New York: Holt, 1993.

Lewis, David Levering. *W. E. B. Du Bois: The Fight for Equality and the American Century, 1919–1963.* New York: Holt, 2000.

Lipsky, Michael. "Protest as a Political Resource." *American Political Science Review* 62 (December 1968): 1144–58.

Locke, Alain. *The New Negro.* New York: A. & C. Boni, 1925.

Logan, Rayford Whittingham. "Introduction." In *The Betrayal of the Negro from Rutherford B. Hayes to Woodrow Wilson;* originally published as *The Negro in American Life and Thought: The Nadir, 1877–1901.* 1965; New York: Da Capo, 1997.

Logan, Rayford Whittingham, ed. *What the Negro Wants.* Chapel Hill: University of North Carolina Press, 1944.

Marable, Manning. *Black American Politics: From the Washington Marches to Jesse Jackson.* London: Verso, 1985.

Martin, Tony. *Race First: The Ideological and Organizational Struggles of Marcus Garvey and the Universal Negro Improvement Association.* Westport, Conn.: Greenwood Press, 1976.

McAdam, Doug. *Political Process and the Development of Black Insurgency, 1930–1970.* Chicago: University of Chicago Press, 1982.

McCartney, John T. *Black Power Ideologies: An Essay in African-American Political Thought.* Philadelphia: Temple University Press, 1992.

McClain, Paula. "Black Politics at the Crossroads? Or in the Cross-Hairs?" *American Political Science Review* 90 (1996): 867–73.

McCormick, Joseph P. "The Messages and the Messengers: Opinions from the Million Men Who Marched." *National Political Science Review* 6 (1997): 142–64.

McLemore, Leslie Burl. "The Mississippi Freedom Democratic Party." Ph.D. diss., University of Massachusetts, 1971.

Merriam, Charles E. *Systematic Politics.* Chicago: University of Chicago Press, 1945.

Moon, Henry Lee. *Balance of Power: The Negro Vote.* Garden City, N.Y.: Doubleday, 1948.

Morris, Aldon D. *The Origins of the Civil Rights Movement: Black Communities Organizing for Change.* New York: Free Press, 1984.

Morris, Lorenzo, ed. *The Social and Political Implications of the 1984 Jesse Jackson Presidential Campaign.* New York: Praeger, 1990.

Morris, Milton D. *The Politics of Black America.* New York: Harper & Row, 1975.

Myrdal, Gunnar. *An American Dilemma: The Negro Problem and Modern Democracy.* New York: Harper, 1944.

"The National Black Political Agenda." Washington, D.C.: The National Black Political Convention, 1972.

Nelson, William. "Black Mayoral Leadership: A Twenty Year Perspective." *National Political Science Review* 2 (1990): 188–95.

Nelson, William E., and Philip J. Meranto. *Electing Black Mayors: Political Action in the Black Community.* Columbus: Ohio State University Press, 1977.

Orfield, Gary, and John Yun. "Resegregation in American Schools." The Civil Rights Project, Harvard University, 1999, viewed on April 11, 2007, http://www.civilrightsproject.harvard.edu/research/deseg/reseg_schools99.php.

Patterson, Ernest. *Black City Politics.* New York: Dodd, Mead, 1974.

Peterson, Paul, and J. David Greenstone. "Racial Change and Citizen Participation: The Mobilization of Low-Income Communities through Community Action." In *A Decade of Federal Antipoverty Programs,* ed. Robert Haveman. New York: Academic Press, 1979.

Political Participation. A Report of the United States Commission on Civil Rights, Washington, D.C., 1968.

"Preserving Democracy: What Went Wrong in Ohio." A Report of the Democratic Staff of the House Judiciary Committee, U.S. House of Representatives, 2004.

Presidential Elections since 1789. 4th edition. Washington, D.C.: Congressional Quarterly, 1987.

Prestage, Jewel. "In Quest of African American Political Women." *Annals of the American Academy of Political and Social Science* 515 (1991): 88–103.

Preston, Michael. "Big City Black Mayors: An Overview." *National Political Science Review* 2 (1990): 131–37.

Preston, Michael B., Lenneal J. Henderson, and Paul Lionel Puryear, eds. *The New Black Politics: The Search for Political Power.* New York: Longman, 1982.

Reed, Adolph. "The Black Urban Regime: Structural Origins and Constraints." In *Power, Community, and the City,* ed. Michael Peter Smith. New Brunswick, N.J.: Transaction, 1988.

Rees, Matthew. *From the Deck to the Sea: Blacks and the Republican Party.* Wakefield, N.H.: Longwood Academics, 1991.

Rein, Lisa. "Mystery of Va.'s First Slaves Is Unlocked 400 Years Later." *Washington Post,* 3 September 2006, A1.

"Report of the National Advisory Commission on Civil Disorders." Republished as *The Kerner Report.* 1968; New York: Pantheon, 1988.

"Reported Voting and Registration by Race, Hispanic Origin, Sex and Age Groups: November 1964–2004." Table A-1. Bureau of the Census, U.S. Department of Commerce, viewed on April 11, 2007, http://www.census.gov/population/socdemo/voting/tabA-1.xls.

Roucek, Joseph S. "Minority-Majority Relations in Their Power Aspects." *Phylon* 15, n0.1 (1956): 24–30.

Schmidt, Peter. "U. of California Ends Affirmative Action Ban." *Chronicle of Higher Education* (May 25, 2001), viewed on April 11, 2007, http://chronicle.com/weekly/v47/i37/37a02301.htm.

Singh, Robert. *The Congressional Black Caucus: Racial Politics in the U.S. Congress.* Thousand Oaks, Calif.: Sage, 1998.

Smith, Robert C. "Black Appointed Officials: A Neglected Area of Research in Black Political Participation." *Journal of Black Studies* 14 (March 1984): 369–88.

Smith, Robert C. "Black Power and the Transformation from Protest to Politics." *Political Science Quarterly* 96, no. 3 (1981): 431–43.

Smith, Robert C. "Ideology as the Enduring Dilemma of Black Politics." In *Dilemmas of Black Politics: Issues of Leadership and Strategy*, ed. Georgia Persons. New York: HarperCollins, 1993.

Smith, Robert C. "'Politics' Is Not Enough: The Institutionalization of the African American Freedom Movement." In *From Exclusion to Inclusion: The Long Struggle for African American Political Power*, ed. Ralph C. Gomes and Linda F. Williams. New York: Greenwood Press, 1992.

Smith, Robert Charles. *Encyclopedia of African-American Politics.* New York: Facts on File, 2003.

Smith, Robert Charles. *We Have No Leaders: African Americans in the Post–Civil Rights Era.* Ithaca: State University of New York Press, 1996.

Smith, Robert Charles, and Hanes Walton Jr. *American Politics and the African American Quest for Universal Freedom.* New York: Longman, 2000.

Stone, Chuck. *Black Political Power in America.* Indianapolis, Ind.: Bobbs-Merrill, 1968.

Swain, Carol. *Black Faces, Black Interests: The Representation of African Americans in Congress.* Cambridge, Mass.: Harvard University Press, 1995.

Tate, Katherine. *From Protest to Politics: The New Black Voters in American Elections.* New York: Russell Sage Foundation, 1993.

Taylor, Alrutheus A. "Negro Congressmen a Generation After." *Journal of Negro History* 7 (April 1922): 127–71.

Tifft, Susan. "A Push toward the Presidency: A Black Convention Urges Jesse Jackson's Candidacy." *Time*, August 8, 1983.

"Voting and Registration in the Election of 2004." Bureau of the Census, U.S. Department of Commerce, viewed on April 11, 2007, http://www.census.gov/prod/2006pubs/p20-556.pdf.

Walker, David. "Walker's Appeal in Four Articles; together with a Preamble to the Colored Citizens of the World, but in Particular, and Very Expressly, to Those of the United States of America." Reprinted as "A Negro on Tyranny and Revolution." In *The Black American*, ed. Leslie H. Fishel and Benjamin Quarles. 1829; New York: Morrow, 1970.

Walters, Ronald. "'The Association Is for the Direct Attack': The Militant Context of the NAACP Challenge to *Plessy*." *Washburn Law Journal* 43 (May 2004): 329–51.

Walters, Ronald W. *Black Presidential Politics in America: A Strategic Approach*. Albany: State University of New York Press, 1988.

Walters, Ronald W. *Freedom Is Not Enough: Black Voters, Black Candidates, and American Presidential Politics*. Lanham, Md.: Rowman & Littlefield, 2005.

Walters, Ronald. "The Great Plains Sit-In Movement, 1958–1960." *Great Plains Quarterly* 16 (Spring 1996): 85–94.

Walters, Ronald. "The Issue Politics of the Jesse Jackson Campaign for President in 1984." In *The Social and Political Implications of the 1984 Jesse Jackson Presidential Campaign*, ed. Lorenzo Morris. New York: Praeger, 1990.

Walters, Ronald. "The New Black Political Culture." *Black World* 21 (October 1972): 4–17.

Walters, Ronald W. *White Nationalism, Black Interests: Conservative Public Policy and the Black Community*. Detroit: Wayne State University Press, 2003.

Walters, Ronald W., and Lucius Jefferson Barker, eds. *Jesse Jackson's 1984 Presidential Campaign: Challenge and Change in American Politics*. Urbana: University of Illinois Press, 1989.

Walters, Ronald W., and Robert Charles Smith. *African American Leadership*. Albany: State University of New York Press, 1999.

Walters, Ronald, with Tamelyn Tucker-Worgs. "Black Churches and Electoral Engagement in the Nation's Capital." In *Black Churches and Local Politics: Clergy Influence, Organizational Partnerships, and Civic Empowerment*, ed. R. Drew Smith and Frederick C. Harris. Lanham, Md.: Rowman & Littlefield, 2005.

Walton, Hanes. *Black Political Parties: An Historical and Political Analysis*. New York: Free Press, 1972.

Walton, Hanes. *Black Politics: A Theoretical and Structural Analysis*. Philadelphia: Lippincott, 1972.

Walton, Hanes, ed. *Black Politics and Black Political Behavior: A Linkage Analysis*. Westport, Conn.: Praeger, 1994.

Walton, Hanes, Shirley M. Geiger, Marion E. Orr, and Mfanya D. Tryman. "The Literature on African American Politics: The Decade of the Nineties." *Politics and Policy* 29 (December 2001): 753–82.

Wesley, Charles H. "The Participation of Negroes in Anti-Slavery Parties." *Journal of Negro History* 29 (January 1944): 45.

Wilkins, Roy, and Ramsey Clark. *Search and Destroy: A Report*. New York: Metropolitan Applied Research Center, 1973.

Williams, Juan. "Direct Attack." In *Thurgood Marshall: American Revolutionary*. New York: Times Books, 1998.

Williams, Linda F. *The Constraint of Race: Legacies of White Skin Privilege in America*. University Park: Pennsylvania State University Press, 2003.

Wilson, James Q. *Negro Politics: The Search for Leadership.* New York: Free Press, 1960.

X, Malcolm. *By Any Means Necessary: Speeches, Interviews, and a Letter.* Edited by George Breitman. New York: Pathfinder, 1970.

X, Malcolm. *Malcolm X Speaks: Selected Speeches and Statements.* Edited by George Breitman. New York: Grove, 1965.

X, Malcolm. *Malcolm X: The Last Speeches.* Edited by Bruce Perry. New York: Pathfinder, 1989.

X, Malcolm, and Alex Haley. *The Autobiography of Malcolm X.* New York: Ballantine, 1965.

CHRONOLOGY

1619   The first Africans arrive in Jamestown; whether they arrived as slaves remains unknown.

1620–70 Legislation within the colonies begins to recognize and define slavery.

1641   Massachusetts enacts the Massachusetts Body of Liberties, stating that "There shall never be any bond slavery . . . unless it be lawful captives taken in just wars, and such strangers as willingly sell themselves or are sold to us."

1661   Virginia passes a law defining Africans as being in bondage "durante vita."

1705   The colonies begin individually to question the legality of maiming or killing a slave. The *Statutes of Virginia* states that it is not a felony to kill a slave during the act of "correction."

1775   The Pennsylvania Society for the Abolition of Slavery is founded. It is the first anti-slavery organization in America.

1780–83 Massachusetts enacts the Declaration of Rights, declaring slavery unconstitutional.

1787   Free blacks, led by Prince Hall, demand equal education in the Massachusetts colony.

1787   The Free African Society, the forerunner to the African Methodist Episcopal Church (1816), is founded by Richard Allen and Absalom Jones.

1789   The U.S. Constitution defines the political representation of a slave as 3/5 that of a white person.

1816   The American Colonization Society is founded. The organization supports the emigration of emancipated blacks to a colony in Liberia.

1829   David Walker's *Appeal to the Coloured Citizens of the World . . .* is published. The distribution of the pamphlet is prohibited in the South.

1830   The National Negro Convention meets in response to sixteen-year-old Hezekial Grice's suggestion that African Americans emigrate to Canada. The American Society of Free People of Colour results; Richard Allen is named president.

1831   Nat Turner's insurrection occurs in Southampton, Virginia.

1841   Frederick Douglass gives his first autobiographical speech to the American Anti-Slavery Society. Listeners are so moved, he becomes a regular agent for the organization.

1843   At the National Negro Convention in Albany, New York, Henry Highland Garnet proposes to end slavery by violence, stating, "You had far better all die—*die immedi-*

ately, than live slaves." A debate ensues between Garnet and Frederick Douglass, and Garnet's proposal fails adoption by one vote.

1840   The Liberty Party is formed in support of antislavery presidential candidates. Between 1840 and 1848, blacks debate joining the party; Henry Highland Garnet is an enthusiastic supporter.

1851   At the Women's Rights Convention in Akron, Ohio, Sojourner Truth delivers her "Ar'n't I a Woman" speech.

1855   John Mercer Langston becomes the first black local elected official; he serves in Ohio.

1857   U.S. Supreme Court rules that Dred Scott is not a citizen of the United States, setting precedent for the denial of citizenship to all African Americans.

1863   The Emancipation Proclamation is issued by Abraham Lincoln.

1865   The 13th Amendment to the U.S. Constitution makes slavery illegal. "Neither slavery nor involuntary servitude, except as a punishment for crime whereof the party shall have been duly convicted, shall exist within the United States, or any place subject to their jurisdiction."

1868   The 14th Amendment to the U.S. Constitution extends citizenship, due process, and equal protection to African Americans.

1870   The 15th Amendment to the U.S. Constitution grants African Americans the right to vote.

1875   The Civil Rights Act grants equal access to public accommodations for blacks.

1877   Rutherford B. Hayes is elected president of the United States as a result of the Hayes Bargain. Granted disputed electoral votes in exchange for such favors as removing federal troops from the South, Hayes effectively ends Reconstruction and restores the political stronghold of white supremacists in the South.

1883   The U.S. Supreme Court overturns the Civil Rights Act of 1875.

1895   Booker T. Washington gives his speech at the Atlanta Exposition, arguing that the majority of African Americans are better suited for physical labor than for academia; W. E. B. Du Bois and other black intellectuals derogatorily call Washington's stance the "Atlanta Compromise."

1896   In the landmark case *Plessy v. Ferguson*, the U.S. Supreme Court reinforces segregation by declaring "separate but equal" facilities for blacks and whites constitutionally acceptable.

1905–10 The Niagara Movement is founded by W. E. B. Du Bois, William Monroe Trotter, and others in opposition to Booker T. Washington's accomodationist philosophies.

1909   The National Association for the Advancement of Colored People (NAACP) is established by W. E. B. Du Bois, Ida B. Wells-Barnett, Mary White Ovington, and other black intellectuals.

1910   The National Urban League (NUL) is founded by George Edmund Haynes and Ruth Standish Baldwin.

1916   Marcus Garvey brings the Universal Negro Improvement Association (UNIA) from Jamaica (where it was founded in 1914) to the United States.

1928 Oscar De Priest is elected to the U.S. Congress from Illinois Congressional District 1; he is the first black to be elected from outside the South.

1930 The Nation of Islam, known collectively and more popularly as the Black Muslims, is founded in the United States by Wallace D. Fard.

1934 The Honorable Elijah Muhammad becomes the leader of the Nation of Islam; Malcolm X becomes a famous spokesman, but later leaves the group in support of a more orthodox strand of Islam.

1935 Mary McLeod Bethune founds the National Council of Negro Women and serves as an adviser to President Franklin D. Roosevelt.

1941 A. Philip Randolph warns President Franklin D. Roosevelt that he will organize a march on Washington to protest segregation in the war industries; Roosevelt issues Executive Order 8802, creating the Committee on Fair Employment Practice and making discrimination in the war industries illegal.

1942 The Congress of Racial Equality (CORE), a civil rights organization based on nonviolence, is founded by James Farmer. The group's first protest is a sit-in in a segregated Chicago coffee shop.

1954 In the case *Brown v. Board of Education of Topeka*, the U.S. Supreme Court declares that separate facilities are inherently unequal and that segregation violates the 14th Amendment.

1955–56 The Montgomery bus boycott occurs.

1957 Conflict occurs in Little Rock, Arkansas, as federal troops escort nine black students during the integration of Central High School; the students become known as the "Little Rock Nine."

1957 The Southern Christian Leadership Conference (SCLC) is formed; it is the first organization to unite civil rights organizations across the South.

1960 The Student Nonviolent Coordinating Committee (SNCC) is founded in Raleigh, North Carolina. The group is dedicated to nonviolent protests such as freedom rides and student sit-ins.

1963 The March on Washington is led by Rev. Martin Luther King Jr.

1964 The Civil Rights Act of 1964 is passed.

1964–65 By an executive order in 1965 following the Civil Rights Act of 1964, the administration of Lyndon B. Johnson begins to enforce affirmative action, providing equal opportunities for African Americans. (Affirmative action is later extended to include other minorities, women, and the disabled.)

1965 Rev. Martin Luther King Jr. leads three marches from Selma, Alabama—the last comprising 25,000 marchers who reach Montgomery less than five months before the Voting Rights Act is passed in August, reinforcing the 15th Amendment right of black Americans to vote. In the first march on Bloody Sunday, March 7, 1965, six hundred marchers are beaten by local police.

1966 The Black Panther Party is founded by Huey Newton and Bobby Seale.

1966–67   In response to the Black Power movement of the mid- to late 1960s, SNCC becomes more militant under the leadership of Stokely Carmichael (SNCC also begins to stand for the Student National Coordinating Committee).

1967   Thurgood Marshall is appointed associate justice of the U.S. Supreme Court. He is the first African American to be appointed to the Supreme Court.

1967   Barbara Jordan is the first black to be elected state senator in Texas since 1883.

1968   Martin Luther King Jr. is assassinated April 4 while standing on his balcony at the Lorraine Motel in Memphis, Tennessee.

1968   Comedian and civil rights activist Dick Gregory and the author Eldridge Cleaver run for president of the United States — the former on the Freedom and Peace Party ticket, the latter on the Peace and Freedom Party ticket. Richard Nixon wins the election; in his "Southern strategy" — to guarantee Southern votes — he promises, among other things, to oppose court-ordered busing and to appoint a Southerner to the Supreme Court.

1968   Shirley Chisholm, a founder of the National Political Caucus of Black Women (1984), is elected to the House of Representatives.

1969   In *Alexander v. Holmes County (Mississippi) Board of Education*, Supreme Court Justice Hugo Black, while affirming a district-court decision to delay implementation of desegregation plans in the county schools, expresses his displeasure with the fourteen-year delay in desegregation since *Brown v. Board of Education of Topeka*, and he reiterates for the second time the Court's 1964 pronouncement that the time for "all deliberate speed" referred to in *Brown* has run out.

1971   Jesse Jackson establishes Operation PUSH (People United to Save Humanity) in order to improve working conditions for African Americans.

1971   April 20. Regarding efforts to desegregate schools, the U.S. Supreme Court rules unanimously that student busing is constitutional, a ruling later complicated by an obiter dictum from Chief Justice Warren Berger suggesting that every school in a community need not reflect the racial composition of the school system.

1971   August 3. In response to federal orders to begin busing in Austin, Texas, President Nixon orders that the busing be limited to the "minimum required by law."

1971   George Jackson, who had become a Black Panther leader while in prison, is killed in San Quentin Prison in what is said to have been an attempted escape. The suspicion surrounding his death leads to an uprising at Attica State Prison in New York three weeks later.

1972   The National Black Political Convention is held in Gary, Indiana.

1972   Shirley Chisholm wins 152 delegates before dropping her campaign for U.S. president.

1972   Barbara Jordan is elected to the U.S. House of Representatives from the 18th District of Texas.

1978   Marion Barry is the first African American to be elected mayor of the District of Columbia.

1978   Allan Bakke is admitted to the University of California Medical School following his appeal to the Supreme Court. A white student, Bakke claims that affirmative action blocked his acceptance to the school; the Court upholds Affirmative Action, but denies the legality of racial quotas.

1979   Patricia Roberts Harris is appointed secretary of Health, Education, and Welfare by President Jimmy Carter, becoming the first black woman in a presidential cabinet post.

1984   Jesse Jackson seeks the Democratic nomination for president. He establishes the National Rainbow Coalition, a civil rights organization dedicated to the equal treatment of blacks, women, and homosexuals.

1984   Shirley Chisholm founds the National Political Caucus of Black Women.

1986   The Employment Equity Act is passed.

1989   Colin Powell becomes the first African American to serve as chairman of the Joint Chiefs of Staff. He holds the position until 1993.

1991   President George Bush appoints Clarence Thomas to the U.S. Supreme Court, replacing Thurgood Marshall with the Court's second African American, and a decidedly conservative associate judge.

1992   Carol Moseley-Braun becomes the first female African American U.S. senator.

1994   The Violent Crime Control Enforcement Act is passed.

1995   Louis Farrakhan organizes the Million Man March. Directed by Benjamin Chavis, the march on Washington, D.C., brings together some 835,000 African American men in a peaceful expression of black solidarity.

1996   Jesse Jackson merges his National Rainbow Coalition with Operation PUSH to form RainbowPUSH.

1996   The Personal Responsibility and Work Opportunity Reconciliation Act is passed.

2001   Condoleezza Rice becomes the first black female U.S. national security advisor.

2001   Retired General Colin Powell is appointed U.S. secretary of state. He is the first African American to hold this position.

2004   Barack Obama becomes the fifth African American to serve in the U.S. Senate.

2004   Colin Powell resigns his position of secretary of state.

2005   Condoleezza Rice becomes the first black female U.S. secretary of state.

GLOSSARY

Affirmative Action. A set of policies and practices designed to effect a compensatory remedy for the past exclusion of blacks from educational and employment opportunities, implemented by an executive order of the administration of President Lyndon B. Johnson in the wake of the Civil Rights Act of 1964.

American Anti-Slavery Society. Founded in 1833 by William Lloyd Garrison, this Philadelphia-based organization advocated the complete abolition of slavery in the United States. The society grew to 2,000 chapters by 1840, with more than 150,000 members, and remained active until 1870. Publications sponsored by the AASS included *The Emancipator* (1833–1850) and *The National Anti-Slavery Standard* (1840–1872).

Black Leadership Forum. This coalition, founded by leaders of the top eleven (now approximately twenty-eight) major black organizations in the political, social, and economic fields, includes representatives from groups such as the Southern Christian Leadership Conference (SCLC), the National Association for the Advancement of Colored People (NAACP), and the National Urban League (NUL).

Black Nationalism. Black nationalism is a political and social movement that emphasizes adherence to a common black identity based on African origins, opposition to racism, unity in the approach to competition for power, and belief in a common destiny. Traceable to the late 1700s in America, black nationalism contributed to such various events as the establishment of the African Methodist Episcopal Church in 1816, to Marcus Garvey's Universal Negro Improvement Association (UNIA) of the 1920s, and to the Black Power movement of the 1960s (including the work of Stokely Carmichael and Malcolm X).

British Colonialism. The British government dominated territories and peoples outside of their own land, subjugating the status and proceeds from colonized lands to the purposes of the British Crown. These territories and peoples, which included the United States, were supported by the British Crown, beginning successfully in the seventeenth century as entities contributing to the mercantile system. The British American colonies were formally recognized as part of the "Kingdom of Great Britain" until the American Revolution, when thirteen of the colonies separated from British rule.

Brown v. Board of Education of Topeka. Case decided by the Supreme Court in May 1954 that combined three other cases: *Briggs v. Elliott* (South Carolina), *Davis v. County School Board of Prince Edward County* (Virginia), and *Gebhart v. Belton* (Delaware). The case declared racial segregation in education unconstitutional, reversing *Plessy v. Ferguson*, the 1896 Supreme Court decision that allowed "separate but equal" facilities.

Civil Rights Act of 1964. Proposed by President John F. Kennedy in 1963 and passed into law on July 2, 1964, by President Lyndon B. Johnson. The Civil Rights Act made it illegal to practice discrimination on the basis of race, gender, national origin, or religion in the provision of public accommodation, in the labor force, and in the use of federal funds. An Equal Employment Opportunity Commission was created to monitor and enforce these provisions. The Civil Rights Act also facilitated equal voting rights and the desegregation of public schools.

Durante Vita. A legal term used in the Charter of the Virginia Colony to define the status of Africans as slaves for life, distinguishing them from persons who were bound to service for a specific period of time.

Hayes Bargain. The result of a tie in the Electoral College in the election of 1876. Negotiations led to the cession of Southern votes to Rutherford B. Hayes in exchange for his promise to remove Union troops from the South.

The Liberty Party. A political party that emerged in 1840 as a result of a split with the American Anti-Slavery Society leader William Lloyd Garrison. The new antislavery party had unsuccessful nominations for president in 1840, 1844, and 1848. In 1848 the party merged with the Whigs to form the Free-Soil Party.

The Nadir. A term coined by Professor Rayford Logan of Howard University to signal a low period in the history of the black community caused by the failure of Reconstruction at the turn of the century.

National Association for the Advancement of Colored People (NAACP). The premier civil rights organization in America, founded in 1909 by Ida B. Wells-Barnett, Mary White Ovington, W. E. B. Du Bois, and others to resist lynching and other aspects of the degradation of blacks through protest demonstrations and legal actions.

National Black Political Convention. A historic convention held in 1972 in the city of Gary, Indiana, bringing together more than 10,000 attendees to develop a Black Political Agenda and a strategy for black political participation for the 1972 elections and beyond.

National Convention of Colored Men. A national association of freedmen who began to meet in 1829 to consider the state of both African slaves and freedmen, and to constitute a voice of opposition to slavery and the pursuit of American citizenship. At the 1843 convention in Buffalo, the group defeated a resolution proposed by Henry Highland Garnet to eliminate slavery by revolutionary means.

National Urban League (NUL). Founded in 1910 by Edmund Hayes, Ruth Standish, and others (including members of three other organizations that merged with the NUL in 1911), the NUL was dedicated to providing assistance for blacks who were transitioning from life in the South to Northern urban living, especially those relocating to New York City. Originally called the National League on Urban Conditions among Negroes, the organization took on the shorter name in 1920.

Niagara Movement (1905–1910). The predecessor to the NAACP, this group of black intellectuals, led by W. E. B. Du Bois and William Monroe Trotter, was founded in opposition to Booker T. Washington's accommodationist philosophy and in favor of the immediate implementation of civil rights for African Americans.

Pan African Movement. A movement initiated in 1900 by H. Sylvester Williams, a Trinidadian lawyer in London, which was taken up by W. E. B. Du Bois, who sponsored conferences in Europe in 1919, 1921, 1923, and in New York City in 1927 and formed the Pan African Association.

Plessy v. Ferguson. Key civil rights case of 1896 in which the concept of "separate but equal" confirmed the lawfulness of segregation as long as the facilities provided to each group were equal.

Political System. The use of social power through rules establishing legitimate patterns of human relationships to make authoritative decisions that result in the distribution of social goods. Such a system claims to be universal, extending to all citizens, claiming a sense of primal authority and the legitimate use of force and coercion to effect decisions bearing the force of law or accepted as legitimate.

Racial Quotas. Any numerical objective established by an institution to achieve the inclusion of blacks or other groups. The conservative definition of Affirmative Action.

RainbowPUSH Coalition. A civil rights organization created in 1996 through a merger of two organizations founded by Rev. Jesse Jackson: Operation PUSH (People United to Save Humanity), a civil rights organization founded in 1971, and the National Rainbow

Coalition, founded in 1985. The economically minded mission of Operation PUSH included increasing job opportunities for African Americans, while the advocacy of the National Rainbow Coalition included social justice for African Americans, women, and homosexuals.

Reconstruction. Period (1865–1877) wherein liberal Republicans sought to foster equal rights for blacks with the enactment of post–Civil War amendments to the Constitution, civil rights laws, and the establishment of the Freedmen's Bureau.

Second Amenia Conference. A conference held in 1933, sponsored by Joel Spingarn, president of the NAACP, to discuss the economic and political plight of blacks during the Great Depression, and to devise a proposal for intervention by the Roosevelt administration.

Second Reconstruction. Period (World War II to 1980) of U.S. social and legal slackening that appears to mirror the minimal enforcement of civil rights laws and the heightened white nationalism of the turn of the twentieth century.

Slave Codes. A comprehensive set of laws passed by slave states before the Civil War to define the status and social relationship of the African slave to his or her environment.

Southern Regional Council. Founded in 1919 as the Commission on Interracial Cooperation and headquartered in Atlanta, Georgia, the Southern Regional Council is a key civil rights organization whose self-stated mission is to "remind the country that racial injustice is the South's unfinished business."

Three Strikes and You're Out. Law enacted in California, for habitual offenders, whereby the conviction of three felonies is punishable by life imprisonment.

Tough-on-Crime Movement. Measures announced by Richard Nixon in 1972 and pursued by subsequent administrations. As a result, the prison population increased fivefold between 1980 and 1995.

U.S. Commission on Civil Rights. An independent agency established in 1957 by Congress to monitor enforcement of civil rights laws by investigating complaints, developing data and reports, and submitting recommendations to Congress.

Voting Rights Act of 1965. Law passed on August 6, 1964, by President Lyndon B. Johnson that endeavored to protect the 15th Amendment right of blacks to vote, by requiring that state laws be approved by the Justice Department, that the vote be meaningful and not diluted, and that language assistance be given to those in need.

Education

Linda M. Perkins

Abstract

The quest for education for African Americans has been one of continuous struggle. From the very beginning, enslaved African Americans recognized the importance of literacy and frequently risked their lives to obtain this often forbidden privilege. During the early nineteenth century, free blacks established schools, as well as other institutions, within their communities. Those who lived in areas where there were few African Americans often went to school with whites. Where the population was large, such as in New York, Philadelphia, and Boston, they attended segregated schools. The issue of integration versus segregation has been a constant debate within the African American community for two centuries. While integration was preferred by most blacks, the cost they paid was the loss of black teachers, community schools, and important cultural programs. After Reconstruction, the focus of black education was in the South with the establishment of hundreds of schools for the newly freed men, women, and children. As in the North, blacks in the South established schools within their communities through their churches and as private individuals. In addition, white religious denominations, individual donors, and the Freedmen's Bureau also aided in the establishment of schools in the South. More than a hundred black colleges were founded from the 1850s through the early twentieth century. The topic of the appropriate curriculum for blacks began in the early- and mid-nineteenth century in the North. These discussions continued in the South with the rise in prominence of conservative educator Booker T. Washington at the end of the nineteenth century.

Blacks viewed education as important for the entire race and educated women and girls as readily as they did men and boys. In an era when women of the larger society were socialized to be dependent and educated solely for motherhood and marriage, African American women were educated to help their race.[1] They recognized an obligation and duty to their race, and thus, "race uplift" was the motto throughout their communities. While black institutions produced outstanding graduates and successful members of the community, after the New Negro Movement, which stressed black pride and culture, many became more vocal about racial injustices. By the 1930s, the National Association for the Advancement of Colored People (NAACP) began its crusade to overturn the "separate but equal" 1896 Supreme Court ruling of *Plessy v. Ferguson*. Through a series of lawsuits challenging the absence of graduate and professional education for African Americans in some states and, later, segregated public schools, in 1954 the Supreme Court overturned the *Plessy* decision with *Brown v. Board of Education*. In the fifty years since *Brown*, blacks have continued the struggle to have the promise of *Brown* realized.

Antebellum Era

In the late eighteenth and early nineteenth centuries, whites educated enslaved Africans and later emancipated Africans primarily for religious and moral reasons. These reasons would persist well into the twentieth century in schools founded by whites for African Americans. While the purposes of education during this period for whites was also religious and moral, a similar education for blacks was perceived as a means of civilizing and making obedient and loyal slaves. For example, in an 1834 article in the *Southern Religious Telegraph*, the author informed Southern slaveholders of the positive benefits of religious education for slaves. Detailed information was given extolling how household servants versus plantation servants should be provided with sermons and oral Bible study. The author wrote that in the western part of North Carolina, slaves who received religious education "are more contented, exemplar and faithful than perhaps in any part of the southern states."[2] This type of oral education was conducted by the slave master. The slave master provided the interpretation of the importance of being an obedient and docile servant. Thus, slaves had no opportunity to read or interpret Scripture for themselves.[3]

While it was permissible for white masters to provide oral "instruction" to their slaves, and such was encouraged for the above stated reasons, literacy was often forbidden. There were scattered opportunities for both free blacks and slaves to become literate prior to the 1830s in the South. However, education was viewed as dangerous after the fiery *Appeal* of David Walker in 1829 and the slave revolt of Nat Turner in 1831, both being literate black men. After the 1830s, all of the Southern states instituted laws prohibiting the education of African Americans, thus forcing such activities underground. Black abolitionist Frederick Douglass recounts in his autobiography the horror and outrage of his owner when he discovered his wife teaching Douglass his alphabet and words. Douglass wrote that his owner, Mr. Auld,

> forbade Mrs. Auld to instruct me further, telling her, among other things, that it was unlawful, as well as unsafe, to teach a slave to read. To use his words, further, he said, "If you give a nigger an inch, he will take an ell. A nigger should know nothing but to obey his master—to do as he is told to do. Learning would *spoil* the best nigger in the world."[4]

Douglass recalled that his owner expressed the fear that most slave owners believed about literate slaves:

> If you teach a nigger (speaking of myself) how to read, there would be no keeping him. It would unfit him to be a slave. He would at once become unmanageable, and of no value to his master. As to himself, it could do him no good, but a great deal of harm. It would make him discontented and unhappy.[5]

The notion that a literate and, later, educated black person was a dangerous and uncontrollable one was a belief that persisted in the minds of many whites over the next two centuries. Despite the laws against blacks becoming literate during this period, Carter G. Woodson found in a study of black education prior to the Civil War that clandestine schools were found in most of the large cities and towns of the South, even though the law prohibited such activities.[6] Numerous such schools were reported in Savannah, Georgia. Julian Froumountaine, a black woman from Santo Domingo, openly conducted a free school for African Americans in Savannah as early as 1819, and secretly after the 1830s when the education of blacks became illegal. Another underground school opened in 1838 and operated for more than twenty-five years without the knowledge of local whites.[7] Susan King Taylor, who served as a nurse and teacher for the Union Army during the Civil War, was educated in several of the "secret" schools of Savannah. In her *Reminiscences,* Taylor recalled the methods devised by the black pupils to deceive the unsuspecting white residents.[8] Similar schools existed in other areas of the South. In Natchez, Mississippi, Milla Granson became literate through the teachings of her master's children and taught other slaves to read and write in what they termed Milla's "midnight" school because the classes were held after midnight. In all of these instances, it is clear that slaves often risked their lives to obtain literacy. Their recollections of these secret schools and literate slaves among them indicate that most slaves who obtained any learning passed on their knowledge to other slaves.[9]

Mandy Jones, a former slave from Mississippi, recalled the manner in which slaves on her plantation gained literacy:

> Dey [slaves] would dig pits, an kiver the spot wid bushes an' vines . . . an' dey had pit schools in slave days . . . way out in the woods . . . an' de slaves would slip out o' de Quarters at night, an go to dese pits, an some niggah dat had some learnin' would have a school.[10]

Thus, in their struggle for freedom, blacks viewed education as one of their greatest forces of liberation and understood its importance in the advancement and "uplift" of their race. Historian V. P. Franklin is one of the many scholars who have noted black enthusiasm for education. He wrote, "Schooling, both formal and informal, was judged to be the main thoroughfare by which blacks could leave 'Babylon' and reach 'Canaan-Land.'"[11] In addition to seeking education for the "uplift" of their race, blacks also sought to dispel the notion that African Americans were intellectually deficient. As noted above, education for blacks was perceived as a threat to white superiority and domination. In his 1829 *Appeal*, militant David Walker wrote to his black audience:

> I would crawl on my hands and knees through mud and mire, to the feet of a learned man, where I would sit and humbly supplicate him to instill into me, that which devils nor tyrants could remove, only with my life—for coloured people to acquire learning in this country, make tyrants quake and tremble on their sandy foundation . . . the bare name of educating the coloured people scares our cruel oppressor almost to death.[12]

While laws and covenants prohibiting their education restricted most blacks in the South, blacks in the North had greater opportunities for formal education. As early as 1704, Elias Neau established a school for slaves in New York, and in 1750, Anthony Benezet, a Quaker, established an evening school for African Americans in Philadelphia. These schools were followed by other private schools for black people, established by various religious organizations and abolitionist societies. These schools, opening and closing sporadically, depending on funding, frequently offered only the rudimentary subjects. For example, the white trustees of the African Free School established by the New York Manumission Society in 1787 discouraged higher education for its students, stating that it was beyond the "sphere" of blacks. David Walker in his *Appeal* reported an incident of a white teacher forbidding a black student to study grammar, because the subject was perceived as one reserved for study by whites. These incidents were connected to the belief in the intellectual inferiority of African Americans.

African American women, in addition to the men, were subject to similar attitudes. Beatrice B. Butcher, in her study of the history of black women's schools in the United States, notes that from 1827 to 1863, sporadic attempts to offer classes to black girls and women were recorded in abolitionist and other New England newspapers. According to Butcher, most of the schools that were established emphasized only the most rudimentary education and handwork.[13] As with black men, when attempts were made to educate African American women similarly to whites, great opposition ensued. When Prudence Crandall, a Quaker, opened a seminary for "genteel" girls in Canterbury, Connecticut, in 1831, an African American girl who wanted to become a teacher for her race was admitted in 1833. The parents of the white students were so outraged that most withdrew their daughters. In addition, public sentiments were so negative towards Crandall that she changed the school to one solely for African American women. When she advertised in the abolitionist newspaper the *Liberator* for "young colored Ladies and Misses" — titles reserved for only white women — this enflamed the white citizens of Canterbury. When fifteen young black women from Philadelphia, Boston, New York, Providence, and Connecticut enrolled in the institution by April 1833, the town instituted a law forbidding the instruction of out-of-state black students. After ignoring this law, Crandall was arrested, and her school burned down.[14]

Opposition and prejudice against advanced education of African Americans was supported through various academic projects. Throughout the nineteenth century, "scientific" studies were produced to confirm, in brain size, lung capacity, and a variety of physiological and psychological traits, the widespread notion of black biological and intellectual inferiority. The American Colonization Society, formed in 1816 to return freed blacks to Africa, reported:

> Educate him [the black man] and you have added little or nothing to his happiness — you have unfitted him for the society and sympathies of his degraded kindred, and yet you have not procured for him and cannot procure for him any admission into the society and sympathy of the white man.[15]

Another publication noted, "After a certain age, [African Americans] did not correspondingly advance in learning — their intellect being apparently incapable of being cultured beyond a particular point."[16]

As a result of these beliefs, African Americans throughout the nineteenth century urged the members of their race to acquire education to prove that they were as capable as whites. In 1829, Samuel Cornish, the editor of the New York black newspaper *The Rights of All*, believed that a demonstration of black intellect would rid the nation of prejudice, and he urged his readers to educate themselves and their children. Writing that "knowledge is power," Cornish stated that when black children were educated, "merit will form the character and respectability. The term Africa will no longer be synonymous with that of degradation."[17]

There was a widely held belief among many African Americans that only through education would racism decrease. This view was repeatedly stated throughout the early years of the nineteenth century. At a black national conference in 1832, the body resolved that "If we [black people] ever expect to see the influence of prejudice decrease and ourselves respected, it must be by the blessings of an enlighten [*sic*] education."[18] At each black convention prior to Emancipation, delegates protested the dearth of educational opportunities available to African Americans.

Unlike whites of the time, African Americans viewed education as important for both men and women. *The Weekly Advocate*, a New York black newspaper, featured an article in 1837 titled "To the Females of Colour." It read:

> In any enterprise for the improvement of our people, either moral or mental, our hands would be palsied without woman's influence. Thus, let our beloved female friends, then, rouse up, and exert all their power, in encouraging, and sustaining this effort [education] which we have made to disabuse the public mind of the misrepresentations made of our character; and to show the world, that there is virtue among us, though concealed; talent, though buried; intelligence, though overlooked.[19]

Education for both girls and boys was so important to African American families that they frequently relocated to areas where their daughters as well as their sons could receive a better education. For example, when Blanche V. Harris was denied entrance to a white seminary in Michigan in the 1850s, her entire family moved to Oberlin, Ohio, where she and her four brothers and sister could attend school in that location. Similarly, the parents of Mary Jane Patterson, who in 1862 became the first black woman to earn a college degree in America, moved from North Carolina in the 1850s to educate their four children (three girls and one boy) in Oberlin.[20] Finally, Fanny Jackson Coppin moved from Washington, D.C., in 1851 to New Bedford, Massachusetts, and later to Newport, Rhode Island, for better educational opportunities. She graduated from Oberlin College in 1865, one of the earliest black women to earn a college degree in the nation.[21] After graduating from Oberlin, Coppin became the principal of the Institute for Colored Youth (ICY), a prestigious Quaker-founded private high school in Philadelphia. Coppin served at ICY from 1865 to 1903. Her philosophy was to produce not "mere scholars," but youth who would serve to "uplift" the race. Throughout her tenure at ICY, Coppin instilled within her students a deep sense of service to the race. In a letter to Frederick Douglass, Coppin articulated her strong sense of commitment of love and service to her race:

> I need not tell you, Mr. Douglass, that this is my desire to see my race lifted out of the mire of ignorance, weakness and degradation; no longer to be the fog end of the American rabble: to sit in obscure corners in public places and devour the scraps of knowledge which his superiors fling him. I want to see him erect himself above the untoward circumstances of his life: I want to see him crowned with strength and dignity: adorned with the enduring grave of intellectual attainments and a love of manly deeds and downright honesty.[22]

Unlike society at large, coeducation was the norm within the African American communities. A perusal of advertisements of schools in the black and abolitionist newspapers indicates that institutions such as "B. H. Hughes School for Coloured Children of Both Sexes" and "Evening School for People of Color of Both Sexes" were typical.[23] The largest black literary society of New York, The Phoenix, organized in 1833, provided lectures, evening schools, and a high school available to members of both genders, and employed black male and female teachers. Through the persuasion of black citizens of Philadelphia, they convinced Quakers to change an institution they established for black boys to a coeducational high school.[24]

Because most white teachers had low expectations for African Americans and believed them to be of low intelligence, black teachers for black students became an important issue during the early decades of the nineteenth century. This is a topic that would be revisited even into the twentieth century. *Freedom's Journal* protested the small number of schools for blacks and the poor quality of teachers provided for them. It wrote, "We cannot believe that almost *anyone* is qualified to keep a school for our children."[25] Most blacks were of the view that white teachers would not encourage black students to "elevate" their race. Expressing this point of view, a report of the 1853 black national convention stated that "their [white teachers'] whole tendency is to change him [the black student], not his condition — to educate him out of his sympathies, not to quicken and warm his sympathies, for all that is of worth to him is his elevation, and the elevation of his people."[26]

African American teachers, prior to the Civil War, were not uncommon. In 1793, the Committee for Improving the Condition of Free Blacks in Pennsylvania opened a school and recommended a qualified black woman as teacher. In that same year, a slave, Catherine Ferguson, purchased her freedom in New York and took forty-eight black and white children from an almshouse and opened Katy Ferguson's School for the Poor. Because blacks were prohibited from attending most white schools, they established their own schools. Prince Hall established a school in Massachusetts in 1798. Similarly, black Philadelphia had ten private schools by 1838, all operated by African American teachers.

Public schools for black students opened in Massachusetts in 1820, and by Emancipation, most New England states provided public education for them. However, the decades prior to Emancipation witnessed much discontent and dissatisfaction among black Northerners concerning education. Segregated schools were the norm in large cities. In 1848, Benjamin Roberts, a black activist of Boston, brought suit against the Boston public schools on behalf of his five-year-old daughter Sarah Roberts. Sarah had to pass five white schools on the way to her black school. Her application to attend a white school had been rejected four times when her father brought suit. The well-known lawyer and abolitionist Charles Sumner argued the case for Roberts. *Roberts v. City of Boston* was the precursor to the landmark school-integration case of *Brown v. Board of Education* a century later. Sumner argued that the segregated schools violated Sarah's right to equality before the law, or "precise equality."[27] The City of Boston argued that the racially segregated schools were legal and did not deny Roberts her legal right to an education. The Massachusetts Supreme Court agreed with the City of Boston. However, in 1855 the Massachusetts legislature agreed with Sumner and struck down the statute that outlawed school integration.[28]

Few Northern states provided public education for black students prior to 1865. For example, Delaware provided no public education to African Americans prior to Emancipation. The Quakers established the Delaware Association for the Moral and Social Improvement of the Colored People in 1866 to assist black education. Over six hundred students enrolled in their fifteen schools. By 1875, blacks were taxed to support their own schools. However, the tax was so meager that it only covered a third of the expenses of the schools. The black community and friends subsequently furnished the remaining amount. Not until 1883 were black schools placed under the supervision of the state superintendent of schools in Delaware.[29] Most Western states also bitterly opposed proposals to educate black students.[30]

After the Fourteenth Amendment was passed in 1868, guaranteeing "equal protection under the law" to black people, public schools were established to accommodate them outside the South. These schools were normally segregated. Protests were often taken to court, but as in the case of *Roberts v. City of Boston*, the courts usually upheld segregated schools.

School segregation varied by states, and even by cities. The most important factor in school segregation was the number of blacks living in a particular city or location.[31] The New England states were largely integrated, except for a few cities in Connecticut and Rhode Island. Parts of Michigan, Wisconsin, Minnesota; northern parts of Illinois, Ohio; and rural areas of New York, Pennsylvania, and New Jersey maintained integrated schools. However, in larger cities, where the greatest population of black people resided, segregated schools were maintained—if any at all.[32]

Southern Illinois and Indiana exempted black citizens from the school tax and excluded them from the public schools entirely. Not until 1870 did Illinois provide education for *all* children, and in 1869, Indiana provided segregated schools for black students.[33] In certain instances, school boards integrated schools because of the financial burden of maintaining dual systems. But most often, integration was the result of black community pressure. Many times, the battle for integration took years. This fact would be repeated in the twentieth century as well. For example, the struggle for the integration of schools in Rhode Island ended in 1866 after a nine-year battle between the black community and the state.[34] Similarly, Ohio abolished separate schools in 1886 after a persistent battle with the African Methodist Episcopal Church, National Colored Convention, and other black organizations.[35] The black press constantly voiced opposition to segregated schools:

> Contrary to all exception the school board has again opened and set in operation two or three little colored schools in different parts of the city and thus again offers insult to every colored resident of the city. We hear of no Irish schools, no German schools, no Swedish schools, No, not one . . . [36]

The price that the black community paid for integrated schools was usually the loss of jobs for black teachers. This remained an issue into the twentieth century and significantly impacted the placement and retention of African American teachers, particularly after the 1954 Supreme Court *Brown* decision. Thus, some blacks advocated separate schools in the nineteenth century. One newspaper article reflected this sentiment:

> We want absolute equality in the public schools—mixed scholars and mixed teachers—and if we can't have it, we want colored schools taught by colored teachers. . . . Show us one black president of a white college in this country; show us one black editor running a white newspaper. On the other hand, we have white presidents of black colleges from Maine to California and from the Pacific to the swamps of Alabama, and white professors in black colleges by the hundreds.[37]

In advocating separate schools, black parents argued that in integrated schools, their children were subjected to the insults of white teachers and students. Again, these issues would be revisited in the next century by black parents.

One black magazine in 1876 stated that white teachers in black schools "take no real interest in their work nor in the [black] scholars but teach and tolerate them in order to . . . draw their money . . . we are tired of white overseers."[38]

The concern over the elimination of black teachers was paramount. When white school officials proposed replacing black teachers with white teachers in the black public schools of New York City in 1865, the *New York Weekly Anglo-African* issued a protest stating:

> We find it difficult to trust white men to educate our youth. It is not because they are not abundantly qualified in the letter, but their defect is in spirit and sympathy. There are many whites among our professed friends who do not believe in the square, civilized doctrine of human equality.[39]

Even within the abolitionist community, racism and condescension were common. Black Quaker abolitionist and schoolteacher Sarah Mapp Douglass of Philadelphia discontinued her membership in the Arch Street Meeting in the 1830s because she was segregated at the services. Of the Quakers, Douglass stated, "I have heard it frequently remarked and have observed it myself, that in proportion as we [blacks] become intellectual and respectable, so in proportion does their [the Quakers] disgust and prejudice increase."[40] In 1860, Frederick Douglass concurred and commented, "Consciously or unconsciously, almost every white man approaches a colored man with an air of superiority and condescension."[41]

Segregation for the purpose of retaining black teachers, versus integration, which insured their dismissal, created heated debates within black communities. In 1849 Benjamin Roberts unsuccessfully brought suit to force integration of the Boston schools, which were segregated because black parents had requested separate schools in the early 1800s. Although their children could attend the common schools during that period, the virulent racism that black students experienced resulted in their parents creating their own schools. By 1818 the Boston School Committee assumed oversight of all private and public schools in the city. Of the 117 primary schools in Boston in the mid-1840s, blacks were confined to one primary school. Blacks made up 2 percent of the Boston population at this time, and some black Bostonians believed that segregated schools were no longer desirable. This issue split the Boston black community. While Roberts went to court to challenge the segregated schools of Boston, another group of black citizens petitioned the school officials for improved physical plants and a black master teacher to replace the white teacher. As in other situations, the black parents stated that the white teacher was cruel and had little confidence in the academic capabilities of their children. [42]

Despite the discriminatory treatment that black students often received in integrated schools and the lack of black teachers as role models, many felt that the loss of African American instructors was the sacrifice to be made for school integration. This issue would also be revisited in the next century. Some black newspapers described those African Americans who expressed a desire for all-black schools as being traitors and retrogressive.[43] Nevertheless, according to Carlton Mabee's study of black education in New York State, despite the debate regarding integrated schools versus all black schools, most of the black leadership of New York State "continued through most of the century to plea for black teachers for black schools."[44]

Black Education in the South after Emancipation

With the end of legal slavery in 1863, education was the primary focus of the newly emancipated slaves. Numerous studies have recounted the enthusiastic efforts of former slaves to become literate. W. E. B. Du Bois reported in his 1901 study of the Negro Common School that two years after Emancipation, fewer than 100,000 black students were in schools in the South. The demand for literacy was so great that by 1900, more than 1.5 million black students were enrolled in schools.[45] With the onset of the Civil War, missionary organizations, the largest of which was the American Missionary Association (AMA); freedman-relief organizations; and later the Freedmen's Bureau (established in 1865 by the federal government) sent teachers and missionaries by the thousands to establish schools and churches in the Union-occupied areas of the South. As noted in Du Bois's report of 1901, the thirst for knowledge was overwhelming. Teachers constantly wrote in their reports of the enthusiasm that blacks exhibited for learning. One teacher of black soldiers reported, "I am sure that I have never witnessed greater eagerness to study . . . a majority of the men seemed to regard their books an indispensable portion of their equipment, and the cartridge-box and spelling book are attached to the same belt."[46] Missionaries reported a desire for learning, more than food, by the freedmen.[47]

While the efforts of the Northern white missionaries were important, black people also made significant contributions to the education of the newly emancipated slaves. When the AMA arrived in Fortress Monroe, Virginia, to open a school in 1861, a black woman, Mary Peake, who secretly taught slaves, already had a school. She was hired by the AMA and became their first teacher in the South.[48] And, despite the fact that various missionary organizations established hundreds of schools and colleges throughout the South, as historian James D. Anderson has noted in his study of the history of black education in the South, the freedmen and -women possessed a profound sense of self-determination and established their own educational associations and schools and staffed them completely with black teachers.[49]

The former slaves were well aware of the power of education and the impact of its absence from their lives. Anderson quotes one freedman as stating, "There is one sin that slavery committed against me which I will never forgive. It robbed me of my education."[50] Similarly, in his study of education in the slave community, Thomas Webber notes the deep desire among the slaves for literacy. Quoting one of the many slaves who desired literacy, Mary Ella Grandberry said, "Dar is one thing I surely did want to do, and dat was to learn to read and write."[51] Anderson notes that white missionaries often came to the South with preconceived notions about the former slaves being uncivilized and spiritually and emotionally broken by slavery. In reality, these former slaves had developed a system of mutuality, self-reliance, and profound sense of self. Webber notes that the punitive and harsh rules of whites against black literacy fueled the slaves' resolve to become educated. The connection between literacy and power was clear to most slaves. One former slave, Thomas Jones, noted:

> I was a slave; and I knew that the whole community was in league to keep
> the poor slave in ignorance and chains. Yet, I longed to be free, and to be

able to move the minds of other men with my thoughts. It seemed to me now, that, if I could learn to read and write, this learning might—nay, I really thought it would, point out to me the way to freedom, influence, and real, secure happiness.[52]

Even before the establishment of the school by Mary Peake, other accounts of educational efforts by blacks to teach other blacks have been noted. As discussed above, even during slavery, secret schools existed throughout the South. John V. Alvord, national superintendent of schools for the Freedmen's Bureau, wrote, in a January 1866 report of the educational activities of African Americans, his observations. He noted the "self-teaching" and "native schools," the term he used to describe the schools established by local blacks. He wrote, "An effort is being made by the colored people to educate themselves."[53] Anderson's research details the push by freedmen and -women for universal education in the South.[54] Throughout the South, Anderson reports the Herculean efforts of poor freedmen to establish and sustain schools. He notes among many organizations that black leaders established the Georgia Educational Association in 1865. Through this organization, blacks maintained either all or partial support of two-thirds of the schools in the state. By 1866, this included 96 of the 123 day and evening schools. The purpose of the organization was "that the freedmen shall establish schools in their own counties and neighborhoods, to be supported entirely by the colored people."[55]

In addition to the significant efforts of African Americans in the South to advance the education of their children and themselves, many blacks from the North migrated south to aid in the massive effort of "race uplift." Among them were African American teachers. Traditional studies consistently cite altruism and abolitionist zeal as the impetus for the thousands of white upper- and middle-class Northern women to answer the call to journey south to teach the freedmen through the American Missionary Association. The AMA is significant because it was the largest of the missionary organizations, employed thousands of teachers, and opened schools in all of the Southern and border states. In 1870, the organizations had 157 common schools. As the public school system began to develop throughout the South, the

This school in the South (photographed in 1870) was attended by freedmen during Reconstruction. After emancipation, freed slaves faced homelessness, unemployment, and poverty, which was exacerbated because they were uneducated. Northern relief societies helped establish schools and sent aid in the form of clothes, food, and teachers. Congress established the Freedman's Bureau, which opened over 1,000 schools to train newly emancipated blacks. However, much of the impetus behind Reconstruction came from African Americans themselves, as many literate black men and women opened and sustained the first free schools.

organization focused more on secondary, normal, and college level institutions. While there were many women who were committed to education of the ex-slaves, the above romanticized interpretation does not reflect the motivation of most of these teachers. The letters of application to the AMA national office in New York reflect the need by many of the women to escape the isolation of living at home. Most of these women were educated for their "proper sphere" to become wives and mothers—and not expected to work unless it was financially necessary. Consequently, many of the young women who applied to teach in the South did so to escape their idle and unfulfilled lives.[56] A letter stating, "My circumstances are such that it is necessary for me to be doing something" carried the common theme. Many widows applied. One applicant to go south to teach the freedmen and women was brief and to the point: "I am a soldier's widow left alone. I desire to be busy-useful."[57]

In a study of the female teachers of the AMA who served in Georgia from 1865 to 1873, Jacqueline Jones found that the white female teachers "joined the cause in order to liberate themselves from the comfort and complacency of a middle-class existence . . . the work fulfilled some of their needs and enabled them to understand their own situation more clearly."[58] In contrast, the African American women and men who applied to be AMA-sponsored teachers expressed a deep desire to help their race. These applicants were poorer than their white counterparts and were often single parents and/or supporting siblings and parents. The theme of race "uplift" and obligation to their race was the common theme of their letters of application. Sara G. Stanley, an Oberlin College graduate, wrote, "I have felt a strong conviction of duty . . . possessing no wealth and having nothing to give but my life to my work," when she sought a position with the AMA. Another black Oberlin graduate, Lucie Stanton Day, also expressed her desire to serve her race: "My sense of duty urges me to write . . . I wish to engage in this work because I desire the elevation of my race."[59] Black male teachers were also inspired to teach because of love and duty to their race. One such applicant, George C. Booth, wrote that he enrolled in the Connecticut Normal School for the "sole purpose of qualifying myself to benefit my race. . . . More than I desire my own life, I desire to elevate these, my people." Another black man, Nathan T. Condol from New York, wrote, "As I am a Coloured man, I feel it my duty [to go South] and take up my cross there among my people."[60] Despite their qualifications, African Americans had great difficulty being accepted as teachers with white missionary organizations due to issues of race and culture.

Although requests for positions from the small cadre of educated black women and men of the North poured into the national office of the AMA in New York, their applications were carefully scrutinized, and often denied because of dependent children as well as other reasons. For example, Lucie Stanton Day, the first black women to complete the Ladies Department at

Oberlin College (1850), was rejected by the AMA because she supported a seven-year-old child. Likewise, a widow, Mary S. Leary of Oberlin, was also refused a position with the AMA because she was a single parent. While these conditions prohibited black women from employment as teachers, they did not exclude white women in similar circumstances from being appointed as matrons in mission houses.[61]

As a whole, officials at the AMA had preconceived notions regarding the abilities and culture of African Americans. In selecting teachers, the organization sought those with "culture and refinement." Thus, this tended to exclude African Americans. In 1863, the AMA selected five African American female teachers as an "experiment" to demonstrate that blacks were as competent as whites. While this was perceived as important to the officials of the AMA, as discussed earlier and as will be demonstrated further, there was never a question in the minds of most African Americans concerning the competence of black teachers. They preferred African American teachers. Also, the five black women selected by the AMA were selected because they culturally and physically resembled whites.[62] The selection of these near-white-looking teachers was a reflection of the AMA's belief that mulattoes were smarter than darker-skinned blacks.[63] Robert Morris notes in his study of freedmen and -women's education that AMA superintendent William T. Richardson was "surprised to find so much intelligence among Savannah's freedmen."[64]

The five black teachers selected as an "experiment" for the AMA are important because they provide an insider's view of the organization. The women were appointed to schools in the Norfolk, Virginia, area. From the moment of their arrival, the women wrote to the national office of the AMA of their observations of the discriminatory manner in which black students and teacher aides were treated (the AMA employed local blacks as teaching assistants and monitors). All of the five black teachers were initially barred from housing with the white AMA teachers. After this situation was rectified, letters were sent to the national office regarding the constant reference of white teachers to the inferiority of blacks, the social distinctions made, and the "Negro-hating principles" of the white AMA staff members in their house. The black AMA teachers also reported that there were white teachers who had "no interest in the cause."[65]

Studies on black education have repeatedly documented the racism of missionary organizations and their hostility toward black independent schools and teachers. Anderson, Morris, Jones, and others have discussed in their writings the repeated belief in white superiority. Attitude toward race was not a criterion for selection of white teachers. It was assumed that their (white) superior intellect and culture was essential to black progress. Morris notes the competition that white religious aid societies felt with black religious denominations for students. As stated before, blacks believed that black teachers were better equipped to teach their own race. Even in their letters of application to white organizations for teaching positions, black applicants frequently stated that blacks would be more successful as teachers. Hezekiah H. Hunter wrote, "I believe *we* best can instruct our own people, in this auspicious and momentous hour as they have just begun to struggle up from chattelism to manhood, from bruised and mangled slaves to good citizens."[66] Sallie Daffin also expressed the same sentiment to the AMA by saying that "none can so fully experience the strength of their needs, nor understand the means necessary to relieve them as we who are identified with them."[67]

Duty and obligation to race was instilled in African Americans throughout the nineteenth century. Fanny Jackson Coppin, who headed the distinguished Quaker-sponsored Institute for Colored Youth in Philadelphia from 1865 to 1903, prepared her students to "serve their race." Coppin educated her students to teach in the worst possible situations—no supplies, overcrowded classes, etc. In an 1879 address to her students, Coppin told them:

> You can do much to alleviate the condition of our people. Do not be discouraged. The very places where you are needed most are those where you will get least pay. Do not resign a position in the South which pays you $12 a month as a teacher for one in Pennsylvania which pays $50.[68]

The desire of the AMA and other white aid societies to dominate the education of blacks in the South resulted in frequent attempts to sabotage black efforts. Jones found in her study of the education of blacks in Georgia[69] that the AMA had "great contempt for independent black teachers" and was also "perverse in [its] attempt to thwart efforts at black self-help in education."[70]

African Americans had great difficulty being accepted as teachers with white missionary organizations due to issues of race. As noted above, the organization also attempted to limit the influence of black teachers on black students by denying teaching positions to literate African Americans.

Historians have concluded that New England ethnocentricism and notions of cultural supremacy, along with the refusal of the white missionary organizations to employ African Americans in prominent positions, resulted in a negative impact on blacks. Carter G. Woodson observed in 1933 that the missionary educators in the South sought to "transform and not develop" blacks.[71] The negative impact was especially reflected in negative self-images of African Americans, which will be discussed in more detail later.

The missionary role in common-school education of African Americans diminished greatly by the end of the nineteenth century with the establishment of the public school system. However, as James Anderson has noted, with the end of Reconstruction, the small gains that African Americans had made with public education eroded with public funds for black students being diverted to whites. As a result, African Americans utilized their meager earnings to establish schools. Thus, they experienced double taxation for education. In addition, most black students, particularly in rural areas, had no access to schooling, public or private. As late as 1910, there was not a rural eight-grade public school for black students, nor was there a black public high school, urban or rural, in the entire South. The white planter class made every attempt to thwart black access to schooling so as to contain their aspirations and mobility. According to Anderson, of the more than 2 million black youth aged five to fourteen in 1900, only 36 percent attended school. Of the more than 1 million black youth aged five to nine at this same time period, only 22 percent attended school. Of those youth with access to education, 86 percent of them went to school for less than six months out of the year. Anderson points out that transportation for black youth was nonexistent, and black students often walked more than a mile and a half each way through difficult roads and weather.[72]

Because of Jim Crow laws, poor education, and better opportunities elsewhere, black migration to the North began during the second decade of the twentieth century. This event alarmed white Southerners, who saw the drain of cheap labor from the region. Anderson notes that a report from the United States Department of Labor asserted that increased opportunities for schooling would "keep the Negroes in the South and make them satisfied with their lot."[73]

While missionary efforts were primarily confined to higher education in the twentieth century, this period witnessed the rise in importance of corporate and foundation support and control of black education. Julius Rosenwald, the president of Sears, Roebuck and Company, funded a massive building project to erect schools for blacks in the rural South. In addition, the Anna T. Jeanes Foundation provided large sums of money to establish the Negro Rural School Fund. The Jeanes Fund helped to fund teachers of industrial education and county supervisors. With these two funding sources, African American parents worked in concert to create a system of schools for their children. Anderson notes that the Rosenwald funding was the dramatic rural school construction program of the period. By 1932, some 4,977 rural black schools, with a capacity for 663,615 students, were built. These schools were located in 883 counties through fifteen Southern states and included teachers' homes and industrial shops.

These schools were funded through a variety of sources: the Julius Rosenwald Fund gave 15.36 percent, and rural black residents gave 16.64 percent; white donations were 4.27 percent, and 63.73 percent came from appropriated public taxes that were collected primarily from African American taxpayers.[74]

Anderson notes that while it is generally believed that the Rosenwald Fund paid fully for the rural schools (because the schools were called Rosenwald schools), in reality this fund never paid even half the cost. Most of the funds came from private contributions, public taxes, and rural black citizens.[75]

Curricular Issues

The greatest issue for the education of the freedmen other than access was that of curriculum. Classical education, which emphasized Greek and Latin, higher mathematics, advanced science, and literature, was viewed as the curriculum of elite white males. This type of education was viewed as inappropriate for blacks and women—who were destined for a life of service and not leadership. In addition, this type of education reflected the curricular offerings of secondary schools and colleges. In the minds of most Southern whites, this was significantly more education than was deemed necessary for African Americans. The preferred type of education for blacks was that of industrial or manual training—and the emphasis was on *training*.

The debate over classical education versus industrial education has usually been confined to the ideological difference between the classically trained W. E. B. Du Bois of Fisk and Harvard universities, and the manually trained Booker T. Washington of Hampton Institute. While these two men brought the discussion of curriculum to a national level, the topic was not a new one.

In the North, throughout the 1880s, African Americans discussed the need for blacks to obtain industrial training for greater employment opportunities. As with the issue of separate versus integrated schools, blacks held diverse opinions on the topic. The black press fully covered the issue. The *People's Advocate* of Washington, D.C., stated:

> While the whites may be in a condition to foster academical training and to require those mental luxuries, it will not be doubted that the colored people as a class are not quite ready for it. . . . We feel that the colored people of the country can expect to rise to permanent equality mainly by industrial education–intelligent labor in every department of industry—and that the public mind should be directed to that end is only too patent.[76]

T. Thomas Fortune, close friend of Booker T. Washington and editor of the *New York Globe*, supported the industrial-educational philosophy:

> The flowery education, the education which develops the mental but neglects the physical man, is not what we need most at this time. Colleges for higher education are good things and necessary, but they presuppose by their existence conditions auxiliary and consonant, conditions of the highest civilization, which give encouragement and support to the polished man.[77]

The opponents of industrial education were also vocal:

> Much is being said at present in favor of industrial training, but it is to be
> hoped that a more intelligent person thinks that we have a sufficient number
> of skilled and professional laborers. There is not any danger of the colored
> race having too many skilled and professional men for *many* years to come,
> such is the demand for them, and so inadequate are the facilities for the
> education of colored youth in general. . . . The skilled laborer should have
> the best common school education, if not a collegiate education, that is
> possible. To make a professional man, it is absolutely necessary that the
> person have the best collegiate education possible. This is apparent to all
> intelligent persons, and it behooves parents to use every effort in giving their
> children a collegiate education, which does not mean simply finishing the
> high school.[78]

This debate continued in the North, where both types of education
were possible. In the South, in the 1880s, very few high schools existed for
African Americans, and the black colleges that were established after the
Civil War throughout the South were of preparatory and high school level.
In 1886, black people in New Jersey established an industrial school, which
the state took over fourteen years later.[79] In Philadelphia, in 1888, Fanny
Jackson Coppin succeeded in having an industrial department added to the
classical Institute for Colored Youth. Inspired by the Centennial Exhibition
in Philadelphia in 1876, Coppin observed exhibits on industries and technology from not only the United States but also from fifty-eight countries of
the world. She recognized that blacks were excluded from jobs in emerging
fields. Coppin, speaking at a meeting at the Philadelphia school board on
the future of industrial education in the public schools, stated that "As I
saw building after building going up in the city [Philadelphia], and not a
single colored hand employed in the construction, it made the occasion a
very serious one to me."[80]

As trade unions grew in power and prominence, blacks found themselves
shut out of opportunities through these groups. Employment was a civil right.
Coppin stated:

We [blacks] shall go forward in asking to enter the same employments which other people enter. Within the past ten years we have made almost no advance in getting our youth into industrial and business occupations. It is just as hard to get a boy into a printing office now as it was ten years ago. It is simply astonishing when we consider how many of the common vocations of life colored people are shut out of. Colored men are not admitted to the Printers' Trade Union, nor, with very rare exceptions, are they employed in any city of the United States in a paid capacity as printers or writers. . . . We are not employed as salesmen, or pharmacists, or saleswomen, or bank clerks, or merchants' clerks, or tradesmen, or mechanics, or telegraph operators, or to any degree as State or Government officials, and I could keep on with the "ors" until tomorrow morning.[81]

Many other blacks in the North advocated "industrial" training and employment for members of the race. Alexander Crummell spoke before the House Committee on Education and Labor in Washington, D.C., in 1880 and expressed urgency for trade education for African Americans. He informed the committee: "They [black] people are servants; and the only employment they can get is that of service. They are shut out from trades."[82]

An article in the *Christian Recorder* in 1881 repeated these feelings:

Our children, who are growing in years, need trades as well as mental culture . . . open the factories, and, in fact, all the department of mechanism, and etc., to our children . . ."union" must be the motto.[83]

Indeed, as the industrial department opened at the Institute for Colored Youth, the board of managers emphasized that the literary department was the "main purpose of the Institute," but stated that the industrial department would "widen their [blacks'] field of usefulness by preparing many of the colored people to become good mechanics, and thus equip them with the same chances of success in life enjoyed by their more favored brethren."[84] The ICY offered courses in plumbing, carpentry, blacksmithing, bricklaying, mechanical drawing, baking, sewing, wood carving, design, typewriting, and telegraphy. All of these courses corresponded to the growth in employment in these areas.[85]

W. E. B. Du Bois, the champion of classical education, also advocated and understood the importance of industrial training. In his study of the Philadelphia Negro in the 1890s, he noted the decline of blacks employed in the trades since the early nineteenth century. Du Bois supported Coppin's advocacy of industrial education. Du Bois noted that benevolent organizations and philanthropists had not encouraged or assisted African Americans in obtaining trade education:

> If now a benevolent despot had seen the development [technical education], he would immediately have sought to remedy the real weakness of the Negro's position, i.e., his lack of training; and he would have swept away any discrimination that compelled men to support as criminals those who might support themselves as workmen. . . . There was, however, no despot, no philanthropist, no far-seeing captain of industry to prevent the Negro from losing even the skill he had learned or to inspire him by opportunities to learn more. As the older Negroes with trades dropped off, there was little to induce younger men to succeed them. On the contrary, special effort was made not to train Negroes for industry or to allow them to enter on such a career.[86]

Industrial Education—Southern Style

While the advocacy for industrial education in the North corresponded directly to the growth of unionized trades, industrial education in the South became identified with a conservative ideology to confine African Americans to "Negro" positions. The institutions most identified with industrial education were Hampton Institute in Virginia, and Tuskegee Institute, funded by the state of Alabama and established under the leadership of well-known educator Booker T. Washington.

James Anderson, who has written extensively on the Hampton model of industrial education, states that the institution's primary objective was to train

MPI / Hulton Archive / Getty Images

This vocational school (Tuskegee Normal and Industrial Institute) was established by the Alabama legislature in 1881 and Booker T. Washington (1856–1915) was its first principal, who ensured its success. At the time of his death in 1915, the Tuskegee Institute had more than 100 buildings, a faculty of around 200, a student body of 1,500, and an endowment of 2 million dollars. One of Tuskegee's most noteworthy faculty members was the botanist George Washington Carver (c.1864–1943), who experimented with peanuts, soybeans, sweet potatoes, and other crops. Pictured here are students in the laboratory in 1884.

a cadre of conservative black teachers who were to help African Americans in the South adjust to a subordinate social and political role.[87] The Hampton Normal and Industrial Institute was founded in 1868 by Samuel Chapman Armstrong, a white son of missionaries, with the assistance of the American Missionary Association to prepare African Americans for their appropriate role in the post-Reconstruction South. This included an emphasis on moral and character training and a shunning of any desire for political equality and activism. Armstrong viewed African Americans as morally inferior to whites, which, according to him, kept them in a degraded state. He stated that white control was necessary because that group surpassed African Americans "in moral strength, in guiding instincts, in power to 'sense things' in the genius for this or that." Armstrong also commented that he believed that the issue with blacks was not intellect, but morality.[88]

Unlike Coppin and other Northern blacks who viewed industrial training as a vehicle for entrepreneurship, Armstrong proposed for Hampton a curriculum that was, according to Anderson, designed to "mainly train black ideologues who were expected to model and transmit Armstrong's philosophy of Southern Reconstruction to the Afro-American working class." This model became known as the Hampton Idea. This philosophy prepared students for the lowest types of employment in the South and also taught them to develop a subservient demeanor. The students at Hampton were trained to be teachers, and not tradesmen and women. Hampton did not offer trade certificates until 1895—and even by 1900, only 45 of its 656 students were enrolled in the trade school.[89] All students at Hampton were required to work. Those in the academic normal-school program worked two ten-hour days, and those in the manual training program worked six ten-hour days.

Booker T. Washington, an 1875 graduate of Hampton, became synonymous with the conservative racial ideology of the Hampton Idea. Anderson notes that Hampton deliberately trained its black students to espouse beliefs that were detrimental to the economic and political well-being of the black community.[90] In his first major speech in 1884, after the Supreme Court declared the Civil Rights Act of 1875 unconstitutional, Washington addressed the National Education Association in Madison, Wisconsin, stating:

> Brains, property and character for the Negro will settle the question of civil rights. The best course to pursue in regard to the civil rights bill in the South is to let it alone and it will settle itself. Good school teachers and plenty of money to pay them will be more potent in settling the race question than many civil rights bills and investigating committees.[91]

Washington established Tuskegee Institute in Alabama in 1881 on the Hampton model. Both institutions drew considerable funding from Northern philanthropists, primarily because these schools advocated blacks remaining in the South and taught their students to aspire to occupations that were considered "honorable" and most often menial.[92] Washington's ridicule of classically trained blacks was legendary. He called them "loafers" and stated that they walked around with "beaver hat, kid gloves, and walking cane" and contributed nothing to the race.[93] Washington's most infamous address was in Atlanta in 1895 at the Cotton Exposition, when he urged blacks not to seek social equality with whites. This lecture coincided with the continued erosion of rights for African Americans. The following year, in 1896, the Supreme Court handed down the *Plessy v. Ferguson* decision, which mandated "separate but equal" treatment of blacks in public accommodations as well as other aspects of public life. This decision resulted in Southern states passing laws prohibiting the integration of public schools.[94] It was not until 1954 that this ruling was reversed.

In a collection of essays on "the Negro problem" in 1903, Washington expounded on his view of industrial education. He wrote:

> No race can be lifted until its mind is awakened and strengthened. By the side of industrial training should always go mental and moral training, but the pushing of mere abstract knowledge into the head means little. We want more than the mere performance of mental gymnastics. Our knowledge must be harnessed to the things of real life. I would encourage the Negro to secure all the mental strength, all the mental culture — whether gleaned from science, mathematics, history, language or literature that his circumstances will allow, but I believe most earnestly that for years to come the education of the people of my race should be so directed that the greatest proportion of the mental strength of the masses will be brought to bear upon the every-day practical things of life.[95]

It was at this point that W. E. B. Du Bois vocalized his opposition to Washington's conservative educational philosophy. In the same volume, Du Bois responded with an essay entitled *The Talented Tenth*. He noted that while industrial education was important, it was essential for African Americans to have liberally trained members who would serve as the leadership of the race. On manual and industrial training, Du Bois wrote:

I am an earnest advocate of manual training and trade teaching for black boys, and for white boys, too. . . . I insist that the object of all true education is not to make men carpenters, it is to make carpenters men.[96]

But despite Du Bois's beliefs, by the beginning of the twentieth century Northern foundations and philanthropists dominated the funding of black education in the South. They were smitten with the Hampton Idea. Prominent among them were the Southern Education Board and the General Education Board. Millionaire Northern industrialists headed both of these groups and were members of the board of trustees at Hampton and Tuskegee' institutes. Prominent among them were Robert C. Ogden, a New York merchant; William H. Baldwin Jr., a railroad entrepreneur; George Foster Peabody, Wall Street banker; and other industrialists, such as William E. Dodge, Collis P. Huntington, John D. Rockefeller, and George Eastman.

The above foundations and philanthropists dominated the shaping of education for blacks in the rural South.[97] The control of rural black education was through three major functions: the establishment of state supervisors for Negro rural schools in all the Southern states; the placing of county-supervising industrial teachers (known as Jeanes teachers) in Southern counties; and the development of county training schools—which was, according to James Anderson, the "most important mechanism for translating the GEB's [General Education Board] educational concerns into institutional action at the local level."[98]

County training schools were essentially elementary schools in rural areas that offered industrial education with a strong emphasis upon agriculture and domestic work. Some became secondary schools for the training of industrial-arts teachers.[99] These schools had a profound effect on black education in the South. Anderson notes that the number of county training schools went from four in 1911, to 356 in 1933. These schools were the only source of secondary education for blacks in 293 of 912 counties in the Southern and border states.[100]

Vanessa Siddle Walker provides an excellent case study of the plight of a rural county training school, the Caswell County Training School.

Walker's chronicle of this school and its supporters reinforces Anderson's research on the significant efforts of African Americans to pay for the education of their children. The Caswell County Training School (CCTS) of Caswell County, North Carolina, was established in 1906 when several prominent blacks purchased a two-story house. By 1924, the school was expanded to a four-room "Rosenwald" school, with black citizens donating $800 for this new structure.[101] Walker notes that the black parents of the students at CCTS had repeatedly been denied a high school prior to 1934. When a new principal arrived in that year, a high school was finally added. Seventy-seven students enrolled in the high school, many of whom traveled for more than twenty miles on an open-air truck, donated by a parent. The black parents paid for the electric bill of the school, provided band uniforms and instruments, science equipment, a piano, workbooks, other equipment for the school, and support for the teachers and pupils throughout the existence of the school. A parent donated nine and a half acres to the county for the expansion of a new school site. White school officials delayed this for thirteen years.[102]

What was significant about CCTS was not that black parents and community greatly subsidized the meagerly funded black school, but the fact that the underfunded school far surpassed the school for whites in the county. When the school closed in 1969, its principal, Nicholas Longworth Dillard, held a master's degree from the University of Michigan. By 1954, 64 percent of the school's teachers had graduate-school training beyond that required for state recertification. CCTS had been accredited since 1934, while the white school was not accredited, was smaller, and had fewer facilities. Despite the training-school label, which was to produce farmers and domestics, CCTS offered a college-prep curriculum and more than fifty-three extracurricular clubs, an award-winning debate team, and a host of other impressive activities. The parents of the students were nearly 60 percent farmers. That these parents made enormous sacrifices to ensure that their children received the best education possible was not unusual for poor African Americans. These sacrifices can be traced from slavery. When the parents at CCTS finally had a new school erected in 1951, they had contributed close to $8,000 of their own money for this accomplishment.[103]

Black Higher Education

The first institution of higher education in the United States was Harvard University in Cambridge, Massachusetts, established in 1636. Higher education grew slowly, and for more than 110 years, there were only three colleges (Harvard, William and Mary, and Yale) in the nation. By the Revolutionary War, six additional colleges existed, all but one (Dartmouth) located in the middle states. However, by the nineteenth century, there was tremendous growth in higher education. Some opportunities for African Americans to attend white institutions of higher education existed in the North in the early nineteenth century. Because the earliest institutions of higher education were established for white males for political leadership and the clergy, few opportunities to attend college were available for black men, and virtually none for African American women. Nevertheless, there are some records of black men attending white institutions of higher education by the 1820s. John Brown Russworm and Edward Jones graduated from Bowdoin College in Maine and Amherst College in Massachusetts, respectively. With their education sponsored by the American Colonization Society, both men were sent to Liberia after their graduation.

In 1833, Oberlin College in Ohio was the first white institution of higher education to admit African American men and women on an equal basis with whites. As a result, most of the earliest black college graduates of the nineteenth century were Oberlin graduates.[104] By the end of the Civil War, twenty-eight blacks (twenty-five men and three women) had earned baccalaureate degrees. Following in the tradition of Oberlin, in 1866 Berea College in Kentucky opened its doors to black students and established a policy of admitting students without regard to racial origin. Berea experienced protest from most of the white students and faculty. In 1904, a state law was passed in Kentucky that forbade the teaching of students in an integrated setting. Thus, blacks could no longer attend Berea until 1950, when the 1904 law was amended.

During Reconstruction, blacks experienced a series of gains and "firsts" in higher education. For example, in 1870 Richard T. Greener successfully completed a degree from Harvard University. Edward A. Bouchet became the first black member of Phi Beta Kappa in the nation in 1874, and in 1876 was awarded a Ph.D. in physics from Yale University.[105] In 1877, Henry O. Flipper, the son of former slaves, became the first black graduate of West Point.[106] Black men attended Harvard Law and Medical schools during the 1870s, and by 1890 W. E. B. Du Bois became the sixth black man to graduate from Harvard, and by 1896 the first to receive a Ph.D.

Despite the presence of small numbers of African Americans in white institutions in the nineteenth and early twentieth centuries, most experienced continuous racism on these campuses. Du Bois, in his study *College-Bred Negro* (1900), noted that black students on white college campuses were "tolerated" and not "welcomed." Discussing the outcome of the Berea College incident, Charles W. Eliot, then president of Harvard University, stated, "Perhaps if there were as many Negroes here as there [Berea] we might think it better for them to be in separate schools. At present, Harvard has about five thousand white students and about thirty of the colored race. The latter are hidden in the great mass and are not noticeable. If they were equal in numbers or in a majority, we might deem a separation necessary."[107]

Most African American students were barred from living on campus, and in the rare instances when they were allowed housing on campus, they were given single rooms. They were routinely denied entrance to most social, athletic, and academic organizations. While black men were often on football and track teams, they were prohibited from basketball, baseball, and swimming teams. The first recorded players on a white basketball team were at the University of Nebraska in 1908–1910. By 1919, Columbia University had one black player, and in the 1920s, Oberlin was represented. Even by 1940, no African American was permitted to play basketball on a Big Ten university team.[108] When questioned regarding the absence of blacks from basketball and swimming, the director of athletics of the University of Illinois stated that blacks were primarily jumpers and sprinters, which explained their presence only in the sports of football and track. [109]

Paul Robeson, the internationally renowned singer and actor, was not allowed to sing in the glee club of Rutgers University, his alma mater. Robeson was All-American at Rutgers and won four varsity letters as an undergraduate. He was Phi Beta Kappa, the organization for high scholastic honors. Jesse

Owens, winner of four gold medals in the 1936 Berlin Olympics, was denied entrance into the honorary athletic society at his alma mater, Ohio State University.[110]

Racism towards African American students increased at places thought to be liberal, such as Oberlin College, after the end of the Civil War and Reconstruction. William E. Bigglestone, former archivist of Oberlin, in an article entitled "Oberlin College and the Negro Student, 1865–1940," notes the change in racial attitudes and behavior of students after the Civil War. He maintains that as the nation moved towards more discriminatory laws against African Americans, so did institutions of higher education. Bigglestone noted the beginning of segregated seating in the dining hall, the barring of black students from literary and other clubs on the Oberlin campus, and segregation in housing. In response, by 1908 black students established their own literary clubs at Oberlin. In a discussion of the exclusion of African Americans from literary clubs at Oberlin, one white member stated that the clubs were both literary and social. Thus, "The presence of a colored man in our ranks would for many of us spoil utterly the social side of society life." He further stated that since blacks were not treated equally outside of Oberlin, it would not be wise to treat them as equals at Oberlin. In other words, it was cruel to give blacks at Oberlin a false sense of social equality with whites. Discrimination at Oberlin continued throughout the twentieth century. The college informed black GIs after World War I that they could not live in the same barracks with white students, and suggested they go to African American colleges such as Howard or Wilberforce (in Ohio).[111]

Institutions of higher education specifically for African Americans were established in the 1850s outside of the South. As with the efforts for rudimentary and secondary education, African Americans were at the forefront of higher education as well. White Methodists established Wilberforce College initially in 1856, and by 1863 the Ohio conference of African Methodists purchased the college. After three years of planning, the college opened in 1866. In 1856 John Miller Dickey, a white Princeton graduate, and his wife Sarah Emlen Cresson founded Ashmun Institute in Pennsylvania for the "male youth of African descent." It was later renamed Lincoln University in 1866 in honor of Abraham Lincoln. As noted previously, African Americans viewed education as important for the entire race. Thus, Wilberforce College was established for the education of black youth, while Lincoln University was established for the education of black males.

Black Higher Education in the South

Twenty-four private colleges for African Americans were established ten years after Emancipation by black denominations, white churches, the Freedmen's Bureau, and the American Missionary Association. By 1890, each Southern and border state received federal funds from the Second Morrill Act, which stated: "The establishment and maintenance of colleges separately for White and colored students will be held in compliance with the provisions of this act if the funds received in such State or Territory be equitably divided as herein after set forth." These institutions were responsible for most of the secondary education available to blacks until the early decades of the twentieth century.

Despite the title of "college," most of these institutions were of elementary and high school grades well into the twentieth century. Anderson notes that even by 1917, a report on black higher education indicated that only one of the sixteen black land-grant institutions offered classes of collegiate level — Florida Agricultural and Mechanical College, with twelve students.[112] In addition to the sixteen black land-grant institutions, seven state-controlled colleges also existed at this time. Of the 7,513 combined enrollments at the land-grant and state-controlled institutions, 2,474 of these students were in elementary courses, 3,400 were in secondary classes, and only twelve, as previously mentioned, were studying college-level courses.[113]

The Northern missionary organizations, prominently among them the AMA, had the most academic institutions and provided collegiate courses. Prominent AMA colleges included Fisk University (Tennessee), Dillard (Louisiana), Talladega College (Alabama), and Tougaloo College (Mississippi). The Freedmen's Aid Society of the Methodist Church included Bennett College (North Carolina), Clark University (Georgia), Claflin College (South Carolina), Meharry Medical College (Tennessee), Morgan College

(Maryland), Philander Smith College (Arkansas), Rust College (Mississippi), and Wiley College (Texas). The American Baptist Home Mission Society established Benedict College (South Carolina), Bishop College (Texas), Morehouse College (Georgia), Shaw University (North Carolina), Spelman College (Georgia), and Virginia Union (Virginia). The Presbyterian Board of Missions established Johnson C. Smith (North Carolina), Knoxville College (Tennessee), and Stillman College (Alabama). Nondenominational institutions included Atlanta University (Georgia), Howard University (Washington, D.C.), and Leland University (Louisiana).[114]

Colleges established by black denominations such as the African Methodist Episcopal Church included Allen University (South Carolina), Morris Brown College (Georgia), Wilberforce (Ohio), Paul Quinn College (Texas), Edward Waters College (Florida), Kittrell College, and Shorter College. The African Methodist Episcopal Zion Church founded Livingston College (North Carolina). Meanwhile, the Colored Methodist Episcopal Church established Lane (Tennessee), Paine (Alabama), Texas (Texas), and Miles Memorial (Alabama). Black Baptist colleges included Arkansas Baptist College, Selma University (Alabama), and Virginia College and Seminary.[115]

As with efforts in establishing the common schools, white missionary founders of colleges were often in conflict with efforts of black educators and parents to establish and control their own institutions. Historian James M. McPherson noted that many blacks resented the patronizing attitude of missionaries towards them and sought independent institutions. While the missionary schools were significantly better funded and staffed, many blacks wanted their own institutions. The push for black institutions with black faculty was particularly important because few blacks served on the faculties of the colleges established by white missionaries. As with the argument for the need for black teachers in the common schools, the same rationale was presented for the importance of their presence in higher education. Francis Grimke stated in 1885 that the development of racial pride should be an essential aspect of black education. He noted that missionary schools with white-only faculties had perpetuated black low self-esteem. Grimke stated, "The intellects of our young people are being educated at the expense of their manhood. In the classroom they see only white professors." The result was, according to Grimke, "to associate these places and the idea and fitness for them only with white men."[116] Grimke's views were shared by many other African Americans. McPherson noted that many blacks in Mississippi were unhappy with the white-controlled Tougaloo College and pressured the white legislature to create a college for blacks that would be controlled by them. As a result, Alcorn College was established and controlled by African Americans. By the end of the century, all black public colleges were headed by African American men.[117]

As mentioned earlier, those institutions established by missionaries offered the classical liberal-arts curriculum. The attitude of most of the missionary founders was that African Americans were hindered by slavery and not intellect. Thus, they believed that with the requisite cultural and religious exposure and teaching, educated blacks would become the leaders of their communities. But the emphasis on European history, culture, and values became an issue for many African Americans. As early as 1900, W. E. B. Du Bois began to study black life, culture, and education at Atlanta University. And Carter G. Woodson, graduate of Berea College and Harvard University, began the *Journal of Negro History* in 1916. Woodson was very critical of the psychological and cultural damage that education minus a cultural and historical context had on African Americans. In an explosive 1933 book entitled *The Mis-Education of the Negro*, Woodson charged that educated blacks would be the least likely to help the race, because they were being educated to hate themselves. He noted that the aim of the missionary educator who established schools for blacks in the South was "to transform the Negroes, not to develop them." Woodson noted that blacks' achievements in literature, science, and history were not studied. Woodson stated that with "mis-educated Negroes" in positions of power, the status quo would not change.[118]

Langston Hughes, the renowned writer of the Harlem Renaissance, attended Lincoln University in Pennsylvania in the 1920s. At that time, the institution barred blacks from the faculty and board of trustees. Hughes conducted a survey of his classmates to discern their feelings about the exclusion of blacks from both of these groups. Hughes was shocked to discover that two-thirds of his classmates indicated that they did not want black professors. The reasons given varied: blacks lacked morality, few blacks were qualified, and it was a white-founded school so whites had a right to control it. Hughes was so outraged by his findings that he wrote an article in *Crisis* magazine (the journal of the NAACP) entitled "Cowards from the Colleges."[119] Hughes wrote that he thought it was the "height of absurdity for an institution designed for the training of the Negro leaders to support and uphold, on its own groups, the unfair and discriminatory practices of the American color line."[120]

In addition to issues regarding white control of black institutions of higher education, the issue of gender emerged as a topic as well. While African American women have always sought, and been encouraged, to obtain an education, the paternalism that existed on black campuses also translated into sexism as well. Lucy Diggs Slowe, the first African American woman dean at Howard University, was a leader and advocate for the voice of the black female student. Slowe was an expert in student personnel development. She served as dean of women at Howard University from 1922–1937. Her leadership in black women's higher education resulted in the establishment of two important organizations for the advocacy of African American women college students—the National Association of College Women (NACW, established in 1923) and the National Association of Women's Deans and Advisors of Colored Schools (NAWDACS, established in 1929). Although black education was seen as preparing black students for leadership and service to their race, Slowe was concerned that African American women did not have the same opportunities for leadership training on black college campuses. In addition, she was very critical of the fact that black female students were channeled into teaching as their primary and almost exclusive career option. During Slowe's tenure as dean of women at Howard, as well as president of the two above women's organizations, she produced research to document the status of black female students in black colleges.[121]

While the colleges established by the missionary philanthropists were criticized for their Eurocentric orientation and exclusion of African Americans from their faculties, the Hampton-Tuskegee model reaped the financial backing of the corporate philanthropists. An organization known as the Conference for Education in the South met in Capon Spring, West Virginia, from 1898 to 1900, and other locations annually throughout the South from 1901 to 1914, to discuss appropriate educational plans for blacks in the region.

This organization included the leaders of the Slater, Jeanes, Phelp-Stokes, and Rosenwald foundations; the Southern Education Board; the Rockefeller General Education Board; and white Southern educational reformers. No blacks were invited to attend the first three meetings, and none of the Northern missionary groups were ever included.[122]

William H. Baldwin, the first chairman of the General Education Board, professed his opposition to "so-called higher education of Negroes" and said that blacks "should not be educated out of [their] environment." Another foundation official also stated, "We have no thought of colonizing teachers from the North, nor of transplanting northern ideas. On the contrary, we believe that the teachers of the South should be the product of the soil of the South, and that your schools should be organized by yourselves in harmony with your traditions and institutions."[123]

Such efforts of the corporate philanthropists combined with the efforts of the state governments to transform the black land-grant colleges into vocational and normal schools. Anderson's work reveals that Southern state officials deliberately contained the academic offerings of black state colleges. He noted in 1904 that Governor James K. Vardaman of Mississippi closed Holly Springs Normal School for blacks, stating that education was "ruining our Negroes . . . they are demanding equality." In 1919, the two black state colleges, Alabama State College and Alabama A and M, were placed under the governance of the Alabama State Board of Education. The board immediately reduced the offerings of these colleges to two-year programs. This resulted in there being no state college in Alabama that offered a four-year course of study. Alabama State College became a four-year institution again in 1931, and Alabama A and M had their four-year status restored in 1940. The continued impoverishment impacted public secondary education as well. W. E. B. Du Bois, in his study *College Bred Negro American* in 1910, noted the number of college-level students and listed the classical courses offered. Du Bois lamented the dearth of public high schools for African Americans in the South, which compelled black colleges to offer elementary and secondary education.[124] By World War I, 99 percent of all students attending black public colleges were enrolled below the college level.[125]

World War I and the New Negro Movement of the 1920s, which emphasized black pride and a heightened political awareness, resulted in blacks
becoming increasingly vocal regarding racism and segregation. While blacks
could attend many white institutions of higher education in the North,
W. E. B. Du Bois chronicled each August in *Crisis* (the NAACP journal) the
progress and challenges of black students in white institutions. Most black
students were segregated in housing and barred from many extracurricular
activities on white campuses. By the 1930s, the NAACP sought to dismantle
the *Plessy* separate-but-equal doctrine. Graduate and professional schools
were challenged first.

A suit against the University of North Carolina Law School was lost in 1933
because the president of the North Carolina Negro College refused to certify
the scholastic record of the plaintiff.[126] To respond to the absence of graduate
and professional education for black students in Southern states, some states
began providing out-of-state scholarships for the remission of transportation
and any tuition charges above that charged by the state universities. The
legality of this method was tested in Maryland in 1935. Three months after
the act for out-of-state scholarship was passed, 284 black students formally applied for these awards. Limited funds provided for only 97 scholarships. Thus,
187 students were left without funds. This resulted in a lawsuit against the
University of Maryland by Donald Murray, a graduate of Amherst College
and a resident of Baltimore. Lawyers for the NAACP argued that Maryland
offered professional training to white students in a tax-supported institution,
but denied such training to black students, thus violating the Fourteenth
Amendment.[127] In 1936, the suit won in the court of appeals, which ruled that
that state was obligated to supply a first-class law school for African Americans
or admit them to the existing law school.[128] Since the latter alternative was
the only option of the state, Murray became the first black graduate of the
University of Maryland in 1938. Although the court avoided redefining *Plessy*,
it opened an important door for blacks by ordering integration as a remedy
when no other solution was readily available.

Several months after the Murray case, a similar suit was filed by Lloyd
Gaines, a graduate of Lincoln University in Missouri, against the University
of Missouri Law School. Gaines refused an out-of-state scholarship to attend

a law school in a neighboring state and argued that this remedy did not satisfy the requirement of equal treatment.[129] This case, which went all the way to the Supreme Court, ruled in Gaines's favor and became a major victory for blacks. The Court ruled:

> The basic consideration is not as to what sort of opportunities other states provide, or whether they are as good as those in Missouri, but as to what opportunities Missouri itself furnishes to white students and denies to Negroes solely upon the ground of color. . . . Manifestly, the obligation of the state to give the protection of equal laws can be performed only where its laws operate, that is, within its own jurisdiction . . . nor can we regard the fact that there is but limited demand in Missouri for the legal education of Negroes as excusing the discrimination in favor of whites. . . . Here petitioner's right was a personal one. It was as an individual that he was entitled to the equal protection of the laws, and the state was bound to furnish him within its borders facilities for legal education substantially equal to those which the state has afforded for persons of the white race.[130]

While this ruling removed the legal basis for providing out-of-state scholarships for black students, it failed to redefine the *Plessy* doctrine. The case was returned to the Missouri courts for execution of the order, when mysteriously Gaines disappeared, never to be found again. As a result, no black person attended a white institution in Missouri for another fifteen years.[131]

After the *Gaines* decision, Southern states established black graduate and professional schools to bar black students from entering white institutions. The next three legal cases proved to be crucial to the decision of blacks entering truly Southern white institutions. In 1946, Ada L. Sipuel brought to court a suit against the University of Oklahoma based on the *Gaines* case.[132] After two years of appeals, the Supreme Court ruled that the state had to provide Sipuel with an opportunity for legal education.[133] Soon afterwards, the university regents announced that Langston University, the state black institution, had established a law school to receive Sipuel in Oklahoma City. Three white lawyers had been assigned to teach her in a room in the state capitol.[134] Refusing to accept a one-room law-school education, the Supreme

Court denied further relief on the technicality that the question of segregation was not before it, and the manner in which its previous mandate was carried out was a matter for the state courts to decide. Starting the legal suit all over again, challenging the segregated one-room school, Sipuel was finally admitted to the University of Oklahoma in 1949.[135]

During the same period as the Sipuel case, another legal attack was being waged at the University of Oklahoma. G. W. McLaurin, a fifty-four-year-old professor emeritus of Langston University, was seeking a doctorate in education. A special three-judge panel held that he was entitled to the only graduate courses in his field offered by the state.[136] As a result, the Oklahoma legislature amended the state law to permit the admission of black students to the university for courses not offered at Langston, but also stipulated that segregation should be maintained on the university's campus. As a result, McLaurin was forced to sit in an adjacent room to "listen in" during the lecture, and to sit at a special table in the cafeteria and library. In 1949 McLaurin returned to court stating that these restrictions violated the equal-protection clauses of the Fourteenth Amendment.[137] Ruling in McLaurin's favor, the Oklahoma State Supreme Court held that the restrictions impaired and inhibited his ability to study, to engage in discussions and exchange views with other students, and further concluded that the "appellant, having been admitted to a state supported school, must receive the same treatment at the hands of the state as students of other races."[138]

The final case was a suit filed by Herman Sweatt in 1946 against the University of Texas Law School. The court ruled that he was entitled to relief. The state was given six months to establish a law school equal to the University of Texas-Austin. While the new law school was completed as scheduled, Sweatt refused to enroll and appealed the case.[139] Sweatt fought through the Texas courts without success, and finally, in 1949, appealed to the Supreme Court. This case was unique in NAACP strategy because this was the first case that attacked segregation head-on. The lawyers not only utilized legal arguments but also provided testimonies from anthropologists, educators, and other scholars who discussed the intellectual capabilities of blacks, the harmful impact of segregation on individuals, and the deleterious effects of classification by race. In summary, the experts stated that no segregated institution could be equal. The Court agreed. It not only found the black law school inferior in terms of faculty, courses, library, and other aspects, but it also noted:

> What is more important, the University of Texas Law School possesses to a far greater degree those qualities which are incapable of objective measurement but which make for greatness in a law school. Such qualities, to name but a few, include reputation of the faculty, experience of the administration, position and influence of the alumni, standing in the community, traditions and prestige.[140]

Thus, the Sipuel, McLaurin, and Sweatt cases, while not overturning the *Plessy* doctrine, did succeed in ruling out segregation in specific instances. These cases resulted in either voluntary or legally enforced desegregation of graduate and professional schools in all the Southern states, with the exception of Alabama, Florida, Georgia, Mississippi, and South Carolina.[141] Although these cases assured the desegregation of graduate and professional education, there remained the question of the segregation of black students from public elementary, secondary, and undergraduate education.

Brown v. Board of Education

In the late 1920s, the NAACP began replacing its white lawyers with a small cadre of brilliant Harvard Law School–trained black lawyers. Charles Hamilton Houston, a distinguished graduate of Amherst and Harvard Law School, as well as the current dean of the Howard University Law School, was hired part-time by the Legal Committee of the NAACP in 1934. From 1935 to 1940, Houston served in a full-time position as special counsel. He had distinguished himself by transforming Howard University's Law School into a training ground for studying the law and race. illiam Hastie and Leon Ransom taught with Houston at Howard and also worked with him at the NAACP. Thurgood Marshall, Houston's former student at Howard Law School, served as assistant special counsel from 1936 to 1938 and special counsel in 1938.[142]

In 1939, the NAACP established the Legal Defense Fund, Inc. as the nonprofit educational and legal agency of the organization. Known as the "Inc. Fund," this entity allowed the organization to receive tax-deductible contributions as well as to separate its activities from the propaganda of the larger organization. In the Inc. Fund's strategy to dismantle *Plessy*, Houston had a three-pronged attack. He viewed education as central to his strategy. Houston noted, "Education . . . is a preparation for the competition of life. . . . [A] poor education handicaps an individual in the competition."[143]

Houston's plan of attack was to pursue lawsuits seeking the desegregation of public graduate and professional schools, suits seeking the equalization of salaries for black and white teachers, and suits challenging the inequalities in physical facilities of black and white elementary and secondary schools.[144]

Houston resigned from his full-time position in 1938 to return to his law practice in Washington, D.C., but worked as an attorney by contract with the Inc. Fund afterwards. Thurgood Marshall succeeded him. (As general counsel, Marshall had won equal-pay agreements from nine of Maryland's school boards by the time he took over his new post.) In 1948, Marshall announced that the Inc. Fund would no longer pursue cases that sought equalization. Rather, the organization would confront segregation head-on.[145]

Five public-school cases, which became consolidated into one, resulted in the historic *Brown v. Board of Education* decision. The first case, *Briggs et al. v. Elliott et al.*, was filed in Clarendon County, South Carolina. Black parents petitioned the local school board in 1947 in a complaint regarding lack of bus transportation for black children equivalent to that of whites. When no response was given, the parents filed a lawsuit in 1948. The suit was dismissed, and a year later, J. A. Delaine, one of the leaders of the protest, met with Thurgood Marshall. Marshall convinced Delaine and other parents that a full-fledged attack on the material inequalities of the schools rather than simply the bus issue should be the strategy.

The second case, *Bolling et al. v. Sharpe et al.*, was filed by James Nabrit of the Inc. Fund in 1951. Nabrit represented plaintiffs who sought to attend the new John Philip Sousa Junior High School in Washington, D.C. Unlike in previous cases, Nabrit did not argue the unequal facilities of the schools available to black students versus white ones. Rather, he attacked segregation directly.

The third case, *Davis v. County School Board of Prince Edward County, Virginia,* sought admission for black children to the county's white high school. Initially, the parents sought equalization of their school with that of the whites. However, the Inc. Fund would only support suits for integration only. Therefore, the suit stated that the parents would accept equalization as an alternative.

The fourth case was *Brown v. Board of Education of Topeka, Kansas.* In this case, plaintiffs sought to prohibit the enforcement of a Kansas statute that allowed cities with a population of more than 15,000 to maintain segregated school facilities for black and white students. The Topeka Board of Education had segregated elementary schools but integrated high schools. Although the District Court found segregation to be detrimental, they denied the plaintiffs relief based on the earlier *Plessy* decision. The court stated that the black and white schools were equal in respect to buildings, transportation, curricula, and educational qualification of teachers.

The final case was *Gerbhart et al. v. Belton et al.* This case was based on elementary- and high-school-aged children, seeking to bar the provision of the Delaware constitution that required segregation of black and white students in public schools. The judge in the lower court found that the schools were inferior and that segregation was detrimental to black children. The Supreme Court of Delaware upheld the court's decision, but left open the door for the defendants to seek modification of the finding once the schools had been equalized.

The Inc. Fund could coordinate all of these cases simultaneously because the organization had acquired a seasoned staff of lawyers who were experienced in complex desegregation cases and could spread out across the country. In addition, the organization employed social scientists to provide expert testimony to complement the legal arguments on segregation's impact on children. Black social psychologist Kenneth B. Clark's research on the psychological damage of segregation on black children was pivotal to the outcome of the *Brown* decision.[146]

The cases in Kansas, Virginia, and South Carolina were decided against the Inc. Fund. In Delaware, the court held that the facilities were substantially unequal and ordered desegregation rather than equalization. The board appealed the decision. In 1951 the NAACP requested that the Supreme Court review the Kansas case. This was delayed until June 1952. On the same day that the Court decided to review the Kansas case, it also accepted the appeal of the *Briggs* case. The *Davis* case was later added to the Supreme Court docket to review along with the other two cases. By October of 1952, the Supreme Court agreed to hear all five of the school-desegregation cases.

A series of arguments were held in 1952 and 1953. On May 17, 1954, in a stunning ruling, the Supreme Court deemed "separate but equal" illegal. In the ruling, it asked, "Does segregation of children in public schools solely on the basis of race . . . deprive the children of the minority group of equal educational opportunities? We believe that it does."[147] The Court continued:

> To separate them from others of similar age and qualifications solely be-
> cause of their race generates a feeling of inferiority as to their status in the
> community that may affect their hearts and minds in a way unlikely ever to
> be undone.[148]

The ruling continued:

> We unanimously conclude that in the field of public education the doctrine
> "separate but equal" has no place. Separate educational facilities are inher-
> ently unequal.[149]

The social-science research of Kenneth B. Clark and others had been central to the ruling and was cited in footnote eleven of the decision.[150]

Bolling et al. v. Sharpe et al. was not part of the original consolidated *Brown* case, because the Fourteenth Amendment is not applicable in the District of Columbia. However, this case was decided the same day. The Court held that racial segregation in the District of Columbia violated the "due process" clause of the Fifth Amendment.

Richard Kluger notes that the reaction to the ruling in the black community was muted. He reports that blacks were cautious, although delighted by the ruling.[151]

Resistance

J. Harvie Wilkerson (1979) observed that there were four stages of response to the *Brown* case: absolute defiance from 1955 to 1959; token compliance from 1959 to the 1964 Civil Rights Act; modest integration from 1964 to 1968; and massive integration after the death of Martin Luther King Jr. in 1968. The current and fifth stage began by the 1980s: resegregation.[152]

Absolute Defiance

The response of white supremacists was swift and condemnatory. Although the remedy for *Brown* would not be decided until a year later (*Brown II*), when the Court stated that desegregation should commence with "all deliberate speed,"[153] state legislatures in Arkansas, Alabama, Georgia, Mississippi, South Carolina, and Virginia adopted resolutions of "interposition and nullification" that declared the Court's ruling null and void. In addition, various Southern legislatures passed laws that would penalize persons who attempted to implement integration laws.[154]

Of the five cases decided by *Brown*, Delaware, Kansas, and the District of Columbia complied with the decision and no further litigation ensued. Prince Edward County, Virginia, exhibited massive resistance to the ruling. It refused any attempts to desegregate, and in 1959 the county refused to finance the public schools for four years. Eight private academies, known collectively as the Prince Edward Academy, enrolled the white students of the county and employed sixty-seven teachers at the same salary that they had received in the public schools. The academies had full accreditation from the Virginia State Department of Education. Black students, on the other hand, were not as fortunate. They had no formal education available to them during this period. The black community responded by opening educational centers that initially were staffed by experienced teachers. These were not schools, but centers that offered arts, crafts, and sports and kept youth off the streets. After the school closure went into its second year, the teachers left for other jobs, and the centers were maintained primarily by housewives

In 1954 the Supreme Court ruled in *Brown v. Board of Education* that segregation in public schools was unlawful. However, Southern state governments were quick to find loopholes in the law to avoid and delay the desegregation of their schools. In 1957 Central High School in Little Rock, Arkansas, was forced to desegregate. The nine black teenagers (the "Little Rock Nine") who were chosen to attend the school were met by considerable resistance from the white population and prevented from entering the building. Federal troops had to be sent to Little Rock to ensure their admittance.

and teenagers. This program was discontinued in 1962. When the schools reopened in 1964, the enrollment was virtually all-black.[155]

The integration in 1957 of Little Rock's Central High School by nine students rivals the Prince Edward County case as the most well-known act of massive resistance by the white populace. The nation watched nightly on television the defiance that was exhibited towards attempts to integrate white public schools. More than a thousand people came to the school on the first day of school to protest the enrollment of the students. President Eisenhower had to resort to federalizing 1,000 troops, who escorted the students to school.[156]

Token Compliance

Since the Supreme Court left the implementation of *Brown* to the local school boards, this resulted in years of delays throughout the South. As late as 1962, no black student attended a school or college in Alabama, Mississippi, or South Carolina. By 1964, only 2.2 percent of blacks in the South attended integrated schools.[157] The emergence of the Civil Rights Movement of the 1960s, the March on Washington in 1963, and the passage of the Civil Rights Act in 1964 resulted in greater efforts to integrate schools. Title IV of the Civil Rights Act authorized the federal government to file school desegregation cases. In addition, Title VI prohibited discrimination in programs and activities, including schools receiving federal financial assistance.[158] By the end of the decade, 404 lawsuits were filed in the South on school desegregation.[159]

Modest Integration

The *Brown* decision mandated that schools could not bar students solely on the grounds of race. However, many school districts found other ways to exclude black students. Districts established neighborhood school plans and "choice" programs to discourage integration. "Freedom of choice" plans allowed students to "choose" which school to attend. These plans were known to achieve only token integration and served to intimidate blacks who were dependent on whites for their jobs. One of the most noted families to exercise their rights by utilizing the "choice" plan in the face of intense racism and danger was the Carter family in Drew, Mississippi.[160]

The Supreme Court resolved this method of resistance in 1968 with the case of *Green et al. v. County Board of New Kent County et al.* The Court ordered states to dismantle segregated school systems "root and branch." It identified five factors to gauge compliance: facilities, staff, faculty, extracurricular activities, and transportation.[161]

When this ruling was applied to Summerton in Clarendon County, South Carolina, in 1970, almost all of the white students withdrew from the public schools. Ten years later, all but one of the 268 whites attending school in the community were enrolled in private academies.[162]

Massive Integration

Residential segregation resulted in blacks and whites often living far apart. As a result, busing was instituted as a remedy to this problem. Most whites opposed "forced busing" mandates by the school districts. Blacks bore the brunt of the busing plans. It was assumed that black schools were inferior and that integration was a one-way street, with blacks going into white schools and neighborhoods. The busing issue was decided unanimously in 1971 by the Supreme Court in the *Swann v. Charlotte-Mecklenburg Board of Education* case. The Court approved busing, magnet schools, compensatory programs, and other remedies to achieve racial integration.[163] Journalist and former clerk to Supreme Court justice Lewis F. Powell, J. Harvie Wilkinson III provides an excellent analysis on the issue of busing in his essay "To Bus or Not to Bus."[164]

Residential patterns and white flight resulted in more whites residing in the suburbs. In an attempt to desegregate the overwhelmingly black Detroit public schools, officials bused students into the suburban districts. By the 1970s, urban schools were still among the most segregated ones in the nation. Without a busing program into the suburbs, Detroit public schools would be from 75 to 90 percent black. The Supreme Court ruled against the busing plan in *Milliken v. Bradley* in 1974. This ruling, decided during the conservative Nixon years, was the first lost for the NAACP in a school desegregation case in the twenty years since the *Brown* decision.

Resegregation

By the 1980s the Supreme Court began releasing school districts from their desegregation plans and returning them to local control.[165] With decades behind them in the *Brown* decision, legal scholars, educators, and African American citizens began to question the victory of this landmark case. While there had been gains, the losses were enormous. As with school integration in the nineteenth century, the loss of black teachers and administrators was a profound one. When the University of Louisville merged with the all-black Louisville Municipal College in 1950, all of the African American faculty and staff at the latter institution were dismissed. As integration of educational institutions grew, in a twenty-year period (1950s–1970s), African American teachers, principals, coaches, counselors, band directors, and cafeteria workers were dismissed throughout the South due to court-ordered desegregation. "Displacement" was the term used to describe the phenomenon. A year after *Brown II*, 144 black teachers and 21 black principals lost their jobs. A report in 1970 discussed the hundreds of black teachers who had been demoted, dismissed, or denied new contracts. The report noted that new hires of black teachers were not replacing the dismissed ones.[166] In an article on the displacement of African American teachers, Michael Fultz notes that in addition to the non-hiring of black instructors, the National Teachers Exam (NTE) was increasingly used as a punitive tool to justify the racial hiring patterns.[167]

In a powerful and controversial essay in the *Yale Law Journal* in 1976, former NAACP attorney Derrick Bell criticized the NAACP. Bell felt that the organization erred in not demanding educational improvement rather than simply racial balance. He questioned the notion that having white children in a classroom was essential to a higher quality education. He wrote:

> In essence the arguments are that blacks must gain access to White schools because "equal educational opportunity" means integrated schools, and because only school integration will make certain that black children will receive the same education as white children. This theory of school desegregation, however, fails to encompass the complexity of achieving equal education for children for whom it so long has been denied.[168]

In the lengthy article, Bell criticizes civil rights groups for their rigidity and emphasis on desegregation and not education. He continued:

> Having convinced themselves that *Brown* stands for desegregation and not education, the established civil rights organizations steadfastly refuse to

recognize reverses in the school desegregation campaign—reverses which, to some extent, have been precipitated by their rigidity. They seem to be reluctant to evaluate objectively the high risks inherent in a continuation of current policies.[169]

Bell cited examples of major metropolitan areas such as Detroit, Atlanta, and Boston where black parents were at odds with the NAACP because of the former's desire for improved educational programming rather than racial balance. Bell ended his argument by quoting W. E. B. Du Bois in his thoughtful piece of 1935 entitled "Does the Negro Need Separate Schools?":

> The Negro needs neither segregated schools nor mixed schools. What he needs is Education. What he must remember is that there is no magic, either in mixed schools or in segregated schools. A mixed school with poor and unsympathetic teachers, with hostile public opinion, and no teaching of truth concerning black folk, is bad. A segregated school with ignorant placeholders, inadequate equipment, poor salaries, and wretched housing, is equally bad. Other things being equal, the mixed school is the broader, more natural basis for the education of all youth. It gives wider contacts; it inspires greater self-confidence; and suppresses the inferiority complex. But other things seldom are equal, and in that case, Sympathy, Knowledge and Truth, outweigh all that the mixed school can offer.[170]

In 1992 another prominent black civil rights attorney and law professor, Drew Days III, discussed rethinking the integrative ideal in a law-review article. Days notes that in the thirty-eight years since the *Brown* decision, many black parents realized that their children have paid a high price for desegregation. Black students are the ones being bused; black teachers and administrators have been dismissed in record numbers; black students receive the most disciplinary actions in schools; and black schools that were the pride of their communities and functioned as community centers have been closed. While it would not be fair to say that integration has not been positive in many instances, Drew agrees with Bell that desegregation did not always result in increased educational quality.[171]

Black Higher Education in the Age of Affirmative Action

Throughout the 1950s and early 1960s, blacks challenged the segregated public universities of the Deep South. Those who attempted to integrate in the lower South did so at great personal risk and with enormous publicity. In 1955, Medgar Evers, field secretary of the NAACP, applied for admission to the law school at the University of Mississippi. His application was rejected and the state board of trustees issued a new policy requiring each applicant to provide five letters of references from alumni in their county of residence. Evers, who was later gunned down by a white supremacist, discontinued his efforts to enroll in the institution.[172]

The push for equal rights was energized by the *Brown* decision and led to more direct protest. In 1955 blacks in Montgomery staged a yearlong boycott of the segregated public buses. In response to black assertiveness, the White Citizens Council was established to make economic reprisals against blacks and to intimidate both blacks and whites who sought to change the status quo. Emmitt Till, a teenage black boy who was visiting from Chicago for the summer in Mississippi, was lynched during this period. The federal government responded by signing into law the Civil Rights Act of 1957, becoming the first Civil Rights Act in the United States since 1875. This Act established the United States Commission on Civil Rights as a temporary, independent, bipartisan federal agency.[173]

Other attempts were made to integrate the University of Mississippi, as well as the Universities of Alabama and Georgia. In July 1959 Charlayne Hunter and Hamilton Holmes applied for admission to the University of Georgia. As was the case in Mississippi, they were told that they needed the signatures of two alumni and the home-county clerk. Both Hunter and Holmes had outstanding scholastic records but were denied admission. The court decided a year and a half later that they had been rejected solely due to their race. In January 1961 both entered the University of Georgia, although Governor Ernest Vandiver threatened to close the institution. The day of registration, Hunter was greeted by more than a thousand angry whites who surrounded her dormitory (Holmes lived off campus). The crowd had to be dispersed by tear gas and fire hoses. The hostility towards blacks attempting to gain entrance to public universities, which their parents' tax dollars supported, mirrored the hostility shown to parents attempting to send their children to public elementary and high schools.[174]

The last university of the decade to dramatically resist admitting black students was the University of Alabama. It started in 1956 when Autherine Lucy was admitted to the university as a result of a class-action lawsuit. Three days later, she was driven off the campus by rioters and later expelled by the board of trustees for accusing them of conspiring with the rioters.[175]

While the University of Alabama was technically and legally desegregated by virtue of Lucy's class-action suit in 1955, Governor George C. Wallace constantly pledged during his 1962 gubernatorial campaign to defy any court order to desegregate education in the state. He further promised to "stand in the school house door in person."[176] The summer of 1963, two black students, Vivian Malone and James Hood, arrived to register, along with 500 Alabama National Guardsmen and 150 state policemen. Upon the arrival of Malone and Hood, Governor Wallace made good on his campaign promises, standing in front of the auditorium where all students were to register and reading a five-page document that concluded, "I denounce and forbid this illegal act." In less than an hour, President Kennedy federalized the Alabama National Guard and also alerted 2,000 federal troops.[177] Malone and Hood returned to campus escorted by the guardsmen and a brigadier general from Birmingham. When Wallace was asked to step aside, he complied with the request, and Malone and Hood were admitted without further incident.[178]

The 1964 Civil Rights Act resulted in massive tokenism of black students on white campuses. It was not until the assassination in 1968 of civil rights leader Dr. Martin Luther King Jr. that white institutions made any serious attempts to attract black students. Special recruitment officers and programs were established in many of these institutions. African Americans fought segregation and racial injustice in the previous decades primarily in the courts. By the 1950s and 1960s, blacks took their grievances to the streets with sit-ins, voter-registration programs, freedom rides, marches, and economic boycotts.

As institutions sought to remedy past discrimination and low minority enrollment by special programs, these efforts were challenged legally by whites who viewed them as "reverse discrimination." In 1971, a white man,

Marco DeFunis Jr., sued the University of Washington Law School, stating that he was denied admission because of his race. He argued that the university violated the Equal Protection Clause of the Fourteenth Amendment. Although the case went to the Supreme Court, the Court ruled the case moot because Defunis, who was admitted to the law school while the case was being decided, would graduate by the time of the decision.[179] Other "reverse discrimination" cases were filed throughout the next two decades. Allan Bakke challenged the affirmative-action admission program at the University of California-Davis Medical School. In 1978, the Supreme Court ruled the special-admission program unconstitutional, but stated that race could be used as a factor in admissions, although not a deciding factor.[180] In a suit against the University of Texas, a federal appeals court ruled in 1996 that race could not be used in admissions decisions, ending affirmative action in Louisiana, Texas, and Mississippi.[181] The anti-affirmative-action sentiment was so strong that in 1996, the state of California passed legislation that prohibited any affirmative action or "preferential treatment" programs in the state.[182] The mood of the nation was one that believed that blacks and other minorities were advancing at the expense of whites. In 2003 the question of affirmative-action programs was addressed again in the Supreme Court. The University of Michigan undergraduate and law-school admissions programs were challenged. The Supreme Court ruled that diversity could be used as a rationale in admissions, but special points could not be given to minority students. [183]

The reduction in opportunities for blacks in higher education extended to black colleges as well. Black public colleges had been fiscally starved by white-controlled state boards of education for a century. In 1969, the Department of Heath, Education and Welfare (HEW) ordered ten states to develop desegregation plans for their public universities. A total of nineteen states were later ordered either by HEW or the federal courts to develop desegregation plans. By 1992, the federal courts ruled in *Knight v. Alabama* and *Ayers v. Fordice* that state policies and practices had perpetuated decades of discriminatory patterns in public higher education. As with *Brown*, black public colleges were reshaped and dismantled to fit into the larger state public university system, due to the *Ayres* ruling. Changes in the admissions standards, which included a higher ACT cutoff score, resulted in a decrease in the number of black students admitted. The final settlement of *Ayres* required the three black state institutions to attract white students to their institutions and provide them with tuition-free admissions, thereby further dismantling the racially identifiable black institutions.[184] One study found that even with free tuition, most whites would not consider attending historically black colleges because they were considered to be inferior institutions. Many dissenters of the agreement note that the inferior K–12 education that black students receive in Mississippi would result in them being significantly disadvantaged in admissions to state colleges and universities. In an important article concerning the *Ayres* case, Elias Blake Jr. questioned if desegregation as a remedy was more important than educational equity. As with the outcome of desegregation with K–12, the *Ayres* case was believed by many in the African American community as not being in the best interest of black students or black public colleges in Mississippi.[185]

Conclusion

The issues facing African American education have been persistent in this nation. Initially it was a matter of access and purpose of education. Blacks in America had to fight for a right to an education. Why would a slave need to learn to read and write? Many slave owners believed that educated blacks represented a danger to the white South. Yet, the desire for learning was paramount among African Americans. Throughout the antebellum era, many slaves risked their lives to learn the alphabet. After Emancipation, schooling became available to African Americans in the South through private sponsorship and later through public schools. The fear of the power of education for blacks continued into the twentieth century. The solution to containing black aspirations for social and political equality was solved with the Hampton-Tuskegee Idea. This type of education reinforced notions of "the dignity of labor" and contentment with the status quo. The Hampton-Tuskegee Idea was heavily supported by Northern industrial philanthropists and supported by the white South. While industrial education per se was not a negative, the conservative ideology that surrounded it resulted in many progressive African Americans rejecting this form of education. The *New York Times'* recent obituary of the psychologist Kenneth B. Clark underscores the deep feelings parents had regarding industrial versus classical education. The article noted Clark's education in Harlem in the 1920s. The article described his integrated elementary education in Harlem. However, it continued,

> By the time Kenneth Clark reached the ninth grade, however, Harlem was changing and most of the students around him were black. At school, he was told to learn a trade and prepare for vocational training. Miriam Clark [Clark's mother] would have none of that. She walked into the school one day, told the counselor what she thought of vocational schools and made it clear that as far as she was concerned, her son was better than that.[186]

There was no question that Mrs. Clark understood the implication of one education path versus another. And, of course, this astute realization of his had lifelong implications for the rest of Kenneth Clark's educational career.

· · · · · · · ·

As the nineteenth century moved to a close, the stigmatizing impact of the 1896 *Plessy v. Ferguson* decision of "separate but equal" resulted in the NAACP laboring for decades in the twentieth century to have this ruling overturned. While most blacks appreciated the need to abolish school segregation, many understood that this would come at great cost to the black community. Some were willing to push for equalization rather than integration. The issues of the nineteenth century on this topic were relived in the twentieth century. By 1954, the landmark *Brown v. Board of Education* decision resulted in the dismantling of legal segregation of public institutions.

While the eradication of legal segregation was a significant milestone in American history, the cost to African Americans was profound. The "displacement" of black teachers, administrators, and other important role models in the community cost blacks dearly. In addition, schools in the black community that served as important centers were closed with the onset of integration. David S. Cecelski's book *Along Freedom Road: Hyde County,*

North Carolina and the Fate of Black Schools in the South details the success-ful efforts of a black community to save their beloved school. Cecelski also demonstrates that school integration eliminated an entire generation of black principals. For instance, the number of black elementary principals in North Carolina dropped from 620 to 170 from 1963 to 1970, and for high school principals from 209 to less than 10 in the same time period.[187]

As blacks gradually won the right to schooling, the topic of curriculum became an important issue within their community. They debated whether education should be liberating or accommodating. Self-determination is a constant theme that runs throughout the history of black education. Blacks desired to control their own destiny and to be the captains of their own ships. The many white missionaries and philanthropists who sought to control black schooling did not always appreciate this. Nor did white public-school officials understand this. Throughout the 1960s and 1970s, blacks boycot-ted, staged walk-outs, filed lawsuits, and had other protests in response to desegregation plans that destroyed black institutions and displaced black teachers. With integration came not only a loss of teachers and important role models and schools in one's own community, but also a decline in black students' motivation, self-esteem, and academic performance. Black students experienced harsh discipline, unfair tracking in classes that placed them on the lowest rung of courses, low academic expectations, and disproportionate placement in special-education courses.[188] Cecelski notes that black parents who supported the courageous efforts of the NAACP to integrate schools in the 1940s and 1950s were ambivalent about the merits of school integration by the 1970s.[189]

By the 1970s, school districts throughout the urban systems outside the South were severely segregated. In 1960, the fifteen largest metropolitan school systems were 79 percent non-white. With white flight and predomi-nately black schools, attempts to integrate schools in the 1970s included magnet schools, busing, school choice, mandatory and voluntary intra- and interdistrict transfers, and consolidation of city districts with suburban dis-tricts. By the 1990s, the courts had dismantled most desegregation plans throughout the country. In the Harvard Project on School Desegregation, Gary Orfield and colleagues reported that both charter schools and private schools were now more segregated than public schools. Public schools both in and outside of the South were resegregated as well. Orfield noted that 96 percent of segregated white schools are middle-class, compared to segregated black and Latino schools, which are dominated by poor children.[190] Schools with poor minority students are characterized by lower academic achievement, higher dropout rates, fewer advanced classes, less qualified teachers, and fewer college attendance rates after graduation.[191] The disappointment in the outcome of the *Brown* decision has been expressed in the fifty years since the ruling. Schools in the South remained segregated for a decade after *Brown*. Segregation in the North was not addressed until the mid-1970s. Northern districts refused to provide racial data to measure segregation, and for nearly two decades after *Brown*, the Supreme Court denied hearings on school desegregation in the North.[192] Robert L. Carter, one of the lead attorneys for the NAACP for the *Brown* case, wrote in 1993:

> With the 1954 declaration in *Brown v. Board of Education*, I believed that the path was then clear for black children to receive an equal education. My confidence in the inevitability of this result now seems naïve. Although I expected the initial hostility to *Brown*, whereby black students were forcibly denied entrance to white schools by racist white parents and public officials, I did not anticipate the stubborn obstacles which have continued to hinder vindication by Black children of their constitutional guarantee of equal educational opportunity now for nearly forty years.[193]

Black education has come full circle. The battle for equity and full entrance into American institutions waged for blacks for more than two centuries is bittersweet. While there is a large and growing black middle class as a result of increased educational opportunities, there is also a vast black underclass. Yet, public education for most minority students remains "separate and equal." Many blacks, frustrated with the failed efforts of desegregation plans, now believe that educational equity, opportunity, and achievement outweigh racial integration. Derrick Bell, in a provocative book on the "unfulfilled hopes of racial reform" and the *Brown* decision, posits that it may have been a better strategy to pursue equalization rather than integration. Noting that segregated black schools have historically produced some of the most successful blacks in the nation, Bell argues that education, and not integration, should be the goal.[194] Proponents of school integration such as Gary Orfield point out that separate schools remain "inherently" unequal because of the huge income gap between predominantly black and predominantly white schools. Yet, current research indicates that even in middle-class integrated schools, blacks often do not reap the benefits of these schools.[195] While the reasons for the lower achievement levels and lower-track courses taken by African American students in "good" schools are still being debated, the lack of role models, low expectations by teachers, and "stereotype threat" are among the issues being discussed.[196] In addition, scholars such as Ogbu argue that there is a culture of academic disengagement that some black students exhibit in suburban schools.[197]

More than fifty years after *Brown*, the Civil Rights Act, affirmative-action initiatives, and other efforts to advance black education, much of K-12 public education is dismal and nonresponsive to the needs of African American students. Recent litigation and legislative actions have resulted in higher education becoming less accessible to African Americans as well. Much of the struggles of the nineteenth and early twentieth centuries remain. African American students are labeled "at risk," and the male students of the race are particularly vulnerable to school failure. Scholars are attempting to explore strategies for enhancing academic success for this student population.[198]

Du Bois's reflection on the topic of what type of education black students need is just as relevant today as it was when he wrote it in 1935:

> A separate Negro school, where children are treated like human beings, trained by teachers of their own race, who know what it means to be black in the year of salvation 1935, is infinitely better than making our boys and girls doormats to be spit and trampled upon and lied to by ignorant social climbers, whose sole claim to superiority is ability to kick "niggers" when they are down. I say, too, that certain studies and discipline necessary to Negroes can seldom be found in white schools . . . theoretically, the Negro needs neither segregated schools nor mixed schools. What he needs is Education.[199]

· ·

NOTES

1. Perkins, "The Impact of the 'Cult of True Womanhood' on the Education of Black Women."
2. "Instruction of Slaves," reprinted in *Colonization and Journal of Freedom.*
3. Ibid.
4. Douglass, *The Narrative of the Life of Frederick Douglass.*
5. Ibid.
6. Woodson, *The African Background Outline.*
7. Alvord, *Fifth Semi-Annual Report on Schools for Freedmen.*
8. Taylor, *Reminiscences of My Life in Camp.*
9. Haviland, *A Woman's Life-Work.*
10. Rawick, *The American Slave.*
11. Franklin, "In Pursuit of Freedom: The Educational Activities of Social Organizations in Philadelphia, 1900–1930," in Franklin and Anderson, eds., *New Perspectives on Black Educational History,* 114.
12. Walker, *David Walker's Appeal to the Coloured Citizens of the World.*
13. Beatrice B. Butcher, "The Evolution of Negro Women's Schools in the United States," master's thesis, Howard University, 1936, p. 24.
14. "Prudance Crandall," in *Notable American Women, 1607–1950.*
15. Colonization Society of the State of Connecticut, *An Address to the Public by the Managers of the Colonization Society of Connecticut.*
16. Hayes, *Negrophobia "On the Brain" in White Men.*
17. *The Rights of All* (New York), 18 September 1829.
18. Minutes and Proceedings of the Second Annual Convention for the Improvement of the Free People of Color in These United States (1832), Philadelphia, 34.
19. *The Weekly Advocate* (New York), 7 January 1837.
20. Ellen Henle and Marlene Merrill, "Antebellum Black Coeds at Oberlin College," *Women's Studies Newsletter* 7, no. 2 (Spring 1979): 10.
21. Fanny Jackson Coppin, *Reminiscences of School Life and Hints on Teaching,* 9–10.
22. Fanny Jackson to Frederick Douglass, 30 March 1876, *Frederick Douglass Papers,* letter no. 8167, Library of Congress.
23. *Freedom's Journal* (New York), 23 March 1827; *The Colored American,* New York, 8 December 1838.
24. *The Colored American* (New York), 14 January 1837; see Perkins, "Quaker Beneficence and Black Control."
25. *Freedom's Journal,* 1 June 1827.

26. *Report of the Committee on Social Relations and Policy in the Proceedings of the Colored National Convention, held in Rochester, July 6th, 7th and 8th, 1853* (Rochester, 1853), p. 23.

27. Martin, *Brown v. Board of Education*, 48–60.

28. Ibid., 48.

29. Harold B. Hancock, "The Status of the Negro in Delaware after the Civil War, 1865–1895," *Delaware History* 13 (April 1968): 57–66.

30. J. Max Bond, "The Negro in Los Angeles, Ph.D. diss., University of Southern California, 1936.

31. Fishel and Quarles, *The Negro American*, 262.

32. Leslie H. Fishel Jr., "The North and the Negro, 1865–1900: A Study in Race Discrimination," Ph.D. diss., Harvard University, 1953.

33. Fishel and Quarles, *The Negro American*, 293.

34. Meier and Rudwick, *From Plantation to Ghetto.*

35. Franklin, "The Persistence of School Segregation in the Urban North."

36. *The Colored Citizen* (Fort Scott, Kansas), 20 September 1878.

37. *The Cleveland Gazette*, 25 August 1883.

38. Quoted in Tyack, *The One Best System*, 110–11.

39. Quoted in Mabee, *Black Education in New York State*, 96.

40. Sarah Mapp Douglass to William Bassett, December 1837, in William Lloyd Garrison Collection, Boston Public Library.

41. Quoted in Pease, *They Who Would Be Free.*

42. Martin, *Brown v. Board of Education*, 47; Tyack, *The One Best System*, 112–13.

43. Fishel, "The North and the Negro," 187.

44. Mabee, *Black Education in New York State*, 97.

45. Du Bois, *The Negro Common School.*

46. Richardson, *Christian Reconstruction*, 25.

47. Ibid.

48. Ibid., 4–5.

49. Anderson, *The Education of Blacks in the South, 1860–1935*, pp. 4–8.

50. Ibid., 5.

51. Webber, *Deep Like the Rivers*, 131.

52. Ibid., 135.

53. Ibid., 6.

54. Ibid.

55. Quoted in Anderson, *The Education of Blacks in the South*, 11.

56. Jones, *Soldiers of Light and Love*, 42.

57. Ibid.

58. Ibid.

59. See Robert Morris's discussion of this topic in "Freedmen's Education."

60. Quoted in Richardson, *Christian Reconstruction*, 192.

61. Ibid.; Mary S. Leary, Oberlin, Ohio, to George Whipple, 17 September 1867, American Missionary Association Papers, Amistad Research Library, New Orleans, Louisiana [hereafter referred to as *AMA Papers*]. During the period that Day sought a position with the AMA, the organization employed a white female with four children to serve as matron of the mission house of Norfolk. See Clara C. Duncan, Norfolk to William Woodbury, 29 August 1864, *AMA Papers*.

62. The women were Blanche Harris, a native of Michigan; Clara Duncan of Pittsfield, Massachusetts; Sara G. Stanley of New Bern, North Carolina; Sallie Daffin, a native of Philadelphia and a graduate of the Institute of Colored Youth, and Edmondia G. Highgate of Syracuse, New York, a graduate of the normal school in New York. Ellen Henle and Marlene Merrill, "Antebellum Black Coeds at Oberlin College," *Women's Studies Newsletter* 7 (Spring 1979): 10; Mrs. M. P. Discomb, Oberlin, Ohio, to George Whipple, 2 March 1864; Edmondia Highgate to the Reverend E. P. Smith, 23 July 1870, *AMA Papers*; Coppin, *Reminiscences*, 147, 184.

63. For a discussion of this, see Richardson, *Christian Reconstruction*, 52.

64. Morris, "Freedmen's Education," 465.

65. See correspondence from Daffin, Stanley, and Highgate to the AMA Executive Committee in 1865, *AMA Papers*.

66. Quoted in Richardson, *Christian Reconstruction*, 192.

67. Ibid.

68. Address published in the Philadelphia Press, July 1, 1879; See also Perkins, "Heed Life's Demands."

69. Jones, *Soldiers of Light and Love*, 206.

70. Lucie Stanton Day, Cleveland, Ohio, to George Whipple, 26 April 1864; Sara G. Stanley, Cleveland, Ohio, to George Whipple, 19 January 1864 and 4 March 1864, *AMA Papers*.

71. Woodson, *Mis-Education of the Negro*, 340–41.

72. Anderson, *The Education of Blacks in the South*, 150.

73. Quoted in Anderson, *The Education of Blacks in the South*, 152.

74. Anderson, *The Education of Blacks in the South*, 153.

75. Ibid.

76. *The People's Advocate* (Washington, D.C.), 18 February 1882.

77. *The New York Globe*, 15 December 1883.

78. *The Cleveland Gazette*, 1 September 1883.

79. Fishel, "The North and the Negro," 193.

80. Coppin, *Reminiscences of School Life*, 28.

81. Ibid., 35.

82. *The People's Advocate*, 14 February 1880.

83. *Christian Recorder*, 21 July 1881.

84. *Institute for Colored Youth Annual Report*, 1888.

85. *Committee on Industrial Education Report in Managers' Minutes*, 20 January 1885, Institute for Colored Youth Papers; 1884 ICY Annual Report.

86. Du Bois, *The Philadelphia Negro.*
87. Anderson, "The Hampton Model of Normal School Industrial Education, 61.
88. Ibid., 65.
89. Ibid., 61, 70.
90. Ibid.
91. Quoted in Hawkins, *Booker T. Washington and His Critics.*
92. Ibid.
93. Ibid.
94. Mangum, *The Legal Status of the Negro.*
95. Washington, "Industrial Education for the Negro," 16–17.
96. Du Bois, "The Talented Tenth," 398.
97. For an extensive discussion of this topic, see Anderson, "Northern Foundations and the Shaping of Southern Black Rural Education, 1902–1935."
98. Ibid., 381.
99. Ibid., 385.
100. Ibid., 391.
101. Walker, "Caswell County Training School," 165.
102. Ibid.
103. Ibid., 166.
104. Du Bois, "The College Bred Negro."
105. Bond, *Black American Scholars.*
106. Mullen, *Blacks in America's War.*
107. Quoted in Bond, *The Education of the Negro in the American Social Order.*
108. Henderson, *The Negro in Sports*; McMillan, "The American Negro in Higher Education."
109. Cathie Huntoon, "The University of Illinois and the Drive for Negro Equality, 1945–1951," unpublished paper, University of Illinois Archives.
110. Robeson, *Here I Stand*; Owens, *Blackthink.*
111. Bigglestone, "Oberlin College and the Negro Student, 1865–1940."
112. Anderson, *The Education of Blacks in the South*, 238.
113. Ibid.
114. Ibid., 240.
115. Ibid.
116. McPherson, "White Liberals and Black Power in Negro Education, 1865–1915," p. 1362.
117. Ibid., 1359.
118. Woodson, *The Mis-Education of the Negro*, reprint of 1933 edition (Trenton: Africa World Press, 1990).
119. Hughes, "Cowards from the Colleges."
120. Ibid.
121. Perkins, "Lucy Diggs Slowe: Champion of the Self-Determination of African-American Women in Higher Education"; Perkins, "The National Association of College Women:

Vanguard of Black Women's Leadership and Education, 1923–1964"; Slowe, "Higher Education of Negro Women."

122. Anderson, *The Education of Blacks in the South*, 83.

123. Quoted in Wolters, *The New Negro on Campus*.

124. Du Bois, *The College-Bred Negro American*.

125. James D. Anderson, "The Evolution of Historically Black Colleges and Universities," in the conference program *Mind on Freedom: Celebrating the History and Culture of America's Black Colleges and Universities* (1–3 February 1996), The Program in African American Culture National Museum of American History, Smithsonian Institutions, Washington, D.C., p. 34.

126. Hill and Greenberg, *Citizen's Guide to Desegregation*.

127. Davie, *Negroes in American Society*.

128. Ibid.

129. Ashmore, *The Negro and the Schools*, 32.

130. *Missouri ex rel. Gaines v. Canada*, 305 U.S. 337.

131. Wiggins, *The Desegregation Era in Higher Education*.

132. Ashmore, *The Negro and the Schools*, 33.

133. Ibid.

134. Ibid.

135. Ibid., 34.

136. Ibid.

137. Ibid.

138. *McLaurin v. Oklahoma State Regents*, 339 U.S. 637

139. *Sweatt v. Painter*, 339 U.S. 629

140. Ibid.

141. Johnson, "Racial Integration in Public Higher Education in the South."

142. "Charles Hamilton Houston," in *Dictionary of American Negro Biography*, ed. Logan and Winston, 328–30; Tushnet, *The NAACP's Legal Strategy against Segregated Education, 1925–1950*, p. 30.

143. McNeil, *Groundwork*, quoted in Tushnet, *The NAACP's Legal Strategy*, 34.

144. Tushnet, *The NAACP's Legal Strategy*, 34.

145. Ibid., 114.

146. Kluger, *Simple Justice*, 315.

147. *Brown v. Board of Education*, 347 U.S. 483 (1954).

148. Ibid.

149. Ibid.

150. Ibid.

151. Kluger, *Simple Justice*, 714.

152. Wilkinson, *From Brown to Bakke*, 78.

153. *Brown v. Board of Education*, 349 U.S. 294 (1955).

154. The four states that abolished their state constitutional requirements for public education were Georgia, Alabama, Mississippi, and South Carolina; the six states that passed

legislation denying funding to desegregated schools were Arkansas, Georgia, Louisiana, Mississippi, South Carolina, and Virginia. See Douglas, "The Rhetoric of Moderation."

155. Wolters, *The Burden of Brown*, 94.

156. Wilkinson, *From Brown to Bakke*, 88–90.

157. Wilkinson, *From Brown to Bakke*.

158. Ibid.

159. Sarratt, *The Ordeal of Desegregation*, 167.

160. See Curry, *Silver Rights*. The story of the Carter family's brave decision to send their children to an all-white school and claim their civil rights.

161. *Green et al. v. County School Board of New Kent County et al.*, 391 U.S. 430

162. Wolters, *The Burden of Brown*, 129.

163. *Swann v. Charlotte-Mecklenberg Board of Education*, 402 U.S. 1 (1971).

164. Wilkinson, *From Brown to Bakke*, 161–92.

165. These cases were *Riddick v. School Board of City of Norfolk, Virginia*, 784 F. 2d 521 (4th Circuit 1986); *Board of Education of Oklahoma v. Dowell*, 498 U.S. 236 (1991); *Freeman v. Pitts*, 503 U.S. 467 (1992).

166. Fultz, "The Displacement of Black Educators Post-Brown," in a special issue on the fiftieth anniversary of the *Brown v. Board of Education* decision, Michael Fultz, guest editor.

167. Ibid., 26.

168. Bell, "Serving Two Masters," 477–78.

169. Ibid., 482.

170. Quoted in ibid., 515.

171. Days, "Brown Blues."

172. Sarratt, *The Ordeal of Desegregation*, 127.

173. U.S. Commission on Civil Rights, *Twenty Years after Brown: The Shadows of the Past* (Washington, D.C.: GPO, 1974), 63.

174. Sarratt, *The Ordeal of Desegregation*, 127.

175. *Southern Education Reporting Service, Statistical Summary, 1964–65*, p. 4.

176. Ibid., 4.

177. Sarratt, *The Ordeal of Desegregation*, 167.

178. Ibid.

179. *Defunis v. Odegaard*, 416 U.S. 312 (1974).

180. *Regents of the University of California v. Bakke*, 438 U.S. 265.

181. *Hopwood v. Texas*, 78 F.3d 932 (5th Cir. 1996).

182. Proposition 209, State of California (1996).

183. *Grutter v. Bollinger*, 539 U.S.; *Gratz v. Bollinger*, 539 U.S.

184. Blake, "Is Higher Education Desegregation a Remedy for Segregation but not Educational Inequality?"

185. Ibid.; Sum et al., "Race, Reform, and Desegregation in Mississippi Higher Education," 403.

186. Richard Severo, "Kenneth Clark, Who Helped End Segregation, Dies," *New York Times*, 2 May 2005, p. 1.
187. Cecelski, *Along Freedom Road.*
188. Ibid., 9–10.
189. Ibid.
190. Orfield and Eaton, *Dismantling Desegregation*, 33.
191. Ibid.
192. Ibid., 7–8.
193. Carter, "Public School Desegregation."
194. Bell, *Silent Covenants.* For research on exemplary segregated black schools, see Perkins, *Fanny Jackson Coppin and the Institute for Colored Youth*; Walker, *Their Highest Potential.* See also Sowell, "Black Excellence."
195. See the controversial work of Ogbu, *Black American Students in an Affluent Suburb.*
196. Stereotype threat is a theory conceived by social psychologist Claude M. Steele. According to Steele, high-achieving middle-class students often do poorly on standardized exams because of the stereotype that they are inferior students. As a result, this becomes a self-fulfilling prophecy. See Steele, "A Threat in the Air"; Steele, "Stereotype Threat and the Intellectual Test Performance of African Americans."
197. Ibid.
198. See Maton et al., "Preparing the Way."
199. Du Bois, "Does the Negro Need Separate Schools?," 287–88.

BIBLIOGRAPHY

Altbach, Philip G., and Kofi Lomotey, eds. *The Racial Crisis in American Higher Education.* New York: State University of New York Press, 1991.

Altman, Robert A., and Patricia O. Snyder, eds. *The Minority Student on the Campus: Expectations and Possibilities.* Berkeley: Center for Research and Development in Higher Education, University of California, 1970.

Alvord, J. W., and the U.S. Bureau of Refugees, Freedmen and Abandoned Lands. *Fifth Semi-Annual Report on Schools for Freedmen.* Washington, D.C.: U.S. Government Printing Office, 1868.

Anderson, James D. . *The Education of Blacks in the South, 1860–1935.* Chapel Hill: University of North Carolina Press, 1988.

Anderson, James D. "The Hampton Model of Normal School Industrial Education, 1868–1915." In *The Education of Blacks in the South, 1860–1935.* Chapel Hill: University of North Carolina Press, 1988.

Anderson, James D. "Northern Foundations and the Shaping of Southern Black Rural Education, 1902–1935." *History of Education Quarterly* 18 (Winter 1978): 371–96.

Armor, David. *Forced Justice: School Desegregation and the Law.* New York: Oxford University Press, 1995.

Armstrong, M. F., and Helen W. Ludlow. *Hampton and Its Students.* 1874; Chicago: Afro-Am Press, 1969.

Ashmore, Harry S. *The Negro and the Schools.* Chapel Hill: University of North Carolina Press, 1954.

Balkin, Jack M. *What* Brown v. Board of Education *Should Have Said: The Nation's Top Legal Experts Rewrite America's Landmark Civil Rights Decision.* New York: New York University Press, 2001.

Ball, Howard. *The Bakke Case: Race, Education, and Affirmative Action.* Lawrence: University Press of Kansas, 2000.

Bass, Jack. *Unlikely Heroes.* New York: Simon and Schuster, 1981.

Beale, Howard K. *A History of Freedom of Teaching in American Schools.* New York: Octagon Books, 1941.

Bell, Derrick A., Jr. "Serving Two Masters: Integration Ideals and Client Interest in School Desegregation Litigation." *Yale Law Journal* 85 (March 1976): 470–516.

Bell, Derrick. *Silent Covenants:* Brown v. Board of Education *and the Unfulfilled Hopes for Racial Reform.* New York: Oxford University Press, 2004.

Bigglestone, W. E. "Oberlin College and the Negro Student, 1865–1940." *Journal of Negro History* 56 (July 1971): 198–219.

Blake, Elias, Jr. "Is Higher Education Desegregation a Remedy for Segregation but not Educational Inequality? A Study of the Ayers v. Mabus Desegregation Case." *Journal of Negro Education* 60 (Fall 1991): 538–65.

Bond, Horace Mann. *Black American Scholars.* Detroit: Belamp Publishing Company, 1972.

Bond, Horace Mann. *The Education of the Negro in the American Social Order.* Rev. ed. New York: Octagon Books, 1966.

Bond, Horace Mann. *Negro Education in Alabama: A Study in Cotton and Steel.* New York: Atheneum, 1939.

Bowen, William G., and Derek Bok. *The Shape of the River: Long-Term Consequences of Considering Race in College and University Admission.* Princeton: Princeton University Press, 1998.

Bowles, Frank, and Frank A. DeCosta. *Between Two Worlds: A Profile of Negro Higher Education.* New York: McGraw-Hill, 1971.

Boyd, William M., II. *Desegregating America's Colleges: A Nationwide Survey of Black Students, 1972–1973.* New York: Praeger, 1974.

Brown et al. v. Board of Education of Topeka, 347 U.S. 483, Supreme Court of the United States, 17 May 1954.

Bullock, Henry Allen. *A History of Negro Education in the South,* Cambridge, Mass.: Harvard University Press, 1967.

Callejo-Perez, David M. *Southern Hospitality: Identity, Schools, and the Civil Rights Movement in Mississippi, 1964–1972.* New York: Peter Lang, 2001.

Carter, Robert L. "Public School Desegregation: A Contemporary Analysis." *Saint Louis University Law Journal* 37 (Summer 1993): 885.

Cecelski, David S. *Along Freedom Road: Hyde County, North Carolina, and the Fate of Black Schools in the South.* Chapel Hill: University of North Carolina Press, 1994.

Colonization Society of the State of Connecticut. *An Address to the Public by the Managers of the Colonization Society of Connecticut*. New Haven: Treadway and Adams, 1828.

Coppin, Fanny Jackson. *Reminiscences of School Life, and Hints on Teaching*. New York: G. K. Hall, 1995.

Cornelius, Janet Duitsman. *"When I Can Read My Title Clear": Literacy, Slavery, and Religion in the Antebellum South*. Columbia: University of South Carolina Press, 1991.

Curry, Constance. *Silver Rights*. Chapel Hill: Algonquin, 1995.

Davie, Maurice R. *Negroes in American Society*. New York: McGraw Hill, 1949.

Davis, Deborah R. *Black Students' Perceptions: The Complexity of Persistence to Graduation at an American University*. New York: Peter Lang, 2004.

Days, Drew S., III. "Brown Blues: Rethinking the Integrative Ideal." *College of William and Mary Law Review* 34 (Fall 1992): 53–74.

Derbigny, Irving A. *General Education in the Negro College*. New York: Negro Universities Press, 1947.

Dougherty, Jack. *More Than One Struggle: The Evolution of Black School Reform in Milwaukee*. Chapel Hill: University of North Carolina Press, 2004.

Douglas, Davison M. *Reading, Writing, and Race: The Desegregation of Charlotte Schools*. Chapel Hill: University of North Carolina Press, 1995.

Douglas, Davison M. "The Rhetoric of Moderation: Desegregating the South during the Decade after Brown." *Northwestern University Law Review* 89, no. 92 (1994): 92–137.

Douglass, Frederick. *The Narrative of the Life of Frederick Douglass, An American Slave, Written by Himself*. New Haven: Yale University Press, 2001.

Drago, Edmund L. *Initiative, Paternalism, and Race Relations: Charleston's Avery Normal Institute*. Athens: University of Georgia Press, 1990.

Du Bois, W. E. B. *The College-Bred Negro*. In *Proceedings of the Fifth Conference for the Study of the Negro Problems*, Atlanta University (May 29–30). Atlanta: Atlanta University Press, 1900.

Du Bois, W. E. B. *The College-Bred Negro American*, Atlanta: Atlanta University Press, 1910.

Du Bois, W. E. B. *The Common School and the Negro American*. Atlanta: Atlanta University Press, 1911.

Du Bois, W. E. B. "Does the Negro Need Separate Schools?" *Journal of Negro Education* 4 (July 1935): 278–88.

Du Bois, W. E. B., ed. *The Negro Common School*. Atlanta: Atlanta University Press, 1901.

Du Bois, W. E. B. *The Philadelphia Negro*. Reprint. New York: Schocken Books, 1970.

Du Bois, W. E. B. "The Talented Tenth." In *The Seventh Son: The Thought and Writings of W.E.B. Du Bois*, ed. Julius Lester. New York: Random House, 1971.

Edwards, Harry. *Black Students*. New York: Free Press, 1970.

Feagan, Joe R., et al. *The Agony of Education: Black Students at White Colleges and Universities*. New York: Routledge, 1996.

Fishel, Leslie H., Jr., and Benjamin Quarles. *The Negro American: A Documentary History*. Glenview, Ill.: Morrow, 1967.

Fleming, John E., et al. *The Case for Affirmative Action for Blacks in Higher Education.* Washington, D.C.: Howard University Press, 1978.

Flemming, Jacqueline. *Blacks in College: A Comparative Study of Students' Success in Black and White Institutions.* San Francisco: Jossey-Bass, 1984.

Fordham, Signithia. *Blacked Out: Dilemmas of Race, Identity, and Success at Capital High.* Chicago: University of Chicago Press, 1996.

Formisano, Ronald. *Boston against Busing. Race, Class, and Ethnicity in the 1960s and 1970s.* Chapel Hill: University of North Carolina Press, 1991.

Franklin, Vincent P. "Education for Colonization: Attempts to Educate Free Blacks in the United States for Emigration to Africa, 1823–1833." *Journal of Negro Education* 43 (Winter 1974): 91–103.

Franklin, Vincent P. "Education for Life: Adult Education Programs for African Americans in Northern Cities, 1900–1942." In *Education of the African American Adult: An Historical Overview,* ed. Harvey G. Neufeldt and Leo McGee. New York: Greenwood, 1990.

Franklin, Vincent P. *The Education of Black Philadelphia: The Social and Educational History of a Minority Community, 1900–1950.* Philadelphia: University of Pennsylvania Press, 1979.

Franklin, Vincent P. "The Persistence of School Segregation in the Urban North: An Historical Perspective." *Journal of Ethnic Studies* 1 (February 1974): 51–68.

Franklin, Vincent P., and James D. Anderson, eds. *New Perspectives on Black Educational History.* Boston: G. K. Hall, 1978.

Freedom's Journal, 18 July 1828, "African Schools."

Freeman, Kassie. *African American Culture and Heritage in Higher Education Research and Practice.* Westport, Conn.: Praeger, 1998.

Friedman, Leon. *Argument: The Oral Argument before the Supreme Court in* Brown v. Board of Education of Topeka, 1952–55. New York: Chelsea House Publishers, 1969.

Fultz, Michael. "The Displacement of Black Educators Post-Brown: An Overview and Analysis." *History of Education Quarterly* 44 (Spring 2004): 11–45.

Garibaldi, Antoine. *Black Colleges and Universities: Challenges for the Future.* Westport, Conn.: Praeger, 1984.

Gillard, Frye. *The Dream Long Deferred.* Chapel Hill: University of North Carolina Press, 1988.

Glasker, Wayne. *Black Students in the Ivory Tower: African American Student Activism at the University of Pennsylvania, 1967–1990.* Boston: University of Massachusetts Press, 2002.

Greenberg, Jack. *Crusaders in the Courts: How a Dedicated Band of Lawyers Fought for the Civil Rights Revolution.* New York: Basic Books, 1994.

Hardin, John A. *Fifty Years of Segregation: Black Higher Education in Kentucky, 1904–1954.* Lexington: University Press of Kentucky, 1997.

Haviland, Laura S. *A Woman's Life-Work: Labors and Experiences of Laura S. Haviland.* 4th ed. Chicago: Publishing Association of Friends, 1889.

Hawkins, Hugh, ed. *Booker T. Washington and his Critics.* Lexington, Mass.: DC Heath, 1974.

Hayes, J. R. . Negrophobia "On the Brain" in White Men, or an Essay upon the Origin and Progress, Both Mental and Physical, of the Negro Race and the Use to be Made of Him by the Politicians in the United States. Washington, D.C.: Powell, Ginck and Co, 1869.

Heintze, Michael R. Private Black Colleges in Texas, 1865–1954. College Station: Texas A&M University Press, 1985.

Henderson, Edwin B. The Negro in Sports. Washington, D.C.: Associated Publishers, 1939.

Hill, Herbert, and Jack Greenberg. Citizen's Guide to Desegregation. Boston: Beacon Press, 1955.

Hochschild, Jennifer. The New American Dilemma: Liberal Democracy and School Desegregation. New Haven: Yale University Press, 1984.

Howard University Institute for the Study of Educational Policy. Equal Educational Opportunity for Blacks in U.S. Higher Education: An Assessment. Washington, D.C.: Howard University Press, 1976.

Hrabowski, Freeman A., III et al. Beating the Odds: Raising Academically Successful African American Males. Oxford: Oxford University Press, 1998.

Hughes, Langston. "Cowards from the Colleges." Crisis 41 (August 1934): 226–28.

Hunter-Gault, Charlayne. In My Place. New York: Farrar, Straus, and Giroux, 1992.

Irons, Peter. Jim Crow's Children: The Broken Promise of the Brown Decision. New York: Viking, 2002.

"Instruction of Slaves." Colonization and Journal of Freedom, 1833–1834 (February 1834): 304.

Irvine, Jacqueline Jordan, and Michèle Foster. Growing Up African American in Catholic Schools. New York: Teachers College Press, 1996.

Jacoway, Elizabeth. Yankee Missionaries in the South: The Penn School Experiment. Baton Rouge: Louisiana State University Press, 1980.

Johnson, Charles S. The Negro College Graduate. Chapel Hill: University of North Carolina Press, 1960.

Johnson, G. B. "Racial Integration in Public Higher Education in the South." Journal of Negro Education 23 (Summer 1975): 317–19.

Johnson, Roosevelt. Black Scholars on Higher Education in the 70's. Columbus, Ohio: ECCA, 1974.

Jones, Jacqueline. Soldiers of Light and Love: Northern Teachers and Georgia Blacks, 1865–1873. Chapel Hill: University of North Carolina Press, 1980.

Kluger, Richard. Simple Justice: The History of Brown v. Board of Education and Black America's Struggle for Equality. New York: Vintage, 2004.

Leloudis, James L. Schooling the New South: Pedagogy, Self, and Society in North Carolina, 1880–1920. Chapel Hill: University of North Carolina Press, 1996.

Levine, Donald M., and Mary Jo Bane. The "Inequality" Controversy: Schooling and Distributive Justice. New York: Basic Books, 1975.

Lomotey, Kofi. Going to School: The African-American Experience. Albany: State University of New York Press, 1990.

Mabee, Carlton. *Black Education in New York State: From Colonial to Modern Times.* Syracuse, N.Y.: Syracuse University Press, 1979.

Mangum, C. S., Jr. *The Legal Status of the Negro.* Chapel Hill: University of North Carolina, 1940.

Markowitz, Gerald, and David Rosner. *Children, Race, and Power: Kenneth and Mamie Clark's Northside Center.* Charlottesville: University Press of Virginia, 1996.

Martin, Waldo E., Jr. Brown v. Board of Education: A *Brief History with Documents.* Bedford/ St. Martin's Press, 1998.

Maton, Kenneth I., et al. "Preparing the Way: A Qualitative Study of High-Achieving African American Males and the Role of Family." *American Journal of Community Psychology* 26 (August 1998): 639–68.

McCaul, Robert L. *The Black Struggle for Public Schooling in Nineteenth-Century Illinois.* Carbondale: Southern Illinois University Press, 1987.

McMillan, Lewis. "The American Negro in Higher Education." *Crisis* 54 (August 1947).

McNeil, Genna Rae. *Groundwork: Charles Hamilton Houston and the Struggle for Civil Rights.* Philadelphia: University of Pennsylvania Press, 1983.

McPherson, James M. *The Abolitionist Legacy: From Reconstruction to the NAACP.* Princeton, N.J.: Princeton University Press, 1975.

McPherson, James M. "White Liberals and Black Power in Negro Education, 1865–1915." *American Historical Review* 75 (June 1970).

Meier, August, and Elliott M. Rudwick. *From Plantation to Ghetto.* New York: Hill and Wang, 1976.

Morris, Robert C. "Freedmen's Education." In *Black Women in America: An Historical Encyclopedia*, vol. 1, ed. Darlene Clark Hine. Brooklyn, N.Y.: Carlson, 1993.

Morris, Robert C. *Reading, 'riting, and Reconstruction: The Education of Freedmen in the South, 1861–1870.* Chicago: University of Chicago Press, 1976.

Moss, Alfred A., Jr. *The American Negro Academy.* Baton Rouge: Louisiana State University Press, 1981.

Motley, Constance Baker. *Equal Justice under the Law: An Autobiography.* New York: Farrar, Straus, and Giroux, 1998.

Mullen, Robert W. *Blacks in America's War.* New York: Monad Press, 1973.

Noble, Jeanne L. *The Negro Woman's College Education.* New York: Teachers College, Columbia University, 1956.

Ogbu, John U. *Black American Students in an Affluent Suburb: A Study of Academic Disengagement.* Mahwah: Lawrence Erlbaum, 2003.

Ogletree, Charles J., Jr. *All Deliberate Speed: Reflections on the First Half of* Brown v. Board of Education. New York: Norton, 2004.

Orfield, Gary, and Susan E. Eaton. *Dismantling Desegregation: The Quiet Reversal of* Brown v. Board of Education. New York: New Press, 1966.

Orr, Marion. *Black Social Capital: The Politics of School Reform in Baltimore, 1986–1998.* Lawrence: University Press of Kansas, 1999.

Owens, Jesse. *Blackthink.* New York: Morrow, 1970.

Patterson, James T. Brown v. Board of Education: A Civil Rights Milestone and Its Troubled Legacy. Oxford: Oxford University Press, 2001.

Pease, Jane H., and William H. Pease. They Who Would Be Free: Blacks' Search for Freedom, 1830–1861. New York: Atheneum, 1974.

Peltason, Jack W. Fifty-Eight Lonely Men. New York: Harcourt, Brace & World, 1961.

Perkins, Alfred. "Welcome Consequences and Fulfilled Promise: Julius Rosenwald Fellows and Brown v. Board of Education." Journal of Negro Education 72 (Summer 2003): 344–56.

Perkins, Linda M. Fanny Jackson Coppin and the Institute for Colored Youth, 1865–1902. New York: Garland, 1987.

Perkins, Linda M. "Heed Life's Demands: The Educational Philosophy of Fanny Jackson Coppin." Journal of Negro Education 51 (Summer 1982): 181–90.

Perkins, Linda M. "The Impact of the 'Cult of True Womanhood' on the Education of Black Women." Journal of Social Issues 39, no. 3 (1983): 17–28.

Perkins, Linda M. "Lucy Diggs Slowe: Champion of the Self-Determination of African-American Women in Higher Education." Journal of Negro History 81, no. 1/4 (1996): 89–104.

Perkins, Linda M. "The National Association of College Women: Vanguard of Black Women's Leadership and Education, 1923–1964." Journal of Education 173, no. 3 (1990): 65–75.

Perkins, Linda Marie. "Quaker Beneficence and Black Control: The Institute for Colored Youth 1852–1903." In New Perspectives on Black Educational History, ed. Vincent P. Franklin and James D. Anderson. Boston: G. K. Hall, 1978.

Perry, Theresa et al. Young, Gifted, and Black: Promoting High Achievement among African-American Students. Boston: Beacon, 2003.

Peterson, Marvin W., et al. Black Students on White Campuses: The Impact of Increased Black Enrollments. Ann Arbor: University of Michigan, 1978.

Polite, Vernon C., and James Earl Davis. African American Males in School and Society: Practices and Policies for Effective Education. New York: Teachers College Press, 1999.

Pratt, Robert A. The Color of Their Skin: Education and Race in Richmond, Virginia, 1954–89. Charlottesville: University Press of Virginia, 1992.

"Prudance Crandall." In Notable American Women, 1607–1950: A Biographical Dictionary, ed. Edward T. James. Cambridge, Mass.: Belknap Press of Harvard University Press, 1975.

Rawick, George P., ed. The American Slave: A Composite Autobiography. Supplement Series 1. Westport, Conn.: Greenwood Press, 1977.

Richardson, Joe M. Christian Reconstruction: The American Missionary Association and Southern Blacks, 1861–1890. Athens: University of Georgia Press, 1986.

Robeson, Paul L. Here I Stand. Boston: Beacon, 1958.

Ross, Lawrence C., Jr. The Divine Nine: The History of African American Fraternities and Sororities. New York: Kensington, 2000.

Samuels, Albert L. Is Separate Unequal? Black Colleges and the Challenge to Desegregation. Lawrence: University Press of Kansas, 2004.

Sarratt, Reed. The Ordeal of Desegregation: The First Decade. New York: Harper and Row, 1966.

Schwartz, Bernard. *Swann's Way: The School Busing Case and the Supreme Court.* Oxford: Oxford University Press, 1986.

Shoemaker, Don, ed. *With All Deliberate Speed.* New York: Harper, 1957.

Sindler, Allan P. *Bakke, DeFunis, and Minority Admissions: The Quest for Equal Opportunity.* New York: Longman, 1978.

Slowe, Lucy D. "Higher Education of Negro Women." *Journal of Negro Education* 2, no. 3 (July 1933): 352–58.

Smith, Bob. *They Closed Their Schools: Prince Edward County, Virginia, 1951–1964.* Chapel Hill: University of North Carolina Press, 1965.

Smith, Charles U. *Student Unrest on Historically Black Campuses.* Silver Springs, Md.: Venture Books, 1994.

Sollors, Werner, et al. *Blacks at Harvard: A Documentary History of African-American Experience at Harvard and Radcliffe.* New York: New York University Press, 1993.

Sowell, Thomas. "Black Excellence: The Case of Dunbar High School." *Public Interest* 35 (Spring 1974): 1–21.

St. John, Nancy H. *School Desegregation: Outcomes for Children.* New York: Wiley, 1975.

Steele, Claude M. "A Threat in the Air: How Stereotypes Shape Intellectual Identity and Performance." *American Psychologist* 52, no. 6 (1997): 613–29.

Steele, Claude M. "Stereotype Threat and the Intellectual Test Performance of African Americans." *Journal of Personality and Social Psychology* 69, no. 5 (1995): 97–111.

Sum, Paul E., Steven Andrew Light, and Ronald F. King. "Race, Reform and Desegregation in Mississippi Higher Education: Historically Black Institutions after *United States v. Fordice.*" *Law and Social Inquiry* 29 (Spring 2004): 403–35.

Tatum, Beverly Daniel. *"Why are All the Black Kids Sitting Together in the Cafeteria?" and Other Conversations about Race.* New York: Basic Books, 1997.

Taylor, Susan King. *Reminiscences of My Life in Camp.* Reprint of the 1902 edition. New York: Arno Press, 1968.

Trillin, Calvin. *An Education in Georgia: Charlayne Hunter, Hamilton Holmes, and the Integration of the University of Georgia.* Athens: University of Georgia Press, 1991.

Tushnet, Mark. *The NAACP's Legal Strategy against Segregated Education, 1925–1950.* Chapel Hill: University of North Carolina Press, 1987.

Tussman, Joseph. *The Supreme Court on Racial Discrimination.* New York: Oxford University Press, 1963.

Tyack, David. *The One Best System: A History of American Urban Education.* Cambridge, Mass.: Harvard University Press, 1974.

Waite, Cally L. *Permission To Remain among Us: Education for Blacks in Oberlin, Ohio, 1880–1914.* Westport, Conn.: Praeger, 2002.

Walker, David. *David Walker's Appeal to the Coloured Citizens of the World.* Reprint of the 1828 edition. New York: Hill and Wang, 1965.

Walker, Vanessa Siddle. "Caswell County Training School: Relationships between Community and School." *Harvard Educational Review* 83 (Summer 1993): 161–82.

Walker, Vanessa Siddle. *Their Highest Potential: An African American School Community in the Segregated South*. Chapel Hill: University of North Carolina Press, 1996.

Washington, Booker T. "Industrial Education for the Negro." In Washington et al., *The Negro Problem*. 1903; Amherst, N.Y.: Humanity Books, 2003.

Washington, Booker T. *Tuskegee and Its People*. New York: Appleton, 1905.

Webber, Thomas L. *Deep Like the Rivers: Education in the Slave Quarter Community: 1831–1865*. New York: Norton, 1978.

Wiggins, Sam P. *The Desegregation Era in Higher Education*. Berkeley: McCutchan, 1966.

Wilkinson, J. Harvie, III. *From Brown to Bakke: The Supreme Court and School Integration, 1954–1978*. New York: Oxford University Press, 1979.

Wilkinson, J. Harvie, III. "To Bus or Not to Bus." In *From Brown to Bakke: The Supreme Court and School Integration, 1954–1978*. New York: Oxford University Press, 1979.

Williamson, Joy Ann. *Black Power on Campus: The University of Illinois, 1965–75*. Urbana: University of Illinois Press, 2003.

Willie, Sarah Susannah. *Acting Black: College, Identity, and the Performance of Race*. New York: Routledge, 2003.

Wolf, Eleanor P. *Trial and Error: The Detroit School Desegregation Case*. Detroit: Wayne State University Press, 1981.

Wolters, Raymond. *The Burden of Brown: Thirty Years of School Desegregation*. Knoxville: University of Tennessee Press, 1984.

Wolters, Raymond. *The New Negro on Campus: Black College Rebellions of the 1920s*. Princeton, N.J.: Princeton University Press, 1975.

Woodson, Carter G. *The African Background Outline; or, Handbook for the Study of the Negro*. New York: Negro Universities Press, 1968.

Woodson, Carter G. "The Educated Negro Leaves the Masses." In *The Mis-Education of the Negro*. Trenton: Africa World Press, 1990.

Woodson, Carter G. *The Education of the Negro Prior to 1861*. New York: G. P. Putnam, 1915.

Woodson, Carter G. *The Mis-Education of the Negro*. Washington, D.C.: Associated Publishers, 1933.

CHRONOLOGY

1816   African free schools are established in New York.

1829   Founding of the St. Frances Academy in Baltimore by the Oblate Order, a group of French-educated black nuns.

1835   Oberlin College opens its doors to blacks and women.

1837   Founding of the Institute for Colored Youth in Philadelphia.

1848   *Roberts v. City of Boston*. The Massachusetts Supreme Court rules that segregated schools are permissible under the state's constitution.

1862   Mary Jane Patterson graduates from Oberlin and becomes the first African American woman to receive a college degree.

1874   Edward Bouchet is the first African American to become a member of Phi Beta Kappa honor society.

1876   Edward Bouchet earns a Ph.D. in physics from Yale University; he is the first black person to receive a doctorate from an American university.

1890   The second Morrill Act establishes state land-grant colleges for blacks.

1899   *Cumming v. Richmond (Ga.) County Board of Education, 175 U.S. 528 (1899)*. The Supreme Court allows a state to levy taxes on black and white citizens while providing public schools only for white children.

1908   *Berea College v. Commonwealth of Kentucky, 211 U.S. 45.* The Supreme Court upholds a state's authority to require a private college to operate as a segregated institution, despite the wishes of the institution.

1921   Eva Dykes (Radcliffe), Sadie Tanner Alexander (University of Pennsylvania), and Georgianna Simpson (University of Chicago) are the first black women in the nation to earn Ph.D.s.

1936   *Murray v. Maryland, 182 A. 590 (1936).* The Maryland Supreme Court orders the state's law school to admit black students.

1938   *Missouri ex rel. Gaines v. Canada, 305 U.S. 337.* The Supreme Court rules that out-of-state scholarships for blacks to attend law schools do not fulfill the "separate but equal" doctrine; the Court orders Missouri to admit black students.

1948   *Sipuel v. Oklahoma State Board of Regents, 332 U.S. 631.* The Supreme Court orders the admission of a black student to the University of Oklahoma School of Law because there is not a law school in the state for blacks.

1950   *Sweatt v. Painter, 339 U.S. 629 (1950).* The Supreme Court rejects Texas's plan to create a new law school for blacks, and orders Herman Marion Sweatt's admission to the University of Texas Law School.

1950   *McLaurin v. Oklahoma State Regents for Higher Education, 339 U.S. 637.* The Supreme Court rules that isolating a black student from his peers in law school is unconstitutional.

1954   *Brown v. Board of Education, 347 U.S. 483.* The Supreme Court rules that the "separate but equal" doctrine is unconstitutional; this landmark ruling reverses the *Plessy v. Ferguson* decision of 1896.

1955   *Brown v. Board of Education, 349 U.S. 295.* In a case known as *Brown II*, the Supreme Court orders the lower courts to require desegregation of schools with "all deliberate speed."

1971   *Swann v. Charlotte-Mecklenburg Board of Education, U.S. 1 (1971).* The Supreme Court approves busing, magnet schools, compensatory education, and other remedies to overcome residential segregation.

1974   *Milliken v. Bradley et al., 433 U.S. 267.* The Supreme Court denies a metropolitan-wide desegregation plan as a mean to desegregate urban schools with large minority populations.

1978   *Regents of the University of California v. Bakke, 438 U.S. 265.* A divided Supreme Court rules that the affirmative-action admissions program for the University of

California-Davis Medical School is unconstitutional because it sets aside a specific number of slots for black and Latino students. The Court rules that race can be a factor in university admissions, but not a deciding factor.

1992   *United States v. Fordice et al.*, 505 U.S. 717. The Supreme Court rules that the adoption of race-neutral measures does not, by itself, fulfill the constitutional obligation to desegregate colleges and universities that were segregated by law.

1996   *Hopwood v. Texas*, 78 F.3d 932 (5th Cir. 1996). A federal appeals court prohibits the use of race in college and university admissions, ending affirmative action in Louisiana, Texas, and Mississippi.

2001   Ruth Simmons becomes president of Brown University, the first African American to head an Ivy League university.

2003   *Grutter v. Bollinger*, 539 U.S.; *Gratz v. Bollinger*, 539 U.S. The Supreme Court upholds diversity as a rationale for affirmative-action programs in higher-education admissions, but concludes that point systems are not appropriate.

2004   The nation celebrates the fiftieth anniversary of *Brown v. Board of Education*.

GLOSSARY

American Missionary Association. A nondenominational society that grew out of a committee organized in 1839 to defend slaves who had seized control of the Spanish slave ship *Amistad*. The AMA was incorporated in 1846 to establish missions for freed slaves overseas, but within a few years it turned its efforts towards abolition. After the Civil War it established 500 public schools for freedmen in the South, although they eventually admitted all students. The AMA also helped found ten predominantly black colleges: Atlanta University, Berea College, Dillard University, Fisk University, Hampton Institute (present-day Hampton University), Howard University, Huston-Tilloston College, Le Moyne College, Talladega College, and Tougaloo College. Today the AMA conducts educational and social programs for other minorities as well.

Atlanta Compromise. Booker T. Washington's statement on race relations made in a speech at the Cotton States and International Exposition in Atlanta, Georgia, on September 18, 1895. Washington, a leading African American educator, believed that vocational education was of more immediate importance to blacks than civil rights and social advancement. He believed that blacks should accept their lot in life and live separately from the white community while they gained economic security. Meanwhile, whites were to accept responsibility for improving the social and economic conditions of all Americans. Under such conditions, Washington believed, racism would eventually wither away. While whites in the North and South applauded Washington's stance, some members of the black community were disturbed by his philosophy of accommodation. His greatest detractor was W. E. B. Du Bois, who maintained that such a policy practically accepted "the alleged inferiority of the Negro races."

Berea College v. Commonwealth of Kentucky. A U.S. Supreme Court decision in 1908 that upheld that a state could impose segregated instruction on chartered private schools.

Brown v. the Board of Education of Topeka, Kansas. A landmark U.S. Supreme Court decision rendered on May 17, 1954. The court ruled unanimously that racial segregation in public schools violated the Equal Protection Clause of the Fourteenth Amendment (no state may "deny to any person within its jurisdiction the equal protection of the laws"). Furthermore, separate facilities were "inherently unequal." This particular case was based on a series of Supreme Court cases argued between 1938 and 1950, and reversed *Plessy v. Ferguson* (1896), which had upheld the doctrine of "separate but equal." Although the 1954 decision was aimed at the public school system, it implied that segregation was illegal in all public facilities. Thurgood Marshall, a founder of the NAACP's Legal Defense and Educational Fund and future Supreme Court justice, helped argue the case for the plaintiff. In a second decision known as *Brown II* (1955), the court ordered the states' compliance to desegregate their school systems "with all deliberate speed."

Cumming v. Richmond County (Ga.) Board of Education. A U.S. Supreme Court case decided on December 18, 1899. This was the court's first decision on racial discrimination in schools. It refused to enforce the "separate but equal" doctrine established by *Plessy v. Ferguson* (1896) and declared that plaintiffs had to prove that a public school board's decision not to support black schools had been motivated solely by a "hostility to the colored population because of their race."

Freedmen's Bureau. Popular name for the U.S. Bureau of Refugees, Freedmen, and Abandoned Lands, established in 1865 to help 4 million African Americans in the transition from slavery to freedom. Headed by Major General Oliver Howard, this federal agency was administered through the War Department and had its own court system. Among its responsibilities was providing medical assistance and temporary food relief, but its most important achievement was in education. By late 1865 it had enrolled some 90,000 blacks in public schools. Overall the bureau spent 5 million dollars in educating African Americans and built around 1,000 schools. (Some of these schools had attendance rates as high as 80 percent.) Nevertheless, the Freedmen's Bureau never reached its full potential because of budget cuts, limited jurisdiction, and the hostility of white Southerners. Congress abolished it in 1872.

Hampton Idea. Samuel Chapman Armstrong's philosophy on how to educate African Americans at Hampton Normal and Agricultural Institute. The son of white missionaries, Armstrong believed that blacks were morally inferior to whites and needed vocational training in order to improve their economic and social condition. Booker T. Washington, a graduate of the institute, was an advocate of the Hampton Idea.

Hampton Institute. A historically black institution of higher education in Hampton, Virginia. It was founded in 1868 as the Hampton Normal and Agricultural Institute by Samuel Chapman Armstrong, a Civil War general and an agent for the Freedmen's Bureau who recognized the need for training African American teachers. In its early years, the institute received land-grant funds. It was accredited as a college in 1933 and a university in 1984. Among the school's famous alumni is Booker T. Washington.

McLaurin v. Oklahoma State Regents for Higher Education. A U.S. Supreme Court case decided on June 5, 1950, it was a companion case to *Sweatt v. Painter* (1950). The court ruled that isolating an African American student from his peers in law school was unconstitutional.

Milliken v. Bradley. A U.S. Supreme Court case decided on July 25, 1974; it declared that segregation in one school district did not warrant relief that included another nonsegregating district.

Missouri ex rel. Gaines v. Canada. A U.S. Supreme Court decision of December 12, 1938. The court declared that scholarships for African Americans to attend law schools outside of a specific state did not fulfill the "separate but equal" doctrine, and the University of Missouri law school was ordered to admit a black student.

Murray v. Maryland. A Maryland Supreme Court decision in 1936 that ordered the state's law school to admit black students.

NAACP Legal Defense and Educational Fund. A civil rights organization founded in 1939 by Thurgood Marshall. Originally a part of the National Association for the Advancement of Colored People (NAACP), the Legal Defense Fund, or Inc. Fund as it is commonly called, became a separate entity in 1957. It has provided legal counsel in education, voting, economic-access, affirmative-action, and criminal-justice matters. The Legal Defense Fund's most famous case was *Brown v. the Board of Education of Topeka, Kansas* (1954), and during the Civil Rights movement of the 1960s it provided assistance to Dr. Martin Luther King Jr. and other black leaders.

Regents of the University of California v. Bakke. A U.S. Supreme Court case decided on June 28, 1978. The court held that a university could consider racial criteria in its admissions process so long as "fixed quotas" were not used.

Roberts v. City of Boston. A Massachusetts Supreme Court decision rendered in 1848; it declared that segregated schools were permissible under the state's constitution.

Second Morrill Act. A federal statute passed in 1890 that clarified the process by which land-grant colleges were founded in the United States (the first Morrill Act was enacted in 1862). This law was aimed at the South and required each state to demonstrate that race was not a factor in admissions; otherwise, the state had to establish a separate land-grant institution for African Americans. Among the seventy institutes of higher learning founded under the Morrill Acts are several leading historically black schools, including Tuskegee University, North Carolina A&T State University, and South Carolina State University.

Sipuel v. Oklahoma State Board of Regents. A U.S. Supreme Court decision rendered on January 12, 1948. The court ordered the admission of a black student to the University of Oklahoma School of Law because the state had no similar, separate facility for African Americans.

Swann v. Charlotte-Mecklenburg Board of Education. A U.S. Supreme Court case decided on April 20, 1971, that approved busing and other measures to achieve desegregation in school districts.

Sweatt v. Painter. A U.S. Supreme Court case decided on June 5, 1950. The court ordered the University of Texas Law School to admit a black student, because a proposed new law school for African Americans would in no way be equal to the existing all-white institute.

Tuskegee Institute. A historically black institution of higher learning in Tuskegee, Alabama. It was established in 1881 as the Tuskegee Normal and Industrial Institute by the Alabama legislature. Educator Booker T. Washington served as its first principal and was the guiding influence until his death in 1915. The institute was initially dedicated to Washington's principles of providing vocational training to African Americans so they could develop economic self-reliance. Renamed Tuskegee Institute in 1937, it received university status in 1985. As head of the agricultural department, the botanist George Washington Carver conducted many of his famous experiments with peanuts, soybeans, and other crops at the school. Frederick Douglass Patterson, founder of the United Negro College Fund (1944), served as the school's third president from 1935 to 1953.

African Americans in the Military

Chad Williams

Abstract

From the War of Independence to the contemporary conflict in Iraq, African Americans have played a central role in United States military history. Reflecting the often warlike nature of American race relations, the military has been a site of fierce political contestation, both figuratively and literally. More than any other segment of American society, the armed forces have encapsulated the tension of demanding that African Americans sacrifice their lives on the behalf of the nation while they are often still denied the fruits of equal citizenship. As a result, African American soldiers have historically held powerful and often competing metonymic values, functioning as symbolic embodiments of issues such as African American citizenship, manhood, civic nationalism, and black radicalism. The figurative resonance of black soldiers, however, frequently overshadows the fact that African Americans have been and remain attracted to the military as a site to make democracy a lived reality and as an opportunity for personal social, educational, and economic advancement, in particular during moments of warfare. The history of African Americans in the military thus encompasses more than dichotomized stories of, on the one hand, unflinching patriotism and, on the other, systemic racial abuse. Shaped by the forces of war, the contextual character of the armed forces, and the evolving nature of race relations, the history of African American servicemen and women reflects the everyday struggles of black people to appropriate the military as an institution to fulfill the promise and potential of their citizenship.

Historiographical Evolution and Trends

The earliest scholars of African American history placed considerable emphasis on the experience of black people in the nation's military. George Washington Williams, himself a soldier and veteran of the Civil War, devoted several hundred pages to the heroism of black servicemen in his landmark study *History of the Negro Race in America, 1619–1880* (1883). His subsequent book, *A History of the Negro Troops in the War of the Rebellion* (1888), placed the participation of black soldiers in the Civil War within the larger historical legacy of black military service in the United States, as well as in other countries. Other early histories of African Americans, such as Booker T. Washington's *The Story of the Negro* (1909), Joseph T. Wilson's *The Black Phalanx* (1888), and Carter G. Woodson's *The Negro in Our History* (1922), likewise stressed the valor of black troops and their contribution to the defense of the nation.

These early histories shared a revisionist desire to insert black soldiers into the military history of the United States and thus demonstrate the unwavering commitment of African Americans to the nation, in spite of slavery, segregation, and racial violence. As symbols of racial heroism and patriotic loyalty, black soldiers functioned to vindicate the race, and black manhood along with it, from assertions that African Americans had played no meaningful role in the nation's historical development and were thus unworthy of recognition as citizens. The politicized nature of this construction imbued black soldiers with a powerful metonymic value in which their courage and sacrifice represented that of African Americans writ large.

The historiography of African Americans in the military has evolved with the trajectory of race relations in the United States and the development

Kean Collection / Hulton Archive / Getty Images

This portrait of the Civil War veteran George Washington Williams dates from 1870 when he was twenty-one years old. Born in Bedford Springs, Pennsylvania, Williams was 14 when he joined the Union forces in 1863, eventually serving as a lieutenant-colonel in the Mexican Army. Upon his return to America, Williams studied at the Newton Theological Seminary and became a Baptist minister in Boston and Cincinnati. Williams also worked as a journalist, writing for a number of leading journals. His first major book, the two-volume *History of the Negro Race in America, 1619–1880: Negroes as Slaves, as Soldiers, and as Citizens, Together with a Preliminary Consideration of the Unity of the Human Family; An Historical Sketch of Africa, and An Account of the Negro Governments of Sierra Leone and Liberia*, was the first formal African American history. He also became the first African American to be elected to the Ohio state legislature, and traveled extensively across Europe attempting to address issues connected to the slave trade and the treatment of Africans in many European colonies. He died in England in 1891.

of African American history as a field of scholarly inquiry. Key texts written during the 1950s and early 1960s, such as *The Negro in the Civil War* (1953) and *The Negro in the American Revolution* (1961) by pioneering historian Benjamin Quarles, and Dudley Taylor Cornish's *The Sable Arm* (1956), remained principally concerned with demonstrating the contribution of black people to the defense of the nation and their triumph in overcoming racism as an implicit argument for full inclusion in the body politic. As the study of African American history became more specialized during the 1970s, a number of works appeared—including Ann Lane's *The Brownsville Affair* (1971), Arthur E. Barbeau and Florette Henri's *The Unknown Soldiers* (1974), Marvin Fletcher's *The Black Soldier and Officer in the United States Army, 1891–1917* (1974), and Richard O. Hope's *Racial Strife in the U.S. Military* (1979)—that placed increased emphasis on the pervasiveness of racial discrimination in the armed forces. This period also marked a temporal and topical broadening of African American military history, as scholars began to examine the experiences of black soldiers beyond the macro level and in a wide variety of historical contexts.

Despite the growth of more specialized studies, surveys of the black military experience did not move significantly beyond the paradigm established by late nineteenth-century historians. Beginning with Jack Foner's *Blacks and the Military in American History* (1974), studies of the larger history of African Americans in the armed forces were shaped by a conceptual framework that asserted institutionalized racism as the defining characteristic of the black military experience, and the steadfast patriotism and determination of African American soldiers to overcome its negative impacts. Scholars viewed the post-segregation military as ahead of its time in confronting racial discrimination—yet far from idyllic, given its troubled history in accepting African Americans on equal terms with whites. Bernard C. Nalty's *Strength for the Fight* (1986) stressed this very point, and is still widely upheld as the standard text on the black military experience.

Beginning in the early 1990s the military, aided by the 1991 Gulf War and the ascent of Colin Powell, successfully cultivated an image of itself as the most racially diverse and equitable institution in American society. Scholars have internalized this theme, which dominates recent studies of African American military history. From this perspective, the history of black people in the nation's armed forces is a success story, representing the advancement of a people from bondage to the highest echelons of the government. Works including Michael Lee Lanning's *The African American Soldier: From Crispus Attucks to Colin Powell* (1997), Gerald Astor's *The Right to Fight* (1998), Robert B. Edgerton's *Hidden Heroism: Black Soldiers in America's Wars* (2001), and Gail Buckley's *American Patriots* (2001) construct black soldiers as symbols of racial perseverance in overcoming virulent racial discrimination, while remaining committed to and embodying the nation's highest ideals. In this sense, African American servicemen and women stand as the ultimate Americans.

This romanticized portrayal of the military reflects the struggle historians face in moving beyond viewing African American soldiers primarily as racialized symbols. Black troops continue to function as synecdoche for a variety of ideologically charged positions used to characterize the historical experience of African Americans, such as the pervasiveness of white supremacy, the indomitable courage of African Americans, and the gradual achievement of true racial equality. The humanity and individual complexity afforded to white soldiers has largely been denied to black soldiers as a result of their metaphoric potency. As the field of African American military history continues to evolve, scholars must delve further into the individual dimensions of the black military experience, its complexity, and how soldiers responded to their service in multiple and often contradictory ways.

Fighting for Freedom: The War of Independence to the Civil War

The evolution of racial slavery in colonial America coincided with the gradual exclusion of peoples of African descent from military service. Reflecting the initially fluid nature of slavery, opportunities for free black people to serve on behalf of the colonies were frequent in early colonial America, but the evolution of racial slavery in the region coincided with the gradual exclusion of peoples of African descent from military service. Although Virginia barred former slaves from militia duty in 1639, the threat of attacks by Native Americans necessitated that colonial militias have a force readily at hand. For this reason, some states allowed slave owners to consign their most trusted chattel for militia service in defense of the colony—including for a brief moment South Carolina in 1703, which promised manumission in return for the killing of a Native American. Such latitude dissipated in the colonial South as the slave population began to outnumber that of whites in many areas and the specter of rebellion became increasingly real. As the September 1739 Stono Rebellion in South Carolina chillingly demonstrated, the maintenance of the "peculiar institution" necessitated that arms remain out of the hands of black people, slave and free.

The War of Independence

The War of Independence exposed the fundamental tension of slavery's presence in the midst of a land steeped in the rhetoric of individual liberty. One of the first martyrs of the Revolution, an escaped slave named Crispus Attucks, killed on March 5, 1770, along with four other men in the Boston Massacre, personified the entrenched nature of race in the very fabric of American freedom. When formal hostilities erupted at Concord and Lexington in April 1775, African American militiamen fought side by side with white men, characterizing the larger military participation of an estimated five thousand black people who risked their lives for both the cause of American independence and the opportunity to make freedom a personal reality.

Racial ideology quickly found its way into the creation of military policy and the formation of the Continental Army. During the initial stages of the war, free black men, predominantly from New England, served in state militia units without opposition. Colonial legislators, however, became alarmed by the growing interracial character of the army and took steps to preserve its racial integrity. On October 8, 1775, the Continental Congress agreed to "reject all slaves, and, by a great majority, to reject Negroes altogether"—an act that explicitly connected whiteness with freedom, as represented by the Continental Army.

Despite this action, slaves did not need the sanction of the Continental Congress to grasp the implications of the war for their future. Black people by the thousands seized the opportunity to obtain their freedom and define independence on their own terms. British military incursions severely destabilized the institution of slavery, especially in the plantation regions of Virginia, Maryland, South Carolina, and Georgia. Estimates of the number of slaves who took it upon themselves to flee from bondage ran as high as 55,000, with Virginia alone losing more than 30,000 slaves throughout the course of the war.[1]

Reflecting an intrinsic desire for freedom, slaves by the thousands flocked to the British army, further exposing the hypocrisy of the American colonists' revolutionary aims. In an effort to undermine the economic and military advantages slavery provided for the colonists, on November 7, 1775, Lord Dunmore, the British royal governor of Virginia, issued a call for slaves to join the British army, with the promise of eventual freedom. In a dramatic display of resistance to their bondage, over three hundred runaway slaves enlisted in Dunmore's forces by December 1 and were eventually organized into the "Ethiopian Regiment," which saw limited action. Despite the Ethiopian Regiment's revolutionary potential, it represented an exception in the larger history of black participation in the British army during the war. Defeating the rebellious colonists stood as the primary concern of the British, and they used escaped African American slaves, first and foremost, to accomplish this goal. As a result, the army of King George was far from an agent of emancipation. Seen as an expendable work force, the vast majority of slaves performed manual-labor duties, were subject to extreme illness, and faced the distinct possibility of being sold into slavery in the West Indies.

The considerable number of slaves entering the British forces alarmed American leaders and forced a revisiting of the policy regarding black military service. On January 17, 1776, at the behest of General George Washington, the Continental Congress amended its previous decision and allowed free black men already serving in the Continental Army to reenlist. Although new African American recruits remained excluded from service, this action recognized the necessity of securing black support for the war effort.

The service of African Americans varied from colony to colony as determined by demographic factors and, most significantly, the entrenchment of slavery. The prolonged nature of the war, combined with mounting casualties, prompted the Continental Congress to turn a blind eye to the continued recruitment of black men. With enlistment of able-bodied whites lagging, individual states began to accept both free blacks and slaves into militia units. Some states took extremely bold measures—such as Rhode Island, which passed a resolution in February 1778 allowing slaves to enlist in the state militia, with the promise of freedom. In addition to fighting in the army, black men by the hundreds served in the Continental Navy as well. In the southern colonies, concerns regarding the preservation of slavery shaped decisions by colonial legislators to circumscribe the large-scale military participation of black people. While individual free black men joined state militias, the risks of mass organization proved too great for southern slave owners. In 1780 Maryland began accepting individual black recruits and considered organizing a regiment of slaves, only to see the proposal languish. The stakes of allowing slaves to enlist were likewise too high for South Carolina and Georgia. In 1779, despite suffering from severe manpower shortages, both states rejected a Continental Congress request to organize three thousand slaves into segregated units.

The War of 1812

The achievement of American independence in 1783 and the ratification of the United States Constitution in 1787 did nothing to alter the racially subjugated status of African Americans. Despite the abolition of the slave trade in 1808, slavery by 1812 had become an even greater aspect of American social, political, and economic life. The War of 1812, sparked by continued British interference with American shipping and increased naval impressments, tested not only the strength of American nationalism, but the place of black people in the new nation as well.

Several parallels existed between the military experience of black servicemen in the War of Independence and the War of 1812. As an opportunity for increased social and economic status, the army remained attractive to free black people, who served in militia units on an individual basis, although the mass recruitment of African Americans did not occur. Unlike the Regular Army and most state militias, the United States Navy did not adopt a policy of excluding African Americans from service following the War of Independence.

As a result, black men continued to compose a sizable segment of the nation's sailors—a significant fact, considering that much of the fighting occurred on the seas. As in the previous war, slavery forced white Americans to confront the majority of black people as potential domestic enemies. The British took advantage of this by offering freedom to slaves who fought against the United States, and organized at least one unit of black soldiers who saw action against American forces. Moreover, thousands of slaves fled their plantations despite the concerted efforts of Chesapeake-region militia units, whose actions demonstrated a greater desire to preserve the institution of slavery than win the war itself.[2]

The defining moment of black participation in the War of 1812 occurred during the Battle of New Orleans. Free men of color in New Orleans, with a history of militia service under Spanish and French rule, pressed for the creation of black militia units at the outbreak of the war. In anticipation of an impending British attack, on September 21, 1814, General Andrew Jackson rallied free men of color to arms, resulting in the creation of two militia companies of approximately six hundred men. When British forces invaded New Orleans on January 8, 1815, black troops contributed to the decisive American victory.

On March 3, 1815, in spite of the service of black men during the recent war, Congress excluded African Americans from the postwar army, now comprising 10,000 men. This repeated a trend that continued into the twentieth century of accepting African Americans for military service, albeit limited, in times of national emergency, but placing restrictions on their enlistment during times of peace. As a result of their exclusion, very few black soldiers fought in the Mexican-American War of 1848.[3] African American military service, while providing occasional opportunities for freedom and social advancement at the individual level, had no explicit association with the collective obtainment of political rights for the race as a whole. This changed with the onset of the Civil War.

The Civil War

The future of slavery in the United States dominated national political discourse in the years preceding the Civil War. Characterized by increasing sectionalism, the expansion of slavery into the new territories acquired during the Mexican-American War gradually widened the regional and ideological divide between the slaveholding South and the free-labor North. Debates regarding the place and social status of African Americans—slave and free—played out on the national stage with pernicious repercussions. The 1850 Fugitive Slave Act, which empowered federal commissioners to pursue escaped slaves and return them to their alleged owners, threatened the fragile stability of free black communities in many Northern states. The 1857 Dred Scott Supreme Court decision, along with ruling the Missouri Compromise unconstitutional, declared that black people had no rights as American citizens. Black and white Northern abolitionists became increasingly militant, as John Brown's failed October 1859 raid at Harpers Ferry demonstrated. In response, Southern politicians and slaveholding elites became increasingly defensive and hostile to any threat, real or perceived, to the maintenance of slavery. The ascendancy of the Republican Party and the election of Abraham Lincoln as president in 1860 proved to be the decisive moment in splitting the Union in two. By February 1861, eleven Southern states had seceded and founded the Confederate States of America on the bedrock principle of preserving slavery. Only two months later, on April 12, war broke out as a result of the Confederate assault on Fort Sumter, South Carolina.

The restoration of the Union, with slavery intact if necessary, stood as the paramount war aim of Abraham Lincoln at the onset of military hostilities. African Americans, however, had no misgivings about the significance of the war as it pertained to their future. Both slaves and free black people saw the war as an opportunity to achieve individual freedom, and potentially to destroy the institution of slavery. Recognition of the value of African Americans to the war effort came not from Washington, but from slaves themselves. They fled Southern plantations by the thousands and attached themselves to nearby Union forces, transforming it into an army of liberation.

By taking freedom into their own hands, slaves forced Union generals to respond, which they did in significant ways. Serving in Virginia, General Benjamin Butler on May 23, 1861, designated slaves seeking refuge behind Union lines as "contraband of war" and refused to return them to the Confederacy, which had made use of slaves as military laborers from the outset of the war. Major General John C. Frémont took matters even further in Missouri. On August 30, Frémont issued a proclamation confiscating and freeing the slaves of Confederate sympathizers in Union-controlled areas of the state. Lincoln, taken aback by Frémont's actions, was not yet prepared to make emancipation and the destruction of slavery a central goal of the war. Concerned with maintaining the tenuous support of border states, such as Missouri, Lincoln revoked Frémont's order and removed the general from command.

Despite Lincoln's initial reticence, the use of African Americans in the Union Army began as early as March 1862. In South Carolina, General Rufus Saxton organized a regiment of runaway slaves into the First South Carolina Volunteers, who saw limited combat action in November of the same year in South Carolina, Georgia, and Florida. While the First South Carolina Volunteers underwent training, in August 1862 Kansas senator James H. Lane began to recruit escaped slaves into a volunteer regiment that became the First Kansas Colored Volunteer Infantry, later renamed the Seventy-ninth Infantry Regiment, United States Colored Troops. The presence of African Americans in the Louisiana Native Guards represented the most systematic organization of black troops prior to 1863. With a legacy of military service stemming from the War of 1812, free men of color initially offered their support in late 1861 as soldiers to the secessionist cause, a gesture that Southern military leaders rejected as antithetical to the white supremacist principles of the Confederacy. After the Union achieved control of Louisiana, however, General Benjamin Butler organized many of the same men to defend New Orleans. The first regiment was sworn into service in September 1862, with two more regiments formed by the end of the year. The three black regiments, labeled the "Corps d'Afrique" while under the command of General Nathaniel Banks, who replaced Butler in December 1862, comprised both free black men and contraband slaves and were distinguished by the presence of thirty-one black officers. The "Corps d'Afrique" fought with distinction at Port Hudson in May and June 1863, the first major battle involving black troops, and produced several future social and political leaders in Reconstruction Louisiana, including P. B. S. Pinchback, who became the first African American to be appointed governor in United States history.

Just as it had during the Revolutionary War and the War of 1812, the navy provided African Americans with opportunities for military service outside of the army. The Union accepted both free black men and contrabands. By the end of the war, an estimated 18,000 black men had served—nearly 25 percent of total enlistees. The heroics of Robert Smalls cemented his status as the most famous African American seaman. On May 13, 1862, the slave from South Carolina commandeered the Confederate battleship the *Planter* and, along with seven other slaves and their wives and children, sailed the vessel out of Charleston Harbor and into the hands of Union naval forces. Abraham Lincoln acknowledged Smalls's daring actions by making him a captain in the navy and giving him command of the *Planter*.

By the summer of 1862, with the end of the war nowhere in sight, President Lincoln could no longer resist the rising tide of pressure brought to bear by Union officers, public sentiment, and, most significantly, slaves themselves, for the destruction of slavery. On September 22, 1862, he issued the Emancipation Proclamation, effective on January 1, 1863, which freed slaves in the Confederate states and authorized the enlistment of former slaves for service in the Union military. Recruitment in New England states began immediately, and on May 22, the War Department created the Bureau of Colored Troops. In recognition of Lincoln's explicit attempt to undermine slavery, Confederate president Jefferson Davis pledged to execute any white officer captured in command of black soldiers on the grounds of "inciting servile insurrection," and to re-enslave black servicemen. Despite this threat, the recruitment of black men for service proceeded, led by General Lorenzo Thomas in the Mississippi Valley, who brought an estimated 76,000 men, 41 percent of total black enlistees, into the Union Army. The incorporation of African American soldiers also created opportunities for black women such as Harriet Tubman, the famed conductor of the Underground Railroad, to serve as scouts and nurses.

The Fifty-fourth and Fifty-fifth Massachusetts Infantry regiments were the first two Northern regiments of black soldiers organized following the Emancipation Proclamation. Northern white radicals and black abolitionists viewed the Fifty-fourth Massachusetts Infantry Regiment in particular as a challenge to the belief that black men could not be effective combat troops.

Robert Smalls (1839–1915) was born a slave and was forced to serve in the Confeder-ate Navy during the Civil War. In 1862, he took command of the Confederate *Planter* in a daring escape, taking his family and a crew of twelve other slaves with him. He subsequently fought on the side of the Union and rose to the rank of captain. After the war Smalls entered political life, serving first as a member of the South Carolina House of Representatives and the South Carolina Senate before being elected to the United States House of Representatives.

Governor John Andrew, an ardent proponent of abolition, received authori-zation from the secretary of war to raise the regiment, and placed it in the command of twenty-five-year-old Robert Gould Shaw. Frederick Douglass, who himself had two sons enlist, actively recruited free black men for the regiment, which consisted almost exclusively of free black men from New England. After initially being assigned to labor duties, the Fifty-fourth saw its first military engagement on July 16, 1863, and on July 18 led the assault on Fort Wagner, South Carolina. Although the fort remained in Confederate hands and the Fifty-fourth suffered extremely high casualties, the regiment's bravery and sacrifice became legendary and, similarly to the Louisiana Native Guards at Port Hudson, increased motivation for the future organization of black units.

The often romanticized Fifty-fourth Massachusetts and their widespread acclaim masked a darker underside of the broader experience of black soldiers in the Civil War. The Union by and large used African American troops disproportionately for labor duties and in rear-support capacities. Black regiments were commanded exclusively by white officers, reflecting a belief that black men could not effectively lead other black men in combat. African American soldiers received ten dollars, as compared to the regular wage of thirteen dollars for white soldiers—a discrepancy that was not rectified until the last days of the war.[4] Black servicemen, as well as their white officers, faced additional risk from Confederate soldiers, many of whom seethed at the sight of a black man in uniform. A number of racial atrocities occurred throughout the war, the most brutal taking place on April 12, 1864, when Confederate forces massacred 231 white and black soldiers following their surrender at Fort Pillow, Tennessee.[5]

Despite enduring innumerable obstacles, the approximately 180,000 black men who donned the Union blue unquestionably changed the course of the war and contributed to the defeat of the Confederacy by distinguishing themselves in numerous battles.[6] The Civil War likewise fundamentally shaped the future meaning and symbolic significance of black military service. Union victory, combined with the destruction of slavery, explicitly linked African American participation in the nation's armed forces with the obtainment of freedom, manhood, and, with the passage of the Fourteenth Amendment, the achievement of nominal citizenship.[7]

Affirming Citizenship, Confronting Hypocrisy: Buffalo Soldiers to Brownsville

Following the Civil War, African American participation in the army functioned as an opportunity for soldiers to infuse meaning, both personal and political, into their hard-fought citizenship status. The service of black men in the Union Army continued to have a powerful symbolic value, for both black and white people. Because they entered the army later than most white Union servicemen, African American soldiers constituted the majority of Federal troops stationed in the South during the early years of Reconstruction—an especially painful reminder for Southern whites of the social, political, and economic revolution brought about by the end of slavery. For black soldiers and veterans, the social and political violence of Reconstruction represented a continuation of the war, most vividly demonstrated in the race riots at Memphis and New Orleans in 1866. Nevertheless, the postwar period solidified the connection between military service and civic participation, as many Union veterans, including P. B. S. Pinchback and Robert Smalls, formed the vanguard of black political leadership during Reconstruction.

A combination of pragmatism and racial liberalism led to the institutionalization of black soldiers in the United States Army. Radical Republicans, led by Massachusetts senator Henry M. Wilson, successfully fought to ensure that African Americans remained represented in a postwar military facing severe troop shortages. In July 1866, when Congress voted to reduce the size of the Regular Army, it reorganized African American soldiers of the former Union Army into the Ninth and Tenth Cavalry and Thirty-eighth, Thirty-ninth, Fortieth, and Forty-first Infantry regiments. In 1869, Congress further downsized the army, resulting in the merger of the four infantry regiments into the Twenty-fourth and Twenty-fifth infantries.

The Buffalo Soldiers

Through the late 1860s to the late 1890s, approximately 12,500 black soldiers of the Regular Army were stationed in the American West and Southwest, serving in nearly every state west of the Mississippi River. Labeled "Buffalo Soldiers" by the Plains Indians, the African American regulars fought in the so-called Indian Wars to make the frontier secure for continued white settlement, and policed the Mexican border in Texas, Arizona, and New Mexico. Throughout the last three decades of the nineteenth century, black soldiers engaged in numerous conflicts with Native American communities that resisted subjugation, including most notoriously the massacre of Sioux Indians in December 1890 at Wounded Knee, South Dakota. Participation of black soldiers in these racist campaigns demonstrated their ironic and conflicted status in the context of American nationalism.

The experience of African American servicemen in the late nineteenth century revealed both the promise and limitations of life in the United States military. In many ways, the "Buffalo Soldiers" were in, but not of, the United States Army. White officials largely marginalized black troops from the rest of the Regular Army by assigning them to the least desirable posts and restricting their service in the South altogether. The War Department justified their decision by employing late nineteenth-century social-scientific constructions of racial difference that posited African American soldiers as possessing an inherent physical capacity to withstand the harsh climate of the Southwest. Additionally, African American troops faced the constant threat of violence from frontier whites. Despite such challenges, the black regulars established an impressive record of service, as evidenced by the seventeen Medals of Honor awarded African American soldiers. As a career, military service provided economic, educational, and social opportunities, however truncated, not available to the vast majority of the black population in late nineteenth-century America. Moreover, the risks of military service in the West for many individuals represented a safer alternative than the terrorist nature of racial violence and white supremacy in the South.

The fact that white officers, with few exceptions, commanded the African American regiments of the Regular Army stemmed directly from the exclusion of black cadets from West Point Military Academy. The very idea of the black officer ran contrary to dominant ideologies of race and masculinity. The historic officer training school carried a vicious legacy of racial intolerance, reflecting the view that black men did not have the intellectual ability to be successful officers and, most significantly, should never be in a position of authority over white men. West Point was a harrowing experience for the handful of black cadets brave enough to endure the physical and psychological abuse of their white colleagues. Three exceptional men managed to survive their years at West Point. After enrolling in 1873, Henry Ossian Flipper became the first African American to graduate from West Point in 1877,

Kean Collection / Hulton Archive / Getty Images

Born into slavery in Georgia in March 1856, Henry Ossian Flipper became the first African American to graduate from West Point Military Academy in 1877, although not the first to attend—there were four other African Americans already at West Point when Flipper arrived in 1872. Upon graduation, Flipper was posted to an African American cavalry unit, the 10th, with the rank of second lieutenant. At the time, the unit was engaged in operations against Native Americans in Texas, who had already dubbed them "Buffalo Soldiers" as a mark of their ferocious determination in combat. He served in Texas for three years, before he was accused of interfering with the mail and was court martialled. Although acquitted of the charge, he was dishonorably discharged from the service. Flipper would contend the decision for the rest of his life, although he quickly found work as a mining engineer in the frontier states. His extensive experience in Texas and later Mexico meant that he was in demand as a mining engineer and advisor on land law, working for the government as a special agent for the Department of Justice in the Court of Private Land Claims between 1893 and 1910, and later working for a Venezuelan oil company. Flipper retired in 1930 and died in 1940; he was posthumously pardoned by President Bill Clinton in 1999.

receiving a commission as a second lieutenant. He was followed by John H. Alexander in 1887 and Charles Young in 1889, who would be the last African American West Point graduate for another fifty years. All three men, for varying lengths of time, served as officers in the Buffalo Soldier regiments.

The Spanish-Cuban-American War and Its Aftermath

The explosion of the *Maine* in Havana, Cuba, on February 15, 1898, which counted twenty-two African Americans among its 266 casualties, prompted the United States to declare war on Spain—an act that simultaneously served as a clear declaration of the government's imperial aspirations. Initial black support for the Spanish-Cuban-American War was not a foregone conclusion. The erosion of African American citizenship rights, and the increasingly brutal nature of Southern race relations prompted many African American social and political leaders, such as Bishop Henry McNeal Turner, to stress America's need first and foremost to tend to its own domestic crises. Isolationist sentiment also reflected a questioning of the imperialist aims of the United States and the expansion of the "white man's burden"—experienced as racial oppression by Native Americans and Mexicans—to the Caribbean and the South Pacific.

African American support for the war ultimately outweighed dissent. Some African American supporters of the war racially identified with the Cubans, in particular Afro-Cuban revolutionary leader Antonio Maceo. The most widely held argument by pro-war African Americans envisioned patriotism and military service as an opportunity to transform white racial attitudes and loosen the grip of systemic discrimination and violence. The potential use of black soldiers presented an opportunity to affirm African American citizenship that by 1898, only two years after the United States Supreme Court legitimization of racial segregation with the *Plessy v. Ferguson* decision, had become essentially nominal in nature.[8]

African Americans responded to the call for volunteers by President McKinley by forming national guard militias in Illinois, Ohio, Massachusetts, Kansas, Indiana, North Carolina, and Virginia, although the short duration of the war prevented their incorporation into the Regular Army. The army also created an experimental regiment of black soldiers in Alabama, who likewise did not serve in the war.[9] The War Department did, however, order the 28,000 black Regular Army soldiers stationed in the West and Southwest to Florida for embarkation to Cuba. The journey of black troops through the South, where they endured virulent racial abuse from whites, revealed the threat that black military service posed to notions of racial hierarchy and customary behavior undergirding Jim Crow segregation and white supremacy.

Black soldiers arrived in Cuba on June 22, 1898. The black Regular Army regiments, in only three days of fighting at El Caney, Las Guásimas, and San Juan Hill, performed extremely well. At Las Guásimas on June 24, the Tenth Cavalry came to the aid of Theodore Roosevelt's famed "Rough Riders" First Volunteer Cavalry Regiment, saving that regiment from more extensive casualties. Black soldiers further made a name for themselves on July 1 at San Juan Hill, a battle that lasted only ninety minutes. It nevertheless held great symbolic importance for African Americans, as black New Yorkers dubbed their growing West Side neighborhood "San Juan Hill."

Black soldiers subsequently fought in the Philippines, acquired from Spain as a result of the Spanish-Cuban-American War, to quell the anti-American insurgency led by Emilio Aguinaldo. The Twenty-fourth and Twenty-fifth Infantry regiments arrived first on the island in June 1899, later joined by the temporary Forty-eighth and Forty-ninth Volunteer infantries, composed predominantly of African American Regular Army soldiers. Black troops faced guerrilla warfare and racism marked by a virulence not experienced before in Cuba. The United States government and armed forces consciously racialized Filipinos in their efforts to undermine the insurgency, and in the process, tested the loyalties of black soldiers.[10] Many African American soldiers sympathized with the Filipinos and their desire for independence from American imperial rule, although only five black servicemen actually responded to calls from insurgents to desert. African Americans, including Booker T. Washington, seriously questioned the legitimacy of Philippine intervention, even more so than Cuban intervention.

Jim Crow segregation, political disenfranchisement, and the looming threat of racial violence characterized social conditions for the vast majority of African Americans in the years immediately following the military conflicts in Cuba and the Philippines. The worsening conditions of African American social and political life in the civilian world paralleled the entrenchment of white supremacy in the military. Segregation took hold of the previously racially integrated navy, which announced its commitment to white supremacy in 1907 with the launching of a new fleet of American battleships—aptly dubbed the "Great White Fleet"—that excluded African Americans from service except in menial capacities. Upon their return to the United States, the black soldiers of the Regular Army performed duty in Texas along the United States–Mexico border, where racial tensions ran high.

The Brownsville Affair

In the context of Southern white supremacy and the continued epidemic of lynching and race riots, most notably the Atlanta Riot of 1906, the Brownsville incident represented an attack on the manhood and political agency associated with African American soldiers. After shots rang out on the night of August 13, 1906, local whites accused black troops of the Twenty-fifth Infantry's First Battalion of killing one man and wounding two others. Although they steadfastly denied involvement in the shooting, President Theodore Roosevelt dishonorably discharged 167 soldiers without a public hearing, eliciting widespread outcry from African Americans of various political persuasions. Roosevelt's actions, however misguided, should not have come as a great surprise. The president firmly rooted his views of military service in an explicit conflation of whiteness and citizenship, as demonstrated years earlier in disparaging remarks he made about the performance of black troops in the Spanish-Cuban-American War. Despite the miscarriage of justice, Brownsville further fueled the perception among whites, particularly in the South, of black soldiers as a source of violent racial unrest.

Affirming Citizenship, Confronting Hypocrisy: World War I to World War II

World War I

When the United States entered World War I in April 1917, Woodrow Wilson's pronouncement that the United States would fight to make the world "safe for democracy" sparked a combination of optimism and activism. A vocal minority of black intellectuals challenged the entire premise of American intervention, arguing that it was hypocritical for the United States to promote democracy throughout the world while it denied African Americans their basic human rights. Nevertheless, the historical legacy and symbolic meaning of black military service spurred the hopes of many African Americans that the conflict would lead to a social and political transformation of American society on a par with Reconstruction following the Civil War. African American political leaders and newspaper editors, such as W. E. B. Du Bois, William Monroe Trotter, Robert Abbott, and James Weldon Johnson, quickly appropriated Wilson's rhetoric of freedom and democracy to connect African American patriotism and, more specifically, the participation of black soldiers to demands for citizenship rights.

Instead of offering hope, the war exacerbated social relations and heightened racial hostilities. Black migration and interracial labor conflict culminated in the East St. Louis racial pogrom on July 1, 1917, where white mobs killed upwards of 125 African Americans. Most significantly, the prospect of black servicemen stationed in the states of the Old Confederacy viscerally disturbed Southern whites and drew vigorous protests. Fears of violence stemming from the presence of African American troops came to fruition in Houston, Texas. The army transferred black soldiers of the Third Battalion of the Twenty-fourth Infantry to Camp Logan, located on the outskirts of Houston, to protect construction of the wartime training facility. On the night of August 23, 1917, after enduring persistent racial abuse and fueled by rumors that Houston police had killed one of their comrades, over one hundred armed black soldiers marched into the city and killed fifteen white men, including four policemen. Following a summary court-martial, Texas law enforcement hastily executed thirteen convicted soldiers without due process, while forty-one others received life-imprisonment sentences.

Houston served as a precursor to the broader treatment of black soldiers, and officers in particular, within the United States military during the war. The question of commissioned black officers, as symbols of racial leadership and manhood, became an issue of considerable importance for members of the Talented Tenth. In response to pressure from the NAACP, the War Department agreed to the creation of a segregated training camp for black officer candidates at Des Moines, Iowa. Of the initial 1,250 candidates, 639 received officer commissions, although none higher than the rank of captain. Throughout the course of the war, racist white military officials, intent on preserving the army's traditional racial hierarchy, made a concerted effort to undermine the performance of black officers and their opportunities to excel, most notably evidenced in the forced retirement of Colonel Charles Young, at the time the highest ranking African American in uniform.

Approximately 387,000 African Americans served in the United States Army during the war. This number did not, however, include the battle-tested black soldiers of the Regular Army, who were stationed in Hawaii and the Philippines throughout the war. The majority of black soldiers toiled in stevedore and other service units in both France and the United States. Of the 200,000 black soldiers who served overseas, approximately 40,000 were combat soldiers, comprising the Ninety-second and Ninety-third divisions. The Ninety-second Division, composed of black drafted men, waged a constant battle against the racism of white officers, and military effectiveness suffered as a result. The Ninety-third Division, made up of mostly national guardsmen, served with the French military, where they received more equitable treatment and fought with distinction.[11] The 369th Infantry from New York performed exceptionally well and earned international acclaim for its regimental band, led by James Reese Europe.[12]

The Interwar Period

Following the November 1918 armistice, the violence of the postwar period shocked African Americans and represented a blatant disregard of wartime patriotism and the military contributions of black soldiers.[13] Despite enduring systemic racial discrimination and disillusionment, the vast majority of black veterans nevertheless remained extremely proud of their service and thankful for the opportunities that it provided.[14] The multifaceted benefits of military service—leaving the South, health and educational advances, racial camaraderie, interaction with other peoples of African descent in France, development of increased maturity—caution against characterizing black service during the war as either strictly positive or negative. African American soldiers interpreted the political dimensions of their army experience and expressed their often heightened racial consciousness in ways that were frequently highly personal. This speaks to the importance of viewing black soldiers not strictly as racial symbols, but as complicated human beings as well.

In the aftermath of World War I, the United States military downsized considerably and, in the process, attempted to cleanse itself of the legacy of black soldiers. The performance of African American combat troops and officers in particular received intense scrutiny and criticism from officials within the War Department and the Army War College. The War Department restricted new enlistments in the four black Regular Army regiments, although it did allow for reenlistments. Despite ample evidence to the contrary, postwar reports deemed the experiment of African American officers a failure and concluded that the success of black combat soldiers depended on white officers to command them. The military prohibited African Americans from officer training camps and in 1931 threatened to eliminate the Tenth and Twenty-fifth Infantry regiments, only to reverse its course following protests by Walter White and the NAACP. Also of significance, the military excluded African Americans from the newly expanded Air Corps.

The Spanish Civil War provided an alternative opportunity for African Americans to use military service as an expression of political consciousness—in this case, international in scope. Spain served as a proxy for Ethiopia, invaded by Italy in October 1935, for the more than eighty black men and women in the 2,800-person Abraham Lincoln Brigade (ALB). Many of the ALB's black participants were members of the Communist Party, which called for volunteers in the fall of 1936 to aid in the fight against European fascism.[15]

One of the brigade's commanders, Oliver Law, became the first black man to ever lead an integrated American military force.

World War II

Preparedness debates concerning America's seemingly inevitable entry into the European war began in mid-1940, when it became increasingly clear that the nation would need to reinstitute the draft. During congressional debates on the issue, World War I veterans Charles Hamilton Houston and Rayford Logan invoked their experiences with army racism and forcefully argued in their testimony for the elimination of discrimination in the nation's armed forces and defense industries. Although the Selective Service Act, passed by Congress on September 16, 1940, prohibited racial discrimination in the raising of the wartime army, segregation remained firmly intact. Unsatisfied with the status quo, A. Philip Randolph, the NAACP, and the Urban League continued to press President Franklin D. Roosevelt, under pressure for reelection to an unprecedented third term, to reform the military and its policies concerning African American enlistment. In an attempt to solidify black electoral support, on October 8 Roosevelt ordered that the number of African Americans in the army correspond to their numerical percentage in the populace, that they be made eligible to serve in all branches of the military, have opportunities for officer training, and receive equal access to civilian employment at military facilities.

African American activism concerning the Selective Service Act reflected a steadfast commitment to hold the nation accountable to its stated democratic principles and avoid the dashed expectations of World War I. While the new global conflict yet again tested the loyalties and patriotism of African Americans, idealism was discernibly muted as the United States readied itself for war. A. Philip Randolph organized a march on Washington, D.C., scheduled for July 1, 1941, intended to pressure President Franklin Roosevelt to end discrimination in wartime contracting. Facing the prospect of some 100,000 African Americans descending upon the nation's capital, on June 25, 1941, one week before the march, Roosevelt issued Executive Order 8802, banning racial discrimination in defense industries, and created the Fair

Employment Practices Commission to enforce his directive. However, with segregation in the armed forces still entrenched, African Americans, and the black press specifically, did not rest on the achievement of Executive Order 8802.[16] In early 1942 the *Pittsburgh Courier* advanced a campaign of "Double V," symbolizing the dual defeat of fascism and American racism, which came to encapsulate African American political activism during the war.

Roughly one million African Americans served in all four branches of the armed forces during World War II, with nearly half engaged in overseas duty. Despite increased participation, many facets of the military did not change from World War I. At the beginning of the war, only five of the military's five thousand officers were African Americans, comprising three chaplains, General Benjamin O. Davis Sr., and his son Benjamin O. Davis Jr., at the time a first lieutenant. Although the Selective Service Act of 1940 forbade racial discrimination, local draft boards regularly turned away African American volunteers and later routinely denied exemption claims when manpower became more vital.[17]

Race colored the service of African American soldiers, both at home and abroad. African Americans remained in segregated units, and military officials continued to question the fighting capabilities of black troops, negatively shaping the views of their British and French hosts in the process.[18] The War Department reactivated the all-black Ninety-second and Ninety-third divisions established during World War I, and combined the Ninth and Tenth cavalries to form the Second Cavalry Division. The Ninety-third Division served in the Pacific theater, along with the Twenty-fourth and Twenty-fifth infantries, but saw little combat. The Second Cavalry Division served in North Africa. The Ninety-second Division served in the Italian campaign, but after performing poorly in their first combat action, racist military officials, mirroring World War I, derided the division for the remainder of the war. On the home front, African American soldiers were subjected to dangerous work conditions. In the summer of 1944, some 258 black dock workers stationed at Port Chicago, California, refused to work following two ammunition explosions resulting in 320 deaths, 202 of which were African American. The Navy court-martialed fifty men, who received dishonorable discharges and sentences of eight to fifteen years hard labor.

While racism proved dogged, military necessity ushered in new opportunities for African Americans during the war that combated traditional
institutional prejudices. Officer training camps allowed African Americans
to enlist, and by the end of the war over seven thousand black men received
commissions. African Americans distinguished themselves in various combat
units, most notably the 761st Tank Battalion. The war saw the organization
of the first unit of black paratroopers, the 555th Parachute Infantry Battalion. The Marines reversed 167 years of exclusion and opened their doors to
black recruits, with 17,000 enlisting by the war's end. On April 7, 1942, the
navy announced that African Americans could enlist in positions other than
mess attendants. Although the navy's legacy of racial discrimination deterred
enlistment, by the end of the war 65,000 African Americans served, and one
ship, the *Mason*, had a majority black crew.[19]

The Tuskegee Airmen emerged as the most famous and symbolically
powerful collection of African American servicemen in World War II. The
fight to include black men in the Air Corps became a central site of political
struggle from the earliest days of American preparedness. In January 1941 the
War Department approved the establishment of a flight training program at
the Tuskegee Institute in Alabama and later created the Ninety-ninth Pursuit
Squadron of the United States Air Force. White officials fully expected the
experiment in black fighter pilots to be a failure. When given the opportunity to perform, however, the Tuskegee Airmen of the Ninety-ninth, which
later became part of the 332nd Fighter Group, dispelled myths that African
Americans could not become effective aviators. Commanded by Benjamin
O. Davis Jr., the Tuskegee Airmen flew over 15,000 combat sorties, downed
111 enemy fighters, and became the only fighter group to never lose an escorted bomber to enemy fire.[20]

The war created increased opportunities for African American women
as well. Thousands of black women entered the industrial work force.[21] As
regards the military, black women served primarily in the Women's Army
Corps (WAC), constituting approximately 4 percent of its 150,000 enlistees.
African American women also fought to be represented in the Navy's Women
Accepted for Volunteer Emergency Services (WAVES), which ended its
policy of racial exclusion in 1944. A double minority, black women faced

Toni Frissell / Hulton Archive / Getty Images

Born in Washington, D.C., in December 1912, Benjamin O. Davis Jr. (pictured here in Rametti, Italy, March 1945) joined the U.S. Army in 1932 and spent four years studying at West Point Military Academy in New York. Throughout the four years spent at the institute, Davis was largely shunned by the other officer trainees as they attempted to drive him out of the academy. The discrimination only made him more determined, and upon graduation in 1936, Davis became one of only two black line officers in the US Army. The other was his father, Benjamin O. Davis, Sr., the first African American general in US military history. In the 60 years since Henry Ossian Flipper had become the first African American officer to graduate from West Point, only three others, Davis included, had followed in his footsteps. After graduating, Davis was posted to the Tuskegee Institute, where he taught military tactics to other African American recruits. At the outbreak of World War II, and with the formation of the 99th Pursuit Squadron at Tuskegee, Captain Davis was assigned to the first training class and earned his wings in March 1942. When the 99th was deployed overseas as part of the North African campaign, Davis was appointed as commanding officer. After four months, Davis was promoted to take command of the newly created 332nd Fighter Group, which was entirely comprised of African American pilots. In all, 200 escort missions were undertaken by the Tuskegee airmen, and not a single bomber was lost. Davis went on to serve in Korea before retiring from the military as a brigadier general. He died in 2002 aged 89.

the sting of both racism and sexism in their various military capacities. The determination of African American women for equal inclusion, on a par with black men, paved the way for their increased service in the years to come.

The Struggle between Ideal and Reality: Desegregation to Vietnam

The Fight for Desegregation

The military continued to serve as a key battleground for combating governmental racial discrimination. Postwar violence against black veterans, in particular the beating and blinding of Isaac Woodard, a uniformed sergeant returning to South Carolina from service in the Pacific, shocked President Harry Truman and emboldened African American civil rights leaders. Led by A. Philip Randolph, political pressure to reform the armed forces continued into the postwar period. In late 1947 and early 1948, Congress debated a peacetime draft bill submitted by President Harry Truman. Randolph vigorously opposed any form of compulsory military service in which African Americans remained segregated, and vowed to protest the proposed law by encouraging black people to resist induction unless the armed forces were formally desegregated. Congress passed the draft law in June 1948, but Truman fully realized the implications of Randolph's threat of black mass resistance. On July 26, 1948, President Truman issued Executive Order 9981, which immediately outlawed racial segregation in the United States armed forces. Black leaders hailed the executive order as a turning point in the fight for African American racial equality and equal citizenship, although it contained no specifications for how desegregation was to proceed.

The Korean War

Against the backdrop of Cold War politics, Korea represented the first test of the United States military's commitment to racial desegregation. When North Korea crossed the Thirty-eighth Parallel into South Korea on June 25, 1950, the United States military hastily assembled its forces, the majority positioned in Eastern Europe. During the war 220,000 black soldiers served in the four branches of the military, representing 13 percent of total American forces. The rapid pace of American mobilization resulted in desegregation occurring only in incremental steps. For example, the Twenty-fourth Infantry, stationed in Japan prior to direct deployment to Korea, remained completely segregated and ostracized, resulting in a lack of preparation and poor leadership. White supremacy proved resolute in the highest echelons of the military establishment. Compounding the resistance of white soldiers to change, General Douglas MacArthur and other top officers took no direct action to enforce integration.

Despite initial resistance, several regiments began to integrate their ranks based on manpower necessity and reported improved military effectiveness. MacArthur's successor General Matthew Ridgway actively enforced Truman's executive order, resulting in 90 percent of the black soldiers in Korea serving in integrated units by the time of the July 27, 1953, cease-fire. The elimination of separate units for black and white soldiers was further spurred by Project Clear, a study initiated by civilian social scientists that concluded that racial integration improved military efficiency and combat performance. On October 30, 1954, the military announced the achievement of complete integration with the abolishment of the last segregated regiment.[22]

The Vietnam War

The activism of African Americans during World War II, and the inspired determination of countless veterans to enact social change provided momentum for the emergence of the modern Civil Rights Movement of the 1950s and 1960s. The combined efforts of African American political leaders and ordinary black people at the grassroots level pushed the reluctant Eisenhower and Kennedy administrations to enforce integration within the armed forces. Thus, by the beginning of American involvement in Vietnam, the army proudly touted itself as the most racially democratic institution in the United States.

Military service in Vietnam initially went hand in hand with the expansion of African American civil rights. The armed forces provided opportunities unavailable to African Americans in the civilian world, and as a result, many black men volunteered for combat units and reenlisted at a higher rate than whites.[23] However, as the war dragged on and black casualties mounted, African Americans became increasingly critical of the war and their participation in it. By 1968, the war had reshaped the tenor of the Civil Rights Movement, as Black Power coincided with the antiwar movement to fuel increased pessimism regarding the high cost of American citizenship.

Approximately 275,000 African Americans served in Vietnam. Race, just as it did in civilian life, remained a persistent feature of the military experience of black soldiers. The racial composition of the military reflected the social and economic disparities black men faced in American society at large. The draft targeted poor and working-class Americans—a disproportionate number of whom were black people—while upper- and middle-class whites obtained deferments or served in National Guard units. In 1967, around 64 percent of eligible African Americans were drafted, as opposed to 31 percent of whites. Faced with troop shortages, the War Department established "Project 100,000"—an effort to enlist men who had previously been declared ineligible because of low intelligence scores. "Project 100,000" indirectly targeted African Americans, and between October 1966 and June 1969, roughly 40 percent of the 246,000 men inducted through the program were black.[24] Higher numbers of African Americans on the frontlines led to disproportionate casualty rates. Between 1965 and 1967, African Americans represented 20 percent of battlefield casualties. Pressure to remove black soldiers from the frontlines resulted in their casualty rate dropping to 13 percent for the entire war. Despite such racial inequities, African Americans, as they had in previous wars, served valiantly, receiving twenty of the 237 Medals of Honor awarded during the conflict.[25]

Following the assassination of Dr. Martin Luther King Jr. in 1968, race relations in the military experienced a downward spiral. While integration occurred on the battlefield, black and white soldiers remained largely segregated behind the lines. The increasing disillusionment of African American troops was accompanied by a belief in the necessity of Black Power racial solidarity in the face of growing hostility from white soldiers.[26] The deterioration of troop morale and the explosive domestic antiwar movement led

These Marines were photographed during the Vietnam War, 1968. The Vietnam War was fought between 1957 and 1975 in South Vietnam and the bordering areas of Cambodia and Laos, against the Viet Cong, North Vietnamese soldiers who were attempting to infiltrate South Vietnam. The United States increased its troops in Vietnam in 1964, and it is traditionally held that this is when the most intense military engagement began. However, Noam Chomsky, a critic of the war, has held that the Americans conducted bombing on a large scale as early as 1962. American casualties for the war totalled 211,529, of which 58,226 were killed in action or classified as missing in action.

President Richard Nixon by late 1969 to adopt a policy of Vietnamization, which entrusted the South Vietnamese with ground security and committed American forces more exclusively to air strikes. This resulted in a gradual reduction of troops in Vietnam and the eventual withdrawal from Southeast Asia in March 1973.

Opportunity or the Only Option? Post-Vietnam to Iraq

In the years following Vietnam, the military transformed itself into an exclusively volunteer force in order to avoid the self-destructive problem of low morale associated with conscription. As early as May 1969, President Richard Nixon took steps to reform the draft in order to make it more socioeconomically equitable. Congress responded in 1973 by eliminating the Selective Service System except in cases of national emergency.

The elimination of the draft shaped the future racial composition of the United States military. The armed forces continued to offer African Americans employment, educational opportunities, and an escape from the postindustrial ravages of inner-city life during the late 1970s and 1980s. This fact, combined with an increased emphasis on the recruitment of potential enlistees, resulted in African Americans constituting nearly 15 percent of the armed forces in 1974. Only four years later the number had increased to over 18 percent, and by 1981 had reached 20 percent. This trend generated fears among military officials that rising numbers of African American enlistees would "blacken" the armed forces and deter whites from enlisting. Although the percentage of whites in the armed forces increased slightly in the 1980s, the rate of black enlistees remained consistent. This phenomenon reflects the reality that young white men and women continue to have greater opportunities for employment in the private sector, while opportunities for African Americans, even those with high-school and college degrees, are limited due to institutionalized racism.

The 1991 Gulf War and the "Powell Phenomenon"

Thus, by the time of the 1991 Gulf War, the face of the military had become increasingly black. African Americans formed nearly 25 percent of the army during Operation Desert Storm. The disproportionate numbers of black men and women in the United States military during the war generated increased public discussion about the relationship between race, military service, and social justice.[27] Nevertheless, the brevity and nationalist fervor of the war, in many respects reminiscent of the Spanish-Cuban-American War, prevented an examination of these issues beyond the level of public discourse.[28] The military glorified the interracial character of its forces in achieving the rapid victory, further proof of the success of the volunteer army and the elimination of racial discrimination.

Arnold Sachs / Hulton Archive / Getty Images

This portrait of Colin Powell was taken during his time as chairman of the U.S. Joint Chiefs of Staff, on January 16, 1991. Born in April 1937 and raised in the South Bronx district of New York City, Powell's parents had emigrated to the U.S. from Jamaica. He was commissioned into the U.S. Army in June 1958, with the rank of second lieutenant, and saw service in Vietnam, an experience that left its mark for the rest of his life; he later rose through the military until he attained the rank of general in April 1989. Subsequently appointed to the U.S. Joint Chiefs-of-Staff, Powell oversaw the U.S. military's response to several major international crises, including the 1990 invasion of Kuwait by Saddam Hussein, and the subsequent military build-up in the region that preceded the beginning of Operation Desert Storm and the liberation of Kuwait. After his retirement, Powell moved into politics, declaring himself a Republican, and was a part of George W. Bush's presidential campaign in 2000. Upon Bush's assumption of the presidency, Powell was appointed secretary of state, the first African American to attain such a high position of political responsibility. He held the position throughout Bush's first term, playing a key role in disseminating information on Iraq's weapons of mass destruction in the run-up to the second Gulf War. Powell resigned as secretary of state at the beginning of Bush's second term of office, in 2005.

General Colin Powell, chairman of the Joint Chiefs of Staff, was arguably the most recognizable face of the war and personified the military's self-promoted image of racial egalitarianism. A veteran of the Vietnam War, Powell experienced an unprecedented ascent through the ranks of the military and defense establishment. After achieving the rank of brigadier general, Powell served as national security advisor under President Ronald Reagan, and in 1989 became the first African American to serve as chairman of the Joint Chiefs of Staff under President George H. W. Bush. Powell presented the white American public with a nonthreatening image of black leadership firmly rooted in dual core traditions of militarism and nationalism. After retiring from active service in 1993, he was widely touted as a viable candidate for president.[29] In 2000 President George W. Bush tapped Powell to serve as secretary of state.

Afghanistan and the War in Iraq

The early years of the twenty-first century have been marked by increased militarism, stemming from the terrorist attacks of September 11, 2001, resulting in approximately three thousand deaths. The following months were characterized by an intense hypernationalism that resulted in a general suspicion of people of color, in particular those of Muslim faith; increased power of the state and government law-enforcement agencies; and the unquestioned legitimization of military force in the so-called "war on terror." On October 7, 2001, the United States launched an attack against Afghanistan in response to the September 11 terrorist attacks, and a year later invaded Iraq on the spurious grounds that former president Saddam Hussein possessed weapons of mass destruction and posed an immediate threat to national security. In this new era in the history of the American empire, black men and women continue to represent a disproportionate segment of the military in relation to their percentage of the American populace.

Military officials attribute the alleged elimination of racial discrimination within the armed forces to better educated and thus more racially enlightened recruits, both black and white. Despite such hyperbole, the problem of race continues to manifest itself, albeit in much more subtle, institutionalized forms. The military's officer corps remains overwhelmingly white, with little sign of improvement. Black men and women remain overrepresented in the army, the least technical of the military's four branches. The "war on terror" and the Bush administration's policy of preemptive war suggest that militarism will continue to shape both domestic social and international political relations for the foreseeable future. While the impact on African Americans remains to be seen, if recent trends are any indication, young black men and women will continue to represent a substantial portion of the United States military.

The United States armed forces recruit disproportionately in low-income sections of the country—areas frequently occupied by people of color, and African Americans specifically. This has prompted many to question the legitimacy of the military as a space of social equality. In January 2003, as the United States prepared for war against Iraq, Congressman Charles Rangel of New York introduced legislation to reinstitute the draft in order to rectify racial and class inequities within the military.

African American military service remains tied to the dilemma of racial equality and the expansion of democratic rights in the United States. The multifaceted experiences of black men and women in the armed forces reflect how the military has historically functioned as a site of both personal and collective opportunity and contestation. At the symbolic level, African American soldiers embody the tangled history of race, gender, citizenship, and nationalism, beginning with slavery in the seventeenth century and extending to modern-day global conflicts. As black men and women continue to search and struggle for the chance to infuse meaning into their identity as Americans, while simultaneously taking pride in their identity as persons of African descent, the historical legacy and contemporary social, political, and economic realities of military service will continue to occupy a dominant place in the lives of African Americans.

NOTES

1. Frey, *Water from the Rock.*
2. Cassell, "Slaves of the Chesapeake Bay Area and the War of 1812."
3. May, "Invisible Men."
4. Jones, "Two Letters in Protest of Race Prejudice in the Army during the American Civil War."
5. Urwin, "'We Cannot Treat Negroes . . . as Prisoners of War.'"
6. Longacre, "Black Troops in the Army of the James, 1863–65."
7. Cullen, "'I's a Man Now.'"
8. Gatewood, "Black Americans and the Quest for Empire, 1898–1903."
9. Gatewood, "Alabama's 'Negro Soldier Experiment,' 1898–1899."
10. Ngozi-Brown, "African American Soldiers and Filipinos."
11. Haywood, *Black Bolshevik.*
12. Du Bois, "An Essay toward a History of the Black Man in the Great War."
13. Norvell and Tuttle, "Views of a Negro during 'The Red Summer' of 1919."
14. May, "World War I Veteran Horace Pippen Used Art to Purge Himself of the Horrors of the Trenches."
15. Kelley, "'This Ain't Ethiopia, But It'll Do.'"
16. McGuire, "Desegregation of the Armed Forces."
17. Franklin, "Their War and Mine."
18. Hachey, "Document: Jim Crow with a British Accent."
19. Modell and Magnusson, "World War II in the Lives of Black Americans."
20. Percy, "Jim Crow and Uncle Sam."
21. Anderson, "Last Hired, First Fired."
22. Mitchell, "The Status of Racial Integration in the Armed Services."
23. Llorens, "Why Negroes Re-Enlist."
24. Hsiao, "Project 100,000."
25. Loeb, "MIA."
26. Gill, "Black Soldiers' Perspectives on the War."
27. Wilkerson, "Blacks Wary of Their Big Role as Troops."
28. Williams, "Race and War in the Persian Gulf."
29. Roberts, "What's next, General Powell?"

BIBLIOGRAPHY

Allen, Robert L. *The Port Chicago Mutiny: The Story of the Largest Mass Mutiny Trial in U.S. Naval History.* New York: Amistad Press, 1993.

Anderson, Karen Tucker. "Last Hired, First Fired: Black Women Workers during World War II." *Journal of American History* 69, no. 1 (June 1982): 82–97.

Astor, Gerald. *The Right to Fight: A History of African Americans in the Military.* Novato, Calif.: Presidio Press, 1998.

Badger, Reid. *A Life in Ragtime: A Biography of James Reese Europe.* Oxford: Oxford University Press, 1995.

Barbeau, Arthur E., and Florette Henri. New introduction by Bernard C. Nalty. *The Unknown Soldiers: Black American Troops in World War I.* Philadelphia: Temple University Press, 1974.

Berlin, Ira, Joseph P. Reidy, and Leslie S. Rowland, eds. *Freedom's Soldiers: The Black Military Experience in the Civil War.* Cambridge: Cambridge University Press, 1998.

Bowers, William T., William Hammond, and George MacGarrigle. *Black Soldier, White Army: The 24th Infantry Regiment in Korea.* Washington, D.C.: Center of Military History, U.S. Army, 1996.

Brandt, Nat. *Harlem at War: The Black Experience in WW II.* Syracuse, N.Y.: Syracuse University Press, 1996.

Buckley, Gail. *American Patriots: The Story of Blacks in the Military from the Revolution to Desert Storm.* New York: Random House, 2001.

Burton, Art T. *Black, Buckskin, and Blue: African American Scouts and Soldiers on the Western Frontier.* Austin, Tex.: Eakin Press, 1999.

Bussey, Charles M. *Firefight at Yechon: Courage and Racism in the Korean War.* Washington, D.C.: Brassey's Inc., 1991.

Callum, Agnes Kane. *Colored Volunteers of Maryland, Civil War, 7th Regiment, United States Colored Troops, 1863–1866.* Baltimore, Md.: Mullac Publishers, 1990.

Carisella, P. J., and James W. Ryan. *The Black Swallow of Death: The Incredible Story of Eugene Jacques Bullard, the World's First Black Combat Aviator.* Boston: Marlborough House, 1972.

Carroll, John M., ed. *The Black Military Experience in the American West.* New York: Liveright, 1971.

Cassell, Frank A. "Slaves of the Chesapeake Bay Area and the War of 1812." *Journal of Negro History* 57, no. 2 (April 1972): 144–55.

Christian, Garna L. *Black Soldiers in Jim Crow Texas, 1899–1917.* College Station: Texas A&M University Press, 1995.

Colley, David. *Blood for Dignity: The Story of the First Integrated Combat Unit in the U.S. Army.* Boston: St. Martin's Press, 2003.

Collum, Danny Duncan, ed. *African Americans in the Spanish Civil War: "This Ain't Ethiopia, But It'll Do."* New York: G. K. Hall & Co., 1992.

Cornish, Dudley Taylor. *The Sable Arm: Negro Troops in the Union Army, 1861–1865.* New York: Longmans, 1956.

Cox, Marcus S. "From Racial Uplift to Personal Advancement: African American Attitudes toward Military Service in the Deep South, 1941–1973." Ph.D. diss., Northwestern University, 1996.

Cullen, Jim. "'I's a Man Now': Gender and African American Men." In *A Question of Manhood: A Reader in U.S. Black Men's History and Masculinity,* ed. Darlene Clark Hine and Earnestine Jenkins. Bloomington: Indiana University Press, 1999.

Daly, James A. *Black Prisoner of War: A Conscientious Objector's Vietnam Memoir.* Lawrence: University Press of Kansas, 2000.

Dobak, William A., and Thomas D. Phillips. *The Black Regulars, 1866–1898.* Norman: University of Oklahoma Press, 2001.

Donaldson, Gary. *The History of African Americans in the Military: Double V.* Malabar, Fla.: Krieger Publishing Company, 1991.

Dryden, Charles W. *A-Train: Memoirs of a Tuskegee Airman.* Tuscaloosa: University of Alabama Press, 1997.

Du Bois, W. E. B. "An Essay toward a History of the Black Man in the Great War." *Crisis* (June 1919): 63–87.

Earley, Charity Adams. *One Woman's Army: A Black Officer Remembers the WAC.* College Station: Texas A&M University Press, 1989.

Edgerton, Robert B. *Hidden Heroism: Black Soldiers in America's Wars.* Boulder, Colo.: Westview Press, 2001.

Ellis, Mark. *Race, War, and Surveillance: African Americans and the United States Government during World War I.* Bloomington: Indiana University Press, 2001.

Emilio, Luis F. *A Brave Black Regiment: History of the Fifty-Fourth Regiment of Massachusetts Volunteer Infantry, 1863–1865.* New York: Arno Press, 1969.

Fletcher, Marvin E. *The Black Soldier and Officer in the United States Army, 1891–1917.* Columbia: University of Missouri Press, 1974.

Fletcher, Marvin E. *America's First Black General: Benjamin O. Davis, Sr., 1880–1970.* Lawrence: University Press of Kansas, 1989.

Flipper, Henry Ossian. *Black Frontiersman: The Memoirs of Henry O. Flipper, First Black Graduate of West Point.* Fort Worth: Texas Christian University Press, 1997.

Foner, Jack D. *Blacks and the Military in American History: A New Perspective.* New York: Praeger, 1974.

Foner, Phillip Sheldon. *Blacks in the American Revolution.* Westport, Conn.: Greenwood Press, 1975.

Franklin, John Hope. "Their War and Mine." *Journal of American History* 77, no. 2 (September 1990): 576–79.

Frey, Sylvia R. "Between Slavery and Freedom: Virginia Blacks in the American Revolution." *Journal of Southern History* 49, no. 3 (August 1983): 375–98.

Frey, Sylvia R. *Water from the Rock: Black Resistance in a Revolutionary Age.* Princeton, N.J.: Princeton University Press, 1991.

Gatewood, Willard B., Jr. *"Smoked Yankees" and the Struggle for Empire: Letters from Negro Soldiers, 1898–1902.* Urbana: University of Illinois Press, 1971.

Gatewood, Willard B., Jr. "Alabama's 'Negro Soldier Experiment,' 1898–1899." *Journal of Negro History* 57 (October 1972): 333–51.

Gatewood, Willard B., Jr. "Black Americans and the Quest for Empire, 1898–1903." *Journal of Southern History* 38 (November 1972): 545–66.

Gibran, Daniel K. *The 92nd Infantry Division and the Italian Campaign in World War II.* Jefferson, N.C.: McFarland Publishers, 2001.

Gill, Gerald. "Black Soldiers' Perspectives on the War." In *A Vietnam Reader*, ed. Walter Capps. London: Routledge, 1991.

Glatthaar, Joseph T. *Forged in Battle: The Civil War Alliance of Black Soldiers and White Officers.* New York: The Free Press, 1990.

Goff, Stanley, and Robert Sanders. *Brothers: Black Soldiers in the Nam.* Novato, Calif.: Presidio Press, 1982.

Graham, Herman, III. *The Brothers' Vietnam War: Black Power, Manhood, and the Military Experience.* Gainesville: University Press of Florida, 2003.

Greene, Robert Ewell, ed. *Black Courage, 1775–1783: Documentation of Black Participation in the American Revolution.* Washington, D.C.: National Society of the Daughters of the American Revolution, 1984.

Hachey, Thomas E. "Document: Jim Crow with a British Accent: Attitudes of London Government Officials toward American Negro Soldiers in England during World War II." *Journal of Negro History* 59, no. 1 (January 1974): 65–77.

Hargrove, Hondon B. *Buffalo Soldiers in Italy: Black Americans in World War II.* Jefferson, N.C.: McFarland Publishers, 1985.

Harris, Stephen L. *Harlem's Hell Fighters: The African American 369th Infantry in World War I.* Washington, D.C.: Brassey's, Inc., 2003.

Haynes, Robert V. *A Night of Violence: The Houston Riot of 1917.* Baton Rouge: Louisiana State University Press, 1976.

Haywood, Harry. *Black Bolshevik: Autobiography of an Afro-American Communist.* Chicago: Liberator Press, 1978.

Heywood, Chester D. *Negro Combat Troops in the World War: The Story of the 371st Infantry.* Worcester, Mass.: Commonwealth Press, 1928.

Hollandsworth, James G., Jr. *The Louisiana Native Guards: The Black Military Experience during the Civil War.* Baton Rouge: Louisiana State University Press, 1995.

Holway, John B. *Red Tails, Black Wings: The Men of America's Black Air Force.* Las Cruces, N.M.: Yucca Tree Press, 1997.

Hope, Richard O. *Racial Strife in the U.S. Military: Toward the Elimination of Discrimination.* New York: Praeger, 1979.

Hsiao, Lisa. "Project 100,000: The Great Society's Answer to Military Manpower Needs in Vietnam." *Vietnam Generation* 1, no. 2 (1989): 14–37.

Hunton, Addie W., and Kathryn M. Johnson. *Two Colored Women with the American Expeditionary Forces.* New York: G. K. Hall & Co., 1997.

Jones, Howard J., and R. H. Isabelle. "Two Letters in Protest of Race Prejudice in the Army during the American Civil War." *Journal of Negro History* 61, no. 1 (January 1976): 97–98.

Kelley, Robin D. G. "'This Ain't Ethiopia, But It'll Do': African Americans and the Spanish Civil War." In *Race Rebels: Culture, Politics, and the Black Working Class.* New York: The Free Press, 1994.

Kenner, Charles L. *Buffalo Soldiers and Officers of the Ninth Cavalry, 1867–1898: Black & White Together.* Norman: University of Oklahoma Press, 1999.

Knoblock, Glenn A. *"Strong and Brave Fellows": New Hampshire's Black Soldiers and Sailors of the American Revolution, 1775–1784.* Jefferson, N.C.: McFarland Publishers, 2003.

Lane, Ann J. *The Brownsville Affair: National Crisis and Black Reaction.* Port Washington, N.Y.: Kennikat Press, 1971.

Lanning, Michael Lee. *The African American Soldier: From Crispus Attucks to Colin Powell.* Secaucus, N.J.: Carol Publishing Group, 1997.

Leckie, William H. *The Buffalo Soldiers: A Narrative of the Negro Cavalry in the West.* Norman: University of Oklahoma Press, 1967.

Leiker, James N. *Racial Borders: Black Soldiers along the Rio Grande.* College Station: Texas A&M University Press, 2002.

Little, Arthur W. *From Harlem to the Rhine: The Story of New York's Colored Volunteers.* New York: Covici, Friede, 1936.

Llorens, David. "Why Negroes Re-Enlist." *Ebony* (August, 1968): 87–92.

Lloyd, Craig, *Eugene Bullard, Black Expatriate in Jazz-Age Paris.* Athens: University of Georgia Press, 2000.

Loeb, Jeff. "MIA: African American Autobiography of the Vietnam War." *African American Review* 31, no. 1 (Spring 1997): 105–23.

Longacre, Edward G. "Black Troops in the Army of the James, 1863–65." *Military Affairs* 45 (February 1981): 1–8.

MacGregor, Morris J., Jr. *Integration of the Armed Forces, 1940–1965.* Washington, D.C.: U.S. Government Printing Office, 1981.

May, Robert E. "Invisible Men: Blacks and the U.S. Army in the Mexican War." *Historian* 49, no. 4 (1987): 463–77.

May, Stephen. "World War I Veteran Horace Pippen Used Art to Purge Himself of the Horrors of the Trenches." *Military History* 14 (February 1998): 14, 16, 18, 80.

McGuire, Phillip. "Desegregation of the Armed Forces: Black Leadership, Protest, and World War II." *Journal of Negro History* 68, no. 2 (Spring 1983): 147–58.

McGuire, Phillip. *He, Too, Spoke for Democracy: Judge Hastie, World War II, and the Black Soldier.* New York: Greenwood Press, 1988.

Mershon, Sherie. *Foxholes and Color Lines: Desegregating the U.S. Armed Forces.* Baltimore: Johns Hopkins University Press, 1998.

Miller, Edward A., Jr. *The Black Civil War Soldiers of Illinois: The Story of the Twenty-Ninth U.S. Colored Infantry.* Columbia: University of South Carolina Press, 1998.

Mitchell, Clarence. "The Status of Racial Integration in the Armed Services." *Journal of Negro Education* 23, no. 3 (Summer 1954): 203–13.

Modell, John, M. Goulden, and S. Magnusson. "World War II in the Lives of Black Americans: Some Findings and Interpretation." *Journal of American History* 76, no. 3 (December 1989): 838–48.

Moore, Brenda L. *To Serve My Country, To Serve My Race: The Story of the Only African American WACS Stationed Overseas during World War II.* New York: New York University Press, 1996.

Morehouse, Maggi M. *Fighting in the Jim Crow Army: Black Men and Women Remember World War II.* Lanham, Md.: Rowman & Littlefield, 2000.

Morrow, Curtis James. *What's a Commie Ever Done to Black People? A Korean War Memoir of Fighting in the U.S. Army's Last All Negro Unit.* Jefferson, N.C.: McFarland Publishers, 1997.

Motley, Mary Penick, ed. *The Invisible Soldier: The Experience of the Black Soldier, World War II.* Detroit: Wayne State University Press, 1975.

Mullen, Robert W. *Blacks and Vietnam.* Washington, D.C.: University Press of America, 1981.

Nalty, Bernard C. *The Right to Fight: African American Marines in World War II.* Washington, D.C.: U.S. Marine Corps, 1995.

Nalty, Bernard C. *Strength for the Fight: A History of Black Americans in the Military.* New York: The Free Press, 1986.

Ngozi-Brown, Scot. "African American Soldiers and Filipinos: Racial Imperialism, Jim Crow, and Social Relations." *Journal of Negro History* 82, no. 1 (Winter 1997): 42–53.

Norvell, Stanley B., and William M. Tuttle, Jr. "Views of a Negro during 'The Red Summer' of 1919." *Journal of Negro History* 51, no. 3 (July 1966): 209–18.

Percy, William Alexander. "Jim Crow and Uncle Sam: The Tuskegee Flying Units and the U.S. Army Air Forces in Europe during World War II." *Journal of Military History* 67 (July 2003): 773–810.

Peters, James S., II. *The Saga of Black Navy Veterans of World War II: An American Triumph.* San Francisco, Calif.: International Scholars Publications, 1996.

Phelps, J. Alfred. *Chappie: America's First Black Four-Star General: The Life and Times of Daniel James, Jr.* Novato, Calif.: Presidio Press, 1991.

Potter, Lou. *Liberators: Fighting on Two Fronts in World War II.* New York: Harcourt Brace Jovanovich, 1992.

Powell, Colin. *My American Journey.* New York: Random House, 1995.

Putney, Martha S. *When the Nation Was in Need: Blacks in the Women's Army Corps during World War II.* Metuchen, N.J.: Scarecrow Press, 1992.

Quarles, Benjamin. *The Negro and the Civil War.* Boston: Little, Brown & Co., 1953.

Quarles, Benjamin. *The Negro in the American Revolution.* Chapel Hill: University of North Carolina Press, 1961.

Redkey, Edwin S., ed. *A Grand Army of Black Men: Letters from African American Soldiers in the Union Army, 1861–1865.* Cambridge: Cambridge University Press, 1993).

Rishell, Lyle. *With a Black Platoon in Combat: A Year in Korea.* College Station: Texas A&M University Press, 1993.

Roberts, Steven V. "What's next, General Powell?" *US News & World Report* (18 March 1991): 50–53.

Roberts, Frank E. *The American Foreign Legion: Black Soldiers of the 93rd in World War I.* Annapolis: Naval Institute Press, 2004.

Schubert, Frank N. *Black Valor: Buffalo Soldiers and the Medal of Honor, 1870–1898.* Wilmington, Del.: Scholarly Resources, 1997.

Schubert, Frank N. *Voices of the Buffalo Soldier: Records, Reports, and Recollections of Military Life and Service in the West.* Albuquerque: University of New Mexico Press, 2003.

Scott, Emmett J. *Scott's Official History of the American Negro in the World War.* Chicago: Homewood Press, 1919.

Scott, Lawrence P. *Double V: The Civil Rights Struggle of the Tuskegee Airmen.* East Lansing: Michigan State University Press, 1994.

Shaffer, Donald R. *After the Glory: The Struggles of Black Civil War Veterans.* Lawrence: University Press of Kansas, 2004.

Shaffer, Donald Robert. "Marching On: African-American Civil War Veterans in Postbellum America, 1865–1951." Ph.D. diss., University of Maryland, 1996.

Smith, John David, ed. *Black Soldiers in Blue: African American Troops in the Civil War Era.* Chapel Hill: University of North Carolina Press, 2002.

Taylor, Susie King. *A Black Woman's Civil War Memoirs: Reminiscences of My Life in Camp with the 33rd U.S. Colored Troops, Late 1st South Carolina Volunteers.* New York: M. Wiener Publishers, 1998.

Terry, Wallace, ed. *Bloods: An Oral History of the Vietnam War.* New York: Random House, 1984.

Trudeau, Noah Andre. *Like Men of War: Black Troops in the Civil War, 1862–1865.* Boston: Little, Brown & Co., 1998.

Urwin, Gregory J. W. "'We Cannot Treat Negroes . . . as Prisoners of War': Racial Atrocities and Reprisals in Civil War Arkansas." *Civil War History* 42 (September 1996): 193–210.

Urwin, Gregory J. W., ed. *Black Flag over Dixie: Racial Atrocities and Reprisals in the Civil War.* Carbondale: Southern Illinois University Press, 2004.

Voelz, Peter M. *Slave and Soldier: The Military Impact of Blacks in the Colonial Americas.* New York: Garland Press, 1993.

Washington, Booker T. *The Story of the Negro: The Rise of the Race from Slavery.* New York: Doubleday, 1909.

Washington, Versalle F. *Eagles on Their Buttons: A Black Infantry Regiment in the Civil War.* Columbia: University of Missouri Press, 1999.

Westheider, James E. *Fighting on Two Fronts: African Americans and the Vietnam War.* New York: New York University Press, 1997.

Westwood, Howard C. *Black Troops, White Commanders, and Freedmen during the Civil War.* Carbondale: Southern Illinois University Press, 1992.

Wilkerson, Isabel. "Blacks Wary of Their Big Role as Troops." *New York Times,* 25 January 1991, A1, A12.

Williams, Chad Louis. "Torchbearers of Democracy: The First World War and the Figure of the African-American Soldier." Ph.D. diss., Princeton University, 2004.

Williams, Charles H. *Sidelights on Negro Soldiers.* Boston: B. J. Brimmer Company, 1923.

Williams, George Washington. *History of the Negro Race in America from 1619 to 1880: Negroes as Slaves, as Soldiers and as Citizens, together with a Preliminary Consideration of the Unity of the Human Family, an Historical Sketch of Africa, and an Account of the Negro Governments of Sierra Leone and Liberia.* New York: G. P. Putnam's Sons, 1883.

Williams, George Washington. *A History of the Negro Troops in the War of the Rebellion, 1861–1865.* New York: Harper & Bros., 1888.

Williams, Juan. "Race and War in the Persian Gulf: Why are Black Leaders Trying to Divide Blacks from the American Mainstream?" *Washington Post,* 20 January 1991, A19.

Wilson, Joseph T. *The Black Phalanx: A History of the Negro Soldiers of the United States in the War of 1775–1812, 1861–65.* Hartford, Conn.: American Publishing Company, 1888.

Wilson, Keith P. *Campfires of Freedom: The Camp Life of Black Soldiers during the Civil War.* Kent, Ohio: Kent State University Press, 2002.

Woodson, Carter G. *The Negro in Our History.* Washington, D.C.: Associated Publishers, 1922.

Wright, Elisse Yvette. "Birds of a Different Feather: African American Support for the Vietnam War in the Johnson Years, 1965–1969." Ph.D. diss., Ohio State University, 1996.

Wynn, Neil A. *The Afro-American and the Second World War.* New York: Holmes and Meier, 1975.

CHRONOLOGY

1639   Virginia passes first legislation excluding African Americans from militia service.

1703   South Carolina enlists slaves in the colonial militia in its efforts to defend against Native American raids. Slaves who kill or capture a Native American in battle are rewarded with manumission.

1719   South Carolina revokes reward of manumission for slaves serving in colonial militia.

1754–63   French-Indian War. Free African Americans serve as soldiers in northern state militias.

1770   March 5: Crispus Attucks, an escaped slave, is among five men who are killed by British soldiers, marking the first African American casualty of the American Revolution.

1775   April 18: Slaves and African-American militiamen participate in the battles of Concord and Lexington, the first formal military engagements of the American Revolution.

1775   October 8: Continental Congress agrees to reject all African Americans from enlistment in the Continental Army.

1775   November 7: Lord Dunmore, British royal governor of Virginia, issues a call for slaves to join the British army, with the promise of freedom. Over three hundred runaway slaves enlist by December 1 and are eventually organized into the "Ethiopian Regiment."

1776   January 16: At General George Washington's behest, the Continental Congress amends its previous decision and allows African Americans already serving in the Continental Army to reenlist.

1778   February: Rhode Island passes resolution allowing slaves to enlist in state militia with the promise of freedom.

1779   Despite a severe manpower shortage, South Carolina and Georgia reject a Continental Congress request to organize 3,000 slaves into segregated units.

1780   Maryland becomes the only southern state to allow slaves to enlist in the militia.

1792   May: Militia law passed by Congress restricting enlistment to white male citizens.

1812   Governor William Claiborne of Louisiana allows free blacks to serve in the state's militia.

1815   January 8: Battle of New Orleans. Two militia companies comprised of 430 free black men from New Orleans help defeat a British invasion of the city.

1815   March 3: Congress excludes African Americans from the postwar army, consisting of 10,000 men.

1846–48   Mexican-American War. African American participation is limited.

1861   April: Free African Americans in New Orleans are granted approval to organize a Native Guard battalion with commissioned black officers.

1861   May 23: General Benjamin Butler labels slaves seeking refuge behind Union lines as "contrabands of war" and refuses to return them to the Confederacy. Escaped slaves in increasingly significant numbers assist Union forces as laborers.

1861   August 6: Abraham Lincoln signs into law the Confiscation Act, authorizing the seizure of all Confederate property, including slaves, used for military purposes in the rebellion.

1861   August 30: In Missouri, Major General John C. Frémont issues a proclamation declaring all slaves in the Union-controlled state free. President Abraham Lincoln revokes the proclamation and removes Frémont from command.

1862   April: The first regiment of runaway slaves, the 1st South Carolina Volunteers, organized under the command of Rufus Saxton.

1862   May: Robert Smalls commandeers the Confederate ship *Planter* in Charleston Harbor and delivers it to Union naval forces.

1862   June: Kansas senator James H. Lane begins to recruit escaped slaves into the 1st Kansas Colored Volunteer Infantry, which becomes the 79th Infantry Regiment, United States Colored Troops.

1862   October: The 79th Infantry Regiment becomes the first regiment of black soldiers to engage in combat in a skirmish with a unit of Confederate guerrillas at Island Mound, Missouri. This results in the first combat death of black soldiers in the Civil War.

1862   December 23: Confederate President Jefferson Davis signs a proclamation authorizing the execution of any white officer captured in command of black soldiers, and the return of captured black soldiers to slavery.

1863   January 1: The Emancipation Proclamation, issued by Abraham Lincoln on September 22, 1862, takes effect, abolishing slavery in the Confederate States and allowing for African Americans to serve in the Union Army.

1863   May 22: General Order No. 143 issued, creating the Bureau of Colored Troops.

1863	July 18: 54th Massachusetts Regiment leads assault on Fort Wagner, South Carolina. Sergeant William H. Carney becomes the first African American recipient of the Congressional Medal of Honor for his service during the battle.
1864	April 13: Confederate forces massacre over 300 white and black soldiers following their surrender at Fort Pillow, Tennessee.
1864	July: United States Attorney General Edward Bates orders that black volunteers who were free men at the onset of the war are entitled to equal pay on a par with white soldiers.
1865	Martin Delany becomes first African American commissioned to the rank of major.
1865	March 13: Confederate President Jefferson Davis authorizes the enlistment of up to 300,000 slaves for military service with the promise of emancipation.
1866	July 28: Congress authorizes creation of six black regiments in the postwar Regular Army: Thirty-eighth, Thirty-ninth, Fortieth, Forty-first Infantry regiments, and the Ninth and Tenth Cavalry regiments.
1869	Congress reorganizes the Regular Army. The Thirty-eighth and Forty-first Infantry regiments are consolidated into the Twenty-fourth Infantry Regiment (Colored), and the Thirty-ninth and the Fortieth Infantry regiments are consolidated into the Twenty-fifth Infantry Regiment (Colored).
1877	June: Henry Ossian Flipper becomes the first African American to graduate from West Point Military Academy.
1898	February 14: American battleship *Maine* explodes while docked in Havana, Cuba. Twenty-two African Americans are listed among the 266 deaths. The explosion, later determined to be accidental, prompts war with Spain.
1898	July 1: Battle of San Juan Hill. The Ninth and Tenth Cavalry regiments fight alongside Theodore Roosevelt's "Rough Riders" and earn widespread acclaim.
1899	February: Beginning of the Philippine Insurrection. The Twenty-fourth and Twenty-fifth Infantry regiments, along with the newly created Forty-eighth and Forty-ninth Volunteer infantries see extensive action in suppressing the insurgency.
1906	August 13: Soldiers of the Twenty-fifth Infantry Regiment are accused of killing a white civilian and wounding two others at Brownsville, Texas. Despite professing their innocence, 167 soldiers receive dishonorable discharges from the military upon the recommendation of President Theodore Roosevelt.
1907	New navy battle fleet, dubbed the "Great White Fleet," sails around the world. African Americans serve only in menial positions, not as sailors.
1916	March. General John "Black Jack" Pershing leads a punitive expedition, which includes the Tenth Cavalry, into Mexico in pursuit of "Pancho" Villa.
1916	October: Expatriate Eugene Jacques Bullard, born in Columbus, Georgia, becomes the first African American to fight in the French Foreign Legion and serve in the French Air Service.
1917	May 19: In response to intense pressure from black social and political leaders, Congress authorizes the first training camp for African American officer candidates at Des Moines, Iowa.

1917	August 23: Black soldiers of the Third Battalion of the Twenty-fourth Infantry storm downtown Houston in retaliation for persistent racial abuse. Two black soldiers and fifteen white men are killed.
1917	September: Emmett J. Scott, former secretary for Booker T. Washington at the Tuskegee Institute, appointed special assistant to the secretary of war.
1917	November 29: The War Department formally establishes the Ninety-second Division (Colored), the only combat division in the American Expeditionary Forces composed of African American drafted men.
1917	December 11: Thirteen black soldiers of the Twenty-fourth Infantry convicted for their role in the Houston Riot are executed without due process.
1918	January: The War Department establishes the Ninety-Third Division (Provisional), composed of African American National Guard units. The Ninety-third Division served in the French army for the duration of America's participation in the war.
1918	September–November: Black soldiers of the Ninety-second Division participate in the Meuse-Argonne Offensive.
1919	July 27: Race riot erupts in Chicago, resulting in thirty-eight deaths before order is restored thirteen days later. Similar riots occur throughout the summer of 1919.
1919	War Department restricts new enlistments in four black Regular Army regiments, but allows reenlistments.
1920	June: Congress passes the National Defense Act, reducing the size of the postwar army to 30,000 men. The four black Regular Army regiments remain intact.
1936–39	Spanish Civil War. African Americans serve in the 2,800-man Abraham Lincoln Brigade, comprised of white and black volunteers.
1936	Benjamin O. Davis Jr. becomes the fourth African American to graduate from West Point.
1940	September 16: Selective Service Act passed by Congress, specifying no racial discrimination and establishing a 10 percent quota for African American enlistment. Segregation, however, remains intact.
1940	October 8: President Roosevelt, under pressure for reelection and needing to solidify black support, revises military racial policy. He orders that the number of African Americans in the army correspond to their numerical percentage in the populace and that they are eligible to serve in all branches of military, are eligible for officer training, and have access to civilian employment at military facilities.
1940	October 25: Benjamin O. Davis Sr. is promoted to rank of brigadier general, at the time the highest military rank ever achieved by an African American serviceman.
1940	November 1: Judge William H. Hastie is appointed to position of civilian aide to the secretary of war in matters of black rights.
1941	January 9: Secretary of War Henry L. Stimson approves establishment of a flight-training program at Tuskegee Institute.
1941	May 8: War Department establishes the 78th Tank Battalion, eventually redesignated as the 758th Tank Battalion, which constituted one of four African American tank battalions during World War II.

1941   June 25: In response to a threatened March on Washington organized by A. Philip Randolph for July 1, Roosevelt issues Executive Order 8802, banning racial discrimination in defense-industry hiring and establishing the Fair Employment Practices Commission to enforce the order.

1942   January 9: Roosevelt orders the navy and the United States Marine Corps to enlist African Americans.

1942   February: For the first time in 167 years, the United States Marine Corps agrees to admit 1,200 African American recruits for training.

1942   May 15: 93rd Infantry Division reactivated at Fort Huachuca, Arizona—the first black division formed during World War II.

1942   May 15: Roosevelt signs legislation creating the Women's Auxiliary Army Corps (WAAC), which enlisted white and black women for volunteer service.

1942   June 1: "51st Composite Defense Battalion" is formed at Camp Lejeune, N.C. Training begins in September 1942.

1942   October 15: 92nd Division reactivated. About 12,000 enlisted men and officers (200 white and 600 black) served in this division in the war.

1943   January 5: William H. Hastie resigns his position as civilian aide to the secretary of war in matters of black rights in response to continued racial discrimination in the armed forces.

1943   May 27: Federal government prohibits all war contractors from discriminating based on race.

1943   June 20: Race riot erupts in Detroit, resulting in thirty-five deaths and property damage in the millions.

1944   July 17: Port Chicago explosion killing 320 men, 202 African Americans; 258 black soldiers refused to return to duty without increased safety precautions; 50 men convicted of mutiny.

1944   October 19: The Women Accepted for Volunteer Emergency Service (WAVES) admits seventy-two black women for training. Two eventually become officers.

1947   November: A. Philip Randolph and Grant Reynolds create the Committee against Jim Crow in Military Service and Training. Randolph pledges that unless a debated selective service act includes a ban on segregation, African Americans will resist induction.

1948   June 24: Truman signs the Selective Service Act, reinstituting the draft, into law. The act contains no provisions banning segregation. A. Philip Randolph repeats pledge to encourage black resistance to induction.

1948   July 26: President Truman signs Executive Order 9981, prohibiting racial discrimination in the United States armed forces.

1949   May 11: The United States Air Force institutes a new policy ensuring equal treatment and opportunity without regard to race, color, religion, or national origin.

1950   March 27: The army eliminates racial quotas from its enlistment procedures.

1951   October 1: The Twenty-fourth Infantry is deactivated, as the army moves towards complete integration of its forces.

1954   October 30: Secretary of defense announces the abolishment of the last racially segregated military unit.

1963   August 28: March on Washington.

1966   Secretary of war institutes Project 100,000, which lowers army enlistment standards to increase the number of socioeconomically disadvantaged recruits, many of whom are African American.

1971   May 2: Race riot erupts at Travis Air Force Base, California, lasting four days and involving over 200 black and white airmen.

1973   Army abandons use of Selective Service and transitions to an all-volunteer force.

1981   African Americans constitute nearly 20 percent of the United States armed forces.

1989   General Colin Powell becomes the first African American chairman of the Joint Chiefs of Staff.

2003   January 7: African American congressman Charles Rangel (D-NY) introduces legislation to reinstitute the draft in response to racial and socioeconomic disparities in the composition of the volunteer army.

GLOSSARY

Battle of Fort Wagner. On July 18, 1863, Union forces under the command of General Quincy Gillmore attacked the Confederate fort Battery Wagner at Morris Island, South Carolina, in Charleston Harbor. Preceded by a heavy naval assault, the Massachusetts Fifty-fourth Infantry led the initial charge on the fort, a decision in part prompted by racial prejudice. Despite fierce fighting, which resulted in the death of Colonel Robert Gould Shaw, the Fifty-fourth temporarily controlled a portion of the fort and planted the regimental flag. The regiment was ordered to withdraw after enduring staggering casualties. While Battery Wagner remained in Confederate hands, the Fifty-fourth achieved mythic status as a result of its bravery and sacrifice.

The Brownsville Affair. The Brownsville affair stemmed from simmering racial tensions between black soldiers of the Regular Army and white Texans. After shots rang out on the night of August 13, 1906, at Brownsville, Texas, local whites accused black soldiers of the Twenty-fifth Infantry's First Battalion of killing one man and wounding two others. Although they steadfastly denied involvement in the shooting, President Theodore Roosevelt dishonorably discharged 167 soldiers without a public hearing. Brownsville further fueled the perception among whites, particularly in the South, of black soldiers as a source of violent racial unrest. In 1972, following an in-depth investigation, the army reversed Roosevelt's order, clearing the soldiers of any wrongdoing and changing their discharge to honorable.

Buffalo Soldiers. The African American soldiers of the Regular Army consisted of Ninth and Tenth Cavalry and Twenty-fourth and Twenty-fifth Infantry regiments, created by Congress following the Civil War. Throughout the late nineteenth century, African Americans represented approximately 10 percent of the country's active soldiers. Labeled "Buffalo Soldiers" by Cheyenne Native Americans, the black regulars served almost exclusively in the American West and Southwest. In addition to fighting in the so-called "Indian Wars" and policing the Mexican–United States border, black soldiers helped lay the foundation for western settlement by building roads, establishing telegraph lines, protecting food and supply routes, and scouting unmarked territory. The four black regiments served in the Spanish-Cuban-American War, the Philippines, and the Mexico punitive expedition. The numerical strength of the "Buffalo Soldier" regiments decreased during the interwar years, when the army restricted new enlistment. The army disbanded the last original "Buffalo Soldier" regiment, the Twenty-fourth Infantry, in October 1951 during the Korean War.

Ethiopian Regiment. Prompted by a shortage of British soldiers, on November 7, 1775, Lord Dunmore, the Crown's colonial governor of Virginia, issued a proclamation granting freedom to any slave or indentured servant who joined the British forces. Within a month, over three hundred slaves had joined Dunmore's regiment. Eventually comprised of an estimated eight hundred runaway slaves, the regiment first saw military action on December 9, 1775. By June 1776 a smallpox epidemic had severely reduced the ranks of the Ethiopian Regiment. Dunmore's success in undermining colonial slavery and attracting black people to the British army prompted the Continental Army to reverse its policy restricting African American enlistment.

Executive Order 8802. In February 1941, A. Philip Randolph organized the March on Washington Movement to pressure President Franklin D. Roosevelt to eliminate racial discrimination in the military and government-contracted defense industries. Scheduled for July 1, 1941, Randolph expected the march to bring at least 10,000 African Americans to the nation's capital. Fearing political repercussions and needing to maintain black support for the war, Roosevelt issued Executive Order 8802 on June 25, 1941, which stated in part, "There shall be no discrimination in the employment of workers in defense industries or government because of race, creed, color, or national origin, and I do hereby declare that it is the duty of employers and of labor organizations, in furtherance of said policy and of this order, to provide for the full and equitable participation of all workers in defense industries, without discrimination because of race, creed, color, or national origin." The order also created the Fair Employment Practices Commission (FEPC) for enforcement. While symbolically important, the FEPC accomplished little due to a lack of authority and resistance on the part of employers.

Executive Order 9981. President Harry Truman issued Executive Order 9981 on July 26, 1948, in response to pressure from A. Philip Randolph, who pledged that African Americans would resist induction under a Selective Service Act that permitted segregation in the military. The executive order stated that "There shall be equality of treatment and opportunity for all persons in the armed services without regard to race, color, religion or national origin," which Truman later affirmed to mean the elimination of segregation in the nation's armed forces. Despite signaling a bold commitment on the part of the federal government to African American civil rights, the order did not specify how desegregation was to be implemented and at what pace. As a result, complete integration of the armed forces did not occur until 1954.

Fifty-fourth Massachusetts Regiment. The Fifty-fourth Massachusetts Regiment was the first unit of black soldiers raised in the North following the Emancipation Proclamation. In January 1863 Governor John A. Andrew of Massachusetts, a staunch proponent of abolition, received permission from Secretary of War Edwin Stanton to raise a regiment of black soldiers under the state flag. With Frederick Douglass spearheading recruitment, free African Americans from throughout the New England region enlisted, including two of Douglass's sons. Governor Andrew personally selected the white officers to command the regiment, including its twenty-five-year-old colonel, Robert Gould Shaw. The army, not yet convinced that African American troops could be effective in combat, initially consigned the Fifty-fourth to labor duties in South Carolina. Pressure on the War Department resulted in the regiment seeing its first action on July 16 at James Island. Two days later, the regiment led a Union attack on the Confederate fort Battery Wagner at Morris Island, South Carolina. Although it briefly planted the regimental flag, the Fifty-fourth incurred staggering casualties, and the fort remained in Confederate hands. Nevertheless, the Fifty-fourth earned widespread praise for its bravery and paved the way for the future organization of African American regiments.

555th Parachute Infantry Regiment. Known as the "Triple Nickels," the 555th Parachute Infantry Regiment was the first all-black airborne unit in the United States military. The 555th later formed the core of the Second Ranger Infantry Company, which fought in the Korean War and made history as the first unit of black soldiers to make a combat jump.

Fort Pillow Massacre. On April 12, 1864, Confederate forces under the command of General Nathan B. Forrest attacked the Union garrison at Fort Pillow, located at Jackson, Tennessee. Forrest's cavalry of approximately 2,500 men encountered a Union force comprised of 262 African American United States Colored Troops and 295 white soldiers from Tennessee under the command of Major Lionel F. Booth. After Booth was killed, Major William F. Bradford assumed command, but refused to surrender. Confederate soldiers launched a final assault that forced Bradford's men to ultimately surrender and throw down their arms. The Confederates, however, ignored the surrender and commenced shooting unarmed Union soldiers, pursuing them out of the fort into a nearby riverbank. Two hundred thirty-one men were killed, the majority African American, in what became one of the worst racial atrocities of the Civil War. The incident shocked Northerners, and Fort Pillow became a Union rallying cry.

Houston Riot. In early August 1917 the War Department assigned the Third Battalion of the Twenty-fourth Infantry Regiment to guard construction of Camp Logan on the outskirts of Houston, Texas. The black men of the regiment endured weeks of persistent racial discrimination and abuse from local whites, and police officers in particular, who resented the real and symbolic challenge black soldiers posed to their authority. On the night of August 23, 1917, rumors spread that Houston police had killed a black soldier, Corporal Charles Baltimore. Although the rumor proved false, it nevertheless pushed the battalion over the edge. After procuring arms and leaving camp, over one hundred black soldiers methodically marched into downtown Houston, shooting white men and police officers who attempted to impede them. The riot resulted in the deaths of fifteen white men, four of whom were policemen, and four black soldiers. Three separate court-martials found 110 men of the battalion guilty of mutiny. Texas law enforcement summarily executed thirteen men without the opportunity to appeal their sentences. The military later executed six additional soldiers and sentenced forty-one to life imprisonment.

Louisiana Native Guards (Corps d'Afrique). The Louisiana Native Guards represented the first regiments of black soldiers officially mustered into the Union Army during the Civil War. They consisted of black free men and former slaves recruited by Union general Benjamin Franklin Butler. The first of three regiments was organized in August 1862 and mustered into service the following month. Dubbed the "Corps d'Afrique" while under the command of General Nathaniel P. Banks, the native guards saw major action during the siege of Port Hudson on May 27, 1863. Many of the soldiers of the Corps d'Afrique became leading political figures in Louisiana Reconstruction politics, most notably future governor P. B. S. Pinchback.

Ninety-second Division. The War Department created the Ninety-second "Buffalo" Division in November 1917 during World War I as a result of pressure to include African Americans as combat troops in the American Expeditionary Forces (AEF). Although commanded by white officers, the division contained black officers commissioned at Des Moines, Iowa, site of the first officers training camp for black enlistees. The Ninety-second remained completely segregated from white divisions of the AEF throughout the war and was singled out for criticism during the Meuse-Argonne offensive. The War Department reactivated the Ninety-second Division during World War II. The division remained segregated and commanded by racist white officers. The Ninety-second served on the front lines in the Italian Campaign and engaged in combat action between August 1944 and May 1945. As in World War I, the men of the division and its black officers received criticism for their battlefield performance.

Ninety-third Division. The War Department established the Ninety-third Division in January 1918 during World War I. Comprised of black National Guard regiments and one regiment of black draftees, the army assigned the Ninety-third a provisional status and incorporated it into the French army, the only American division to serve with foreign forces during the war. As a result, the men of the Ninety-third had a much different social and military experience than that of other American soldiers, white and black. Overall the Ninety-third served with distinction, in particular the 369th Infantry Regiment. Reactivated during World War II, the Ninety-third Division was stationed in the Pacific Theater and performed primarily mop-up duty following major combat operations.

Port Chicago Mutiny. On July 17, 1944, two ships carrying munitions exploded at Port Chicago, California, resulting in 320 deaths, 202 African American. After being ordered to resume loading ammunition weeks later under still dangerous conditions, 258 black sailors refused to work and were subsequently arrested. The military court-martialed 50 men who refused to return to work and sentenced them to eight to fifteen years hard labor and dishonorable discharges. Despite the efforts of the NAACP and Thurgood Marshall, who successfully reduced the sentences of some of the convicted men, they have yet to receive full exoneration from the military and the federal government.

369th Infantry Regiment (New York Fifteenth National Guard). The New York Fifteenth National Guard was created in 1916 by Governor Charles Whitman and commanded by Colonel William Hayward. The Fifteenth became the first New York National Guard unit recruited to war strength following America's entry into World War I. The black national guardsmen were assigned to the Ninety-third Division, where they were redesignated as the 369th Infantry Regiment. The 369th's band, led by the acclaimed James Reese Europe, enhanced the status and visibility of the regiment. Serving in the French army, the 369th fought for 191 days under fire and never lost any ground to the enemy, earning the nickname the "Harlem Hellfighters." The 369th returned to Harlem in February 1919 as racial heroes.

Tuskegee Airmen (332nd Fighter Group). In January 1941 the War Department approved the establishment of a flight training program at the Tuskegee Institute in Alabama and later created the Ninety-ninth Pursuit Squadron of the United States Air Force. White officials fully expected the experiment in black fighter pilots to be a failure. When given the opportunity to perform, however, the "Tuskegee Airmen" dispelled myths that African Americans could not become effective aviators. After being sent to North Africa, the Ninety-ninth was joined by the 100th, 301st and 302nd Fighter Squadrons, which together made up the 332nd Fighter Group. Commanded by Benjamin O. Davis Jr., the "Tuskegee Airmen" flew over 15,000 combat sorties, downed 111 enemy fighters, and became the only fighter group to never lose an escorted bomber to enemy fire.

African American Religious Experience: An Overview

Michael A. Gomez

Abstract

This essay will broadly interpret the phrase "African American" as generally applicable to people of African descent throughout the Americas. Drawing upon publications in English, Spanish, French, Portuguese, and even a few Arabic documents, the essay will explore the vast religious experience of African Americans. Some discussion of religions in Africa, both before and contemporary with the transatlantic slave trade, will be required, followed by analyses of both the resilience of those religions and the transformations they necessarily underwent during American slavery. The question of religious experience during slavery was a pivotal one, as it held substantial implications for all that followed. This discussion will, of course, take into consideration the impact of Christianity upon the African-descended, and vice versa, during slavery (and among both enslaved and "free"). The narrative strand will continue through post-slavery, a differentiated period that is essentially coterminous with the second half of the nineteenth century. Here, the focus turns to the use of religion in the struggle for worker and peasant rights, and the effort to enter into mainstream societies.

The essay's second major focus (after slavery) will be the explosion of religious activity in the first half of the twentieth century. A myriad of religious organizations and doctrinal elocutions mark the era, as religion was a principal means by which the African-descended addressed the challenges of unrelenting racial discrimination throughout the Americas, the continuation of empire (especially in the Caribbean), and the onset of colonialism (particularly in Africa). Beyond the roles of religion within the various diasporic communities, the phenomenon of black missionary activity, especially in Africa, merits special attention as one of the most intriguing examples of the effects of slavery/imperialism and the attempt to remedy them (e.g., Pan-Africanism).

The Variety of African American Religious Experience

What follows is a historian's perspective on the African American religious experience. The essay does not enter into discussions of doctrinal explications and disputes, or the histories thereof, best addressed by theologians. Rather, this essay attempts to identify and contextualize literatures that exemplify the relational quality of the religious experience; that is, the ways in which religion has informed, infused, and liberated, and undoubtedly bounded, the lives of the African-descended peoples. Conceptually, "African American" is rather broadly configured here, incorporating persons of African descent and their respective communities throughout the Americas.

With the lines of interrogation placed in this way, it is clear that the range of religious experiences of the African-descended in the Americas is quite vast. Our principal premise is that this experience, or more accurately set of experiences, cannot be understood outside the complex of African religions that contributed fundamentally to African cultures and societies that adhered both before and during the transatlantic slave trade. Indeed, religion held historical African communities together. Such was the force and resilience of African religions that the study of African American religions is arguably, and to a considerable degree, the review of African-descended communities who have either struggled to retain connections with African antecedents, or who have expended considerable energy to escape those connections. The essay will also (and obviously) take into consideration the impact of Christianity upon the African-descended, and vice versa, during slavery, and will continue through post-slavery, a differentiated period that is essentially coterminous with the second half of the nineteenth century. Here, the focus turns to the use of religion in the struggle for worker and peasant rights, and the effort to enter into mainstream societies. The first half of the twentieth century, in turn, witnessed an explosion of religious activity. A myriad of religious organizations and doctrinal elocutions mark the era, as religion was an important means by which the African-descended addressed the challenges of unrelenting racial discrimination throughout the Americas, the continuation of empire (especially in the Caribbean), and the onset of colonialism (particularly in Africa). Beyond the roles of religion within various diasporic communities, the phenomenon of black missionary activity, especially in Africa, merits attention as one of the most intriguing examples of the effects of slavery and imperialism, and the attempt to achieve their remedy.

Africans transported to the Americas via the transatlantic slave trade were incontrovertibly deracinated, but were far from culturally vacant. Rather, they brought with them a number of belief systems that would in all instances undergo at least some modification under New World conditions. As such, African religions have historically functioned no differently than religions in any other part of the world; to remain viable, they necessarily adapted to changing circumstances, exhibiting a malleability that simultaneously allowed for certain core principles or conceptualizations of the divine, and the human response to the divine, to be continually renewed. In fact, changes were already underway in Africa itself, both antedating and coterminously unfolding with the transatlantic slave trade.

Religion was a cultural fundamental, and all African religions posited belief in a supreme being, with whom were associated lesser deities as well as the spirits of departed human beings who remained active in the world. Many African religions also practiced spirit possession. As culture bearers, Africans throughout the Americas transformed the Christianity of whites by bringing such antecedent beliefs and practices into its practice—precisely what whites had done in Europeanizing a faith originating in the Middle East. In North

America, for example, the African-descended gradually adopted a Protestant Christianity consistent with their own conceptual framework. The concept of a Trinity was not shocking or beyond consideration, nor was the idea of an indwelling Holy Spirit. The stiff, placid liturgical styles of the various churches were altered substantially, however, to accommodate the full expression of the Holy Ghost, within which dance and ceremony was in every way consistent with African notions of spirit possession. The ring shout, featuring worshipers moving counterclockwise in an ever-quickening circle, was derivative of West Central African and West African practice, and was widespread in North America. In these and other ways, Christianity itself was first adapted, facilitating the subsequent conversion of Africans to its main tenets.

The literature on African religions is quite extensive. For our purposes, it is best to focus on those materials that marshal the requisite African context to elucidate effectively the American revelation, and to that end, those studies that elaborate on the African antecedent for the express purpose of examining culture in the Americas are of greatest relevance (although reading through the study of African religions for their own sake will also and obviously benefit such examination). There are a number of publications that, together, create a rich tapestry of information about African religions as they relate to the Americas. Written by scholars in anthropology, history, art history, sociology, and religious studies, these studies adopt varying methodologies. What often happens is that scholars locate a practice in the Americas in which they have interest, and attempt to trace the origins of the practice in Africa by way of reference to any materials related to the topic. This can result in a hodgepodge of sources that are drawn upon in an uncritical fashion. Eyewitness testimony, travelers' accounts, colonial records, folklore, anthropological findings, and first-hand information gathered by the scholars themselves are at times thrown together without regard to the critical assessment of each category. The most common result is what historians refer to as the "ethnographic present," a reference to the sense of a static, unchanging African cultural landscape that has persisted from time immemorial to the moment of the written record. In this most ahistoric of approaches, African religions assume a timeless quality, when in fact they have undergone significant and demonstrable change over the centuries, both before and during the transatlantic slave trade.

The Influence of African Religions

With these reservations in mind, we can turn to some of the representative literature that has affected our understanding of African religions in the Americas during slavery. With respect to North America, there have been several early studies focusing on the various practices of black Southerners that appear to have been influenced by African cultural antecedents. While Luther Jackson's famous "Religious Development of the Negro in Virginia" addresses conversion to Christianity, it indirectly comments on African religious elements in the American South. Those elements are more directly discussed in Zora Neale Hurston's "Hoodoo in America," a remarkable collection of data relating to varying interests, including pharmacopeia. Similar kinds of discussions can be found in Newbell Puckett's *Folk Beliefs of the Southern Negro.*

The significance of the foregoing could be readily dismissed as folkloric trivia and innocuous anecdotes of a time long gone, and in any event of little consequence, bereft of qualities of serious scholarship (though the scholarship was quite serious). However, the publication of Melville Herskovits's *Myth of the Negro Past,* among his many other publications, challenged that assertion. Here was a formidable orchestration of the data for the purpose of illustrating that even in North America, where the African-descended were viewed as furthest from their African roots in cultural terms vis-à-vis other black populations throughout the Americas, there exists significant evidence for African-derived cultural forms, with religion as a major component. The discourse was then charged with references to "Africanisms" and "retentions" and "survivals," often references to discrete objects or words. Herskovits would face criticism in E. Franklin Frazier's magisterial *Negro in the United States,* in which the retention argument was downplayed (or dismissed). In some ways the debate reflects the differing methodologies of a path-breaking anthropologist (Herskovits) and a similarly positioned sociologist (Frazier). The debate may also incorporate the politics of the day, with African retentions viewed as antithetical to integrationist aspirations. However this initial dispute is characterized, subsequent scholarship positing ongoing cultural connections between Africa and the Americas remains tethered, even when engaged in refutation, to Herskovits's pioneering work.

Probably one of the more significant publications to emphasize the influence of African religion among the enslaved in the Americas is Margaret Washington Creel's A *"Peculiar People": Slave Religion and Community-Culture among the Gullahs.* Creel breaks new ground in the history of African Americans by demonstrating the connections between cultural precursors in Sierra Leone and consequent expressions among the Gullah of South Carolina and Georgia, and among her most important findings were identifications of configurations within slave society that continued to adhere to the contours of secret societies in Sierra Leone. Heretofore, the African secret society as an organizing principle in North America was not a feature about which many scholars could comment in any detail, and for most, it was not even conceptualized. To be sure, Creel's work operates within a context of a developing Christian tradition among the Gullah, but her work shows how what is ostensibly (and arguably substantively) Christian had in fact been Africanized notionally, organizationally, and liturgically. In some ways Creel is responding to the pioneering work of Albert Raboteau, whose *Slave Religion: The "Invisible Institution" in the Antebellum South,* though very important, tends to discount or understate the influence of African religions in North America. As such, her work is consistent with that of Gwendolyn Midlo Hall's *Africans in Colonial Louisiana,* which, although it does not dwell on religion, nevertheless effectively underscores African cultural influences in the lower Mississippi during the colonial period. It can be said that Hall and Creel promote what can be called "the African thesis" as it applies to the subject of religion; that is, African religions as they were formulated within Africa have been crucial to the subsequent emergence of religious expressions in the Americas. Generally, the African thesis takes two forms: either African religions are reconstituted in altered but recognizable forms in the Americas and remain essentially African religions, or Christianity, as practiced by the enslaved, is so imbued with African sensibilities and ontological meaning that Christianity itself is altered, or Africanized. The African thesis gives way to such anthropologically explicatory strategies as "syncretisms" and "dualisms," both of which view the relationship between African religions and Christianity as processual.

Other critical works that address the question of African influence upon the religion of the enslaved in North America include the seminal *Slave*

Culture by Sterling Stuckey, and Michael Gomez's *Exchanging Our Country Marks*.[1] The latter is very much indebted to the former, in particular the first chapter, "Slavery and the Circle of Culture." That chapter lays out a careful argument, buttressed by documentation from a variety of disciplinary categories, about the ring shout—a worship style among the enslaved, originating in West Central and West Africa. Gomez shows that most participants in the shout were not Christians, but practitioners of African religions who brought their own meanings to the experience. *Exchanging Our Country Marks* seeks to build upon this foundation by looking at specific ethnolinguistic provenances and their impact upon North America. Another important, yet overlooked, contribution to this discussion is the scholarship of Theophus Smith, whose *Conjuring Culture* is an imaginative rethinking of the ways in which the enslaved (and their descendants) engaged with Christianity and the Bible through African cultural lenses. All this, of course, is part of a larger debate over the significance of African culture in the Americas—see Michael A. Gomez's other contribution to this series, "Slavery in the Americas."

There are many references to the religious experiences of the enslaved in the Caribbean and Latin America in histories devoted to those regions, but among those works whose impact on the subject of religion has been most influential, the periodization is not necessarily confined to slavery, but projects forward from that moment to explain phenomena that may yet be observable at the time of publication. Examples include the work of Lydia Cabrera on Cuba, such as *El Monte: Igbo–Fina Ewe Orisha, Vititinfinda; La Sociedad Secreta Abakuá*; and *Anaforuana: Ritual y símbolos de la iniciación en la sociedad Abakuá*, the latter of which in many ways relates to the interests of Creel in secret societies. Cabrera can be employed in conjunction with Fernando Ortiz, *Hampa Afro-Cubano: Los Negros Brujos*, for varying interpretations of related phenomena by studies conducted for very different reasons. For Haiti, key works include Alfred Métraux's *Voodoo in Haiti* and Maya Deren's *Divine Horseman: Voodoo Gods of Haiti*, both of which expanded Jean Price-Mars's "Lemba-Petro: Un culte secret." Herskovits's *Life in a Haitian Valley* remains a useful source.

Bridging the Caribbean and Latin America are works such as William Bascom's *Shango in the New World*, Roger Bastide's *African Civilizations in the New World*, and G. E. Simpson's *Black Religions in the New World*.[2] The latter's *Religious Cults of the Caribbean* is more country and region specific, as is Bastide's *African Religions of Brazil*. Kim Butler's *Freedoms Given, Freedoms Won*, though a study of post-slavery Brazil, nonetheless contains critical insights into the ways in which African-informed religion was socially organized, as does Rachel E. Harding's A *Refuge in Thunder*. The work of Robert Farris Thompson, especially his *Flash of the Spirit*, has been critical to the process by which art historians, historians, anthropologists, artists of every description, philosophers, and so on, have been able to learn of one another's work and see the correlations.[3] Thompson effectively merges all these worlds in his analysis of the contributions of African culture, organized into Mande, Kongo, Yoruba, and Ejagham units, to settings throughout the Americas.

An overview of the ways in which African religions took root in the Americas both during and immediately following slavery, as well as their interaction with Christianity there, is in order. To begin, it is certain that in the Americas the African-born continued to practice religions developed in Africa for significant periods, varying in length of time and in fidelity from locale to locale. Such religions tended to revolve around ethnolinguistic relations, and therefore lacked the more expansive aspirations of monotheisms. Aggregations of the same or similar ethnolinguistic groupings, in conjunction with several other variables such as planter policy and attitude, the nature of the work regime, rural versus town contexts, the continuing arrival of newly captured Africans, etc., could help to maintain the integrity of African religions and facilitate their transfer to successive generations. In many if not most instances, however, the enslaved were eventually forced to confront the meaning of Christianity.

One consequence of that encounter saw a Europeanized Christianity steadily Africanized in worship and perspective. Invariably, therefore, and across the expanse of the Americas, the Christianity practiced by slaves contained a range of African influences often inversely proportionate to status (later, class): the higher the status (class), the less the African influence. In most circumstances, the form of Christianity embraced by the enslaved was one developed for their own purposes, as opposed to an indoctrination imposed by slaving interests. This would depend upon the slaving power in question, however, and what is meant by "Christianization." The Portuguese, for example, regularly baptized captives in West Central Africa and gave them Christian names, without necessarily explaining the meaning of these rituals. This observation is also related to the thesis most notably promoted by John Thornton that many in West Central Africa had been Christians, as part of the Kongo kingdom, for centuries, and long before their exportation to the Americas.[4] If accurate, such an argument would not be inconsistent with Ira Berlin's notion of a "charter generation" of Africans enslaved in the sixteenth and seventeenth centuries, who in many instances had been enculturated in European languages and religion.[5] Even if accepted, such a position does not come to terms with the subsequent arrival of many more Africans in the eighteenth and nineteenth centuries who were not so enculturated — millions of people who came practicing their own religions. As a result, the practices of hoodoo and voodoo, analogues derivative of West and West Central African religions, extended from times of slavery and permeated the beliefs of peasant and working-class black Christians in the American South, whose religious services were in any event charged with song and dance and possession by the Holy Ghost. In the English-speaking Caribbean, Christianity was often infused with substantial African content and connected with *obeah* and *myalism.* The religions of *convince* and *kumina* also developed, the former involving respect for the Christian deity, but also an active veneration of the spirits of African and maroon ancestors by practitioners known as Bongo men. *Kumina,* otherwise known as *pukumina* or *pocomania,* also venerates ancestors, who rank after sky gods and earth deities.

In Brazil and Cuba, on the other hand, expressions of African religions were often articulated with a degree of specificity in which connections with West Africa were undeniably demonstrable. While African religions were certainly carried into Brazil, for example, during the period of enslavement, J. Lorand Matory, in "The English Professors of Brazil," has argued that practices documented in the twentieth century were not necessarily transferred pristinely across successive generations within Brazil, but were instead affected by interventions that saw Brazilians return to West Africa, where they acquired knowledge and skills that were then redeployed in Brazil. This is an important argument that goes beyond religion per se and contests standing assumptions about the linear nature of the African Diaspora's unfolding, but it does not disrupt the perspective that enslaved Africans entering Brazil maintained the concept of distinct ethnolinguistic groupings by pursuing, as one strategy, religious traditions peculiar to their lands of origin. At the same time, and in the complex society that would become Brazil, the reality was that groups intermingled, borrowing ideas from one another while retaining the concept of distinct communities, or *nações* ("nations"). As the black population became predominantly *crioulo* (Brazilian-born) and stratified along lines of color gradation during the nineteenth century (with *prêtos*, or "blacks," and *pardos*, or intermediate shades, as the basic divisions), persons born in Bahia and elsewhere began to choose a *nação*. This was significant, as those who made such choices were also choosing an African identity and an African religion. The various *nações*, such as the Nagôs (Yoruba) and Jêjes (Aja-Ewe-Fon), maintained distinctive religious traditions, which can collectively be referred to as *candomblé*. The various African traditions, associated with specific *nações*, were centered upon *terreiros*, large round spaces surrounded by wooden seats and covered with palm-leaf roofs. Originating in private houses, the *terreiros* expanded to separate plots of land during the first half of the twentieth century, facilitating the pursuit of *candomblé* as a way of life with minimal outside interference. As such, the *terreiros* became centers not only of African religion but also of African culture. As Kim Butler's *Freedoms Given, Freedoms Won* makes clear, women were the principal leaders of *candomblé*; perhaps the most famous of the *terreiros* in Bahia, Ilê Iyá Nassô or Engenho Velho, was founded around 1830 by women from the Yoruba town of Ketu. *Terreiros* were established in the late nineteenth and early twentieth centuries by women of considerable financial means, including Eugenia Anna dos Santos, or Aninha, who founded the *terreiro* of Ilê do Axe Opô Afonjá in 1910. Hers is a fascinating example of the mutability of ethnic identity in Bahia, as she was initiated into the Nagô tradition at Ilê Iyá Nassô, but her African-born parents were non-Yoruba.

The Social Rule of Religion

All these various *candomblé* houses were associated with *irmandades*, providing burial benefits and unemployment assistance at a time when state relief either did not exist or was woefully insufficient. Examples include the Bôa Morte ("Good Death") sisterhood and the Senhor dos Martírios ("Lord of the Martyrs") brotherhood of the Nagôs, and the Bom Jesus das Necessidades e Redenção dos Homens Prêtos ("Good Jesus of the Needs and Redemption of Black Men") of the Jêjes. The affiliation of the brotherhoods/sisterhoods with specific *terreiros* underscores an important feature of *candomblé*: its connection to the Catholic church. Indeed, the multiple *orishas* or deities of *candomblé*, such as Eshu, Yemanja, Oshun, and Shango, are associated with the various saints and principal figures of Catholicism, useful when *candomblé* needed concealment.

Other African-centered religions include West Central African *macumba* near Rio de Janeiro, and elsewhere the practice of *umbanda*. Together with *convince*, *kumina*, and *candomblé*, these religions feature the common elements of African spiritual entities, sacrifice, drumming and singing, and spirit possession. They parallel the Cuban experience, where research is revealing the importance of such clandestine religious organizations as the *abukuá*, a society originating in the Cross River area of southeastern Nigeria and Cameroon. Cuba is also a center of Yoruba or *lucumí* influence, apparent in the practice of *santería*. Divisions among the African-born and their descendants, which as in Brazil eventually became a matter of choice, were equally preserved in Cuba's system of *naciones*, supported as they were by the respective *cabildos*, the functional equivalents of the Brazilian *irmandades*. Yoruba-based religion can also be found in Trinidad in the religion of *Shango*, in which the Yoruba gods Shango, Yemanja, Eshu, and Ogun are worshiped along with deities of Trinidadian origin.

Of course, an important relational quality of religion was its role in either fortifying or debilitating slavery. Arguably, it did both. For those enslaved persons who embraced a version of Christianity sanctioned by the planter class, the status quo could not have been safer. For those whose orientation toward the divine was informed by African sensibilities, however, whether in conversation with Christianity or not, religion could be a formidable tool of resistance. The very practice of religions that significantly diverged from planter Christianity arguably represents a refutation of the cultural imperatives of an emerging West. The embrace of the *orishas* in Brazil, or even stealing away to conduct a clandestine, Africanized worship service in the wilderness of North America, constituted resistance, as did the employment of charms to ward off disease and punishment, a ubiquitous practice throughout the Americas.

Religion's role in resistance becomes strikingly clear in the instance of servile insurrection. One of the best known examples is that of François Makandal, the illustrious maroon leader in Saint Domingue. His background is rather curious, as he was supposedly born into an Islamic society in West Africa, raised as a Muslim, and literate in Arabic (which raises the question of Islam's presence in the Americas, which will be addressed shortly). Captured at the age of twelve and shipped to Saint Domingue, his grounding in Islam may have been incomplete, for by the time we encounter him on the island, Makandal is a fully emerged voodoo priest. Voodoo, *vodu*, and *vodun* derive from Dahomean words for "gods"; the religion as practiced in Haiti, Martinique, Louisiana, and Mississippi represents both a transformation and amalgamation of various religions from West and West Central Africa, specifically Fon-Ewe-Yoruba influences from the former and Bakongo elements from the latter. An eloquent man with extensive knowledge of both medicinal and injurious properties of plants and herbs, Makandal developed a following of undetermined size. In concert with those who systematically pillaged estates, he developed a conspiracy to destroy slavery as an institution, and recruited from the plantations. As Carolyn Fick's *The Making of Haiti: The Saint Domingue Revolution from Below* makes clear, the blow for freedom was to begin with a general poisoning of the water in the town of Le Cap, highlighting poisoning as a weapon of choice among the enslaved in Saint Domingue. A member of Makandal's group betrayed him before a large-scale revolt could begin. Makandal was arrested in early 1758, and after a brief but sensational escape, he was recaptured and burned at the stake. His career was an indication, however, of epic events to come forty years later. The revolution that would ultimately arrive saw the forces of marronage combine with those on the plantation to effect sweeping change. Central to the revolution was the role of religion. As C. L. R. James's *The Black Jacobins: Toussaint L'Ouverture and the San Domingo Revolution* has so eloquently demonstrated, the Haitian Revolution was launched with a voodoo ceremony. The leaders of the conspiracy included Dutty Boukman, a voodoo priest, and Cécile Fatiman, a voodoo high priestess or *mambo* described as a "green-eyed mulatto woman with long silken black hair." In the dense forest of Bois-Caïman, she and Boukman officiated at a solemn voodoo ceremony for the conspirators that was not unlike the "Damnation Oath" in Antigua, to which we now turn our attention.

According to David Barry Gaspar's *Bondsmen and Rebels*, the 1736 conspiracy that engulfed the whole of Antigua was led by Court (or Tackey), along with Tomboy. An Akan speaker and a creole, respectively, they were assisted by Obbah (Aba) and Queen, both Akan women who provided critical leadership in facilitating the "Damnation Oath," a ceremony derived from Akan traditions in which the insurrectionists committed themselves by drinking rooster blood, cemetery dirt, and rum, among other elements. Court had been crowned by two thousand of the enslaved as the "king of the Coromantees," the basis of which was the Akan *ikem* ceremony, a tradition preparing participants for war. Queen, in turn, may have been Court's principal advisor, playing the same role as the queen-mother or *ohemaa* in Akan society. While the conspiracy was exposed before it could be executed, planters were astonished that not only the enslaved, but many free blacks and "mulattoes" were also implicated. Again, African religion was central to the conspiracy.

In North America, Vincent Harding, in *There is a River: The Black Struggle for Freedom in America*, has examined slave revolts and their relationship to religion in a comparative fashion. According to Pearson's *Designs against Charleston*, the Denmark Vesey conspiracy of 1822 developed in the urban setting of Charleston and demonstrates both the importance of religion as well as the interconnectedness of the African Diaspora by the early nineteenth century. A fifty-five-year-old seafarer who purchased his freedom in 1800, Vesey, born either in the Caribbean or Africa, organized a revolt that took into consideration differences among the enslaved. He formed columns of distinct groups, such as the Igbo and Gullah (West Central Africans and/

or Gola from West Africa). African religious practices and Christianity were both observed out of respect for diversity, as Vesey himself was both conversant with the Bible and a class leader (religious instructor) in the African Church at Charleston. In fact, most of the conspiracy leaders were also class leaders. Having "studied the Bible a great deal," Vesey on the one hand premised his antislavery arguments upon that holy document, and on the other demonstrated his own respect for African culture by his elevation of Gullah Jack, a "conjure man," as his lieutenant. Vesey also invoked the Haitian Revolution, maintaining that help would arrive from that island and from Africa itself, if only those in and around Charleston would take the initiative. All this suggests that Vesey's followers, possibly as many as nine thousand, could grasp his vision of a black world in which the cause of freedom transcended divisions of birthplace and language, but also in which religion was a crucial element.

Anyone familiar with David Walker's 1829 *Appeal . . . to the Coloured Citizens of the World* can attest to the religious content and underpinning of not only his antislavery sentiment but also his call for insurrection. He may also even have been in Charleston at the time of the Vesey conspiracy. Walker died in Boston under very suspicious circumstances the following year, but Nat Turner answered his summons, launching a large-scale revolt in August 1831 in Southampton, Virginia. A religious man and mystic, Turner interpreted that year's solar eclipse in February as the divine signal for the apocalypse and launched the revolt on August 21. Within twenty-four hours, some sixty whites were killed, including Turner's owner and family. When the smoke cleared, an estimated two hundred blacks, many of whom had nothing to do with the revolt, had been killed. Captured on October 30, Turner was executed on November 11. Scot French has written on Turner in his *The Rebellious Slave*, and Kenneth Greenberg—in *The Confessions of Nat Turner and Related Documents*, and *Nat Turner: A Slave Rebellion in History and Memory*—has assembled useful documents and commentary.

Certainly one of the most important slave insurrections in Latin American history was that which occurred in Brazil. The 1835 Malê (Muslim) revolt, written about exhaustively by João José Reis—see *Slave Rebellion in Brazil*—involved Muslims from what are now northern and southwestern

HORRID MASSACRE IN VIRGINIA.

The Scenes which the above Plate is designed to represent are—Fig. 1, a Mother intreating for the lives of her children.—2. Mr. Travis, cruelly murdered by his own Slaves.—3. Mr. Barrow, who bravely defended himself until his wife escaped.—4. A comp. of mounted Dragoons in pursuit of the Blacks.

A newspaper print graphically details the murder of white plantation owners, and the hunting down of the perpetrators by dragoons, during Nat Turner's Rebellion in Virginia, 1831. Turner, a thirty-one-year-old preacher and slave, claimed he had received visions urging him to rise up. Turner and seven of his fellow slaves stole into his master's house on the night of August 21, and killed the entire family. When they had finished, the gang moved on to the next house, their numbers eventually growing to around seventy-five. Some sixty white people were killed before Turner and his associates were hunted down by militia. Many people in authority blamed the killings on the spread of seditious ideas from outside of the Southern states, and introduced strict laws forbidding slaves from receiving any form of education, including teaching them to read or write. Turner himself was hanged on November 11, 1831.

Nigeria who had been imported into the province of Bahia. The Hausa ethnolinguistic group had long been Muslims in northern Nigeria, and had been implicated in revolts in Bahia dating back to 1807. Enslaved and free Hausa plotted together, and the two leaders of the conspiracy were executed. Two years later, in January 1809, almost three hundred slaves, again mostly Hausa, attacked the town of Nazaré das Farinhas in search of food and weapons. The

1809 revolt saw increased non-Hausa participation, so-called *Jêje*, or Aja-Fon-Ewe, from Dahomey, and *Nagôs*, or Yoruba, from what is now southwestern Nigeria. Between 1810 and 1818 there were three more revolts of significance, the second of which involved Nagôs under Hausa leadership headed by a *malomi* or *malaam*, a Muslim religious leader. The revolts continued with regularity through the 1820s to 1835.

It was in 1835 that the insurrection took place of the so-called *Malês*, a term referring to African Muslims who were by then mostly Nagôs rather than Hausa. Islam had become an important religion in Bahia, but it was not the dominant religion among blacks, nor were all Nagôs Muslim. In January of 1835, up to five hundred Africans, enslaved and free, mostly Muslim, took to the streets of Salvador. The plan called for the conspirators to link with the enslaved in the surrounding plantations, but betrayal forced them to begin the uprising prematurely. Brutally repressed, with over seventy killed, the Malê revolt revealed the importance of Islam and an impressive level of Arabic literacy among the participants, who wore distinctive clothing, maintained their own religious schools, and observed Islamic rituals such as fasting during Ramadan. The 1835 revolt also suggests that participating Africans rejected the notion of race, preferring their own ethnolinguistic identities. The rebels sought to kill not only whites, but also "mulattoes" and *crioulos* (creoles, or Brazilian-born blacks), a reflection not only of racial ambiguities but also of significant cultural differences. The 1835 revolt, therefore, was a Muslim-led, mostly Nagô effort that targeted whites and Brazilian blacks while also rejecting Africans from Congo and Angola for cultural and religious reasons. In the end, hundreds were sent to the galleys, imprisoned, lashed, or expelled from Bahia, some returning to West Africa.

Reference to enslaved Muslims in Brazil raises the question of their presence elsewhere in the Americas, and indeed they were virtually everywhere, in varying numbers and significance, relative to place and period. There were significant Muslim communities in such places as Jamaica, Trinidad, and Saint Domingue. Regarding the first two islands, evidence suggests that Muslim communities were well formed and had become closely knit by the early decades of the nineteenth century, and that many had purchased their freedom through the collective efforts and resource-pooling strategies of the community. In fact, some Muslims were themselves slaveholders and, with the approach of Apprenticeship in the British-held Caribbean in 1834, repeatedly sought to return to West Africa. Yacine Daddi Addoun and Paul Lovejoy have edited an extant record written by a Jamaican Muslim in Jamaica—"The Arabic Manuscript of Muhammad Kaba Saghanughu of Jamaica, c. 1823," while Carl Campbell has written about Muslims in Trinidad in his "John Mohammed Bath." In Saint Domingue, however, Muslims appear in the sixteenth and seventeenth centuries as rebels and maroons, often making common cause with the indigenous population. There is also some evidence of Muslim participation in the Haitian Revolution. Muslims were also present in North America and were concentrated along the Georgia-Carolina coast and Sea Islands, as Michael A. Gomez's "Muslims in Early America" attests. Like their coreligionists in Trinidad and Jamaica, these Muslims were associated with relatively quietist activities rather than rebellion. Interestingly, the Islamic tradition would somehow survive and return to prominence in North America in the twentieth century.

The Role of Non-African Religions

Of course, religion played an important role in the abolition movements throughout the Americas. Religious treatises, such as James G. Birney's *Letter to the Churches: to the Ministers and Elders of the Presbyterian Church in Kentucky on the Sin of Holding Slaves and the Duty of Immediate Emancipation,* and Theodore Weld's *The Bible against Slavery: An Inquiry into the Patriarchal and Mosaic Systems on the Subject of Human Rights* railed against the institution. Black abolitionists also had their own newspapers, including the first black newspaper, *Freedom's Journal,* published in 1827 by John Russwurm and Samuel Cornish.

Religion would continue to serve as a basis for revolt in the post-slavery period. Perhaps the best example of this is the account of Paul Bogle in Jamaica. In 1865, the people of Stony Gut, a St. Thomas Parish farming village located on land leased by blacks following Apprenticeship, refused to continue paying rent to Morant Bay magistrates, claiming squatters' rights instead—a decision informed by desperate economic times that were exacerbated by royal and colonial government indifference. When local planters tried to evict them, Bogle, a deacon in the Native Baptist Church of the Stony Gut community, called for revolt. Following the rescue of a fellow farmer on trial in Morant Bay, members of Stony Gut violently resisted the arrest of the rescuers. Bogle's response was not only shaped by Christian beliefs, but by an apparent residual African spirituality as well, as he and his followers took an oath with clear resemblances to the Akan-based rituals observable during slave uprisings. On October 10 they marched into Morant Bay, vowing to kill repressive whites while saving white sympathizers, and took control of St. Thomas Parish for three days. Bogle would be captured and hanged on a British gunboat on October 24, along with over one thousand other blacks.

Speaking of another form of resistance, many of the leaders of an inchoative Pan-Africanism were Christian ministers. They include Henry Highland Garnet, whose grandfather was Mandinka and whose immediate family escaped slavery in Maryland in the 1820s. In his "Address to the Slaves of the United States," Garnet called for armed revolt against the slaveocracy, citing Toussaint L'Ouverture as an example to be emulated. (Frederick Douglass, who initially opposed Garnet's call for revolt, later reversed his position.) Garnet further revealed a diasporic perspective in predicting that the islands of the Caribbean would eventually be "ours" (a reference to blacks in the Caribbean, not North America), and by his organization of the Cuban Anti-Slavery Committee in 1873. He completed the circle in his voyage to West Africa in 1882, where he died and remains buried. His contemporaries Alexander Crummell, Martin R. Delany, and Henry McNeal Turner all favored black emigration to either Africa or Central and South America, convinced that they would never be fully free in the United States. Edward W. Blyden, born in St. Thomas, Virgin Islands, was also a minister who repatriated to West Africa in the 1860s, becoming a leading force in establishing educational institutions in Liberia and Sierra Leone. Blyden, a brilliant scholar and wonderful writer, was something of an enigma. It may be that his experience in West Africa changed him, for although he remained a Christian minister, his regard for Islam was considerable, as his writings attest. In touting Islam as the means through which Africa would achieve "civilization," his conviction that Islam would also bring Africans to Christianity may have been lacking in depth. Sterling Stuckey, in *The Ideological Origins of Black Nationalism,* and Hollis Lynch, in *Edward Wilmot Blyden: Pan-Negro Patriot, 1832–1912,* have written important and foundational works on these individuals and their ideas.

The early Pan-Africanists, however, were mired in something of a profound contradiction over the matter of religion. Despite their professed (and no doubt genuine) love of their fellow black people and concern for the continent of Africa, they saw the latter in cultural terms that were nearly identical to the perspective of most whites. That is, Africa was perceived as benighted and in need of cultural transformation through its Christianization. Individuals such as Garnet, who had initially opposed the American Colonization Society (founded in 1816), later grew to favor black emigration to Africa (or elsewhere outside the United States) and founded the African Civilization Society in 1859 to such an end. Crummell supported him, with Douglass in dissent. The civilizing mission among the African-descended reveals a profound disconnection between the African religions of the folk and the religions of the more erudite, who embraced the folk while eschewing their culture. Tunde Adeleke, in *UnAfrican Americans: Nineteenth-Century Black Nationalists and the Civilizing Mission,* has contributed significant commentary on this matter.

The dawn of the twentieth century therefore saw the maturation of multiple expressions of religion among the African-descended in the Americas. In English-speaking countries, the more Western-educated tended to favor forms of Protestantism free of African influences, as the latter were seen as backward, whereas the lower strata embraced variants of an Africanized Protestantism without always being aware of the African influences. Concomitantly, in places such as Haiti and Louisiana, the presence of the Catholic Church facilitated an ongoing and conscious engagement with the *loas,* an amalgam of deities from West and West Central Africa. Worship of the *orishas* in Cuba and Brazil was equally facilitated and just as powerful, if not more so. The African deities had successfully survived slavery.

It was also the case, however, that the early twentieth century saw the rise of new religions in the Americas, typically taken from the fabrics of Islamic-Judeo-Christian traditions and woven into entirely novel patterns, informed by a vision of Africa as a historical power and, at least in one instance, a future destination. Perhaps its most innovative example is the Rastafarian movement. Useful sources on the Rastafari include Ennis Barrington Edmonds's *Rastafari: From Outcasts to Culture Bearers*, Barry Chevanne's *Rastafari: Roots and Ideology*, and Nathaniel Samuel Murrell et al.'s *Chanting Down Babylon: The Rastafari Reader*. Horace Campbell's *Rasta and Resistance* covers territory that extends beyond Rastafarianism, and does so from a Marxist perspective—see the chapter "Man in the Hills: Rasta, the Jamaican State, and the Ganja Trade"—whereas Velma Pollard's *Dread Talk: The Language of Rastafari* focuses on its language.

The onerous economic struggle in the Caribbean not only produced emigration, labor unionism, and social unrest, but also conditions in which the sufferers reenvisioned themselves within an international context. Incessant emigration and subordination to colonial empire generated within the Caribbean a transnational perspective, contributing specifically to the belief among the downtrodden in Jamaica that there was a special connection between the Diaspora and Ethiopia. Leonard Percival Howell, experienced in foreign travel, returned to Jamaica in 1932 to proclaim that black Jamaicans should no longer offer their loyalty to England, but to the emperor of Ethiopia, Ras ("Lord") Tafari Makonnen, crowned in November of 1932 and given the throne name Haile Selassie I. The idea that a black man was a sovereign ruler, at a time when most of African descent were under colonial rule in both Africa and the Americas, stirred the collective African imagination. Howell, Archibald Dunkley, and Joseph Hibbert further held that because black Jamaicans belonged to an African nation under Haile Selassie, they should not pay taxes to England.

The 1935 Italian invasion of Ethiopia was a watershed event in the history of the African Diaspora. All around the world, people of African descent were scandalized by the occupation of this ancient, biblically related land and rallied to support the Ethiopian cause. A remarkable, formative moment, the response to the invasion demonstrated the importance of Africa to the struggles of persons thousands of miles and hundreds of years removed from its shores. The invasion also strengthened the position of Howell and his associates. In 1937 the Ethiopian World Federation was founded by a Dr. Malaku Bayen in

Robert Nesta Marley was born in Saint Ann, Jamaica, in February of 1945. When he died of a malignant melanoma in May 1981, aged 36, Marley had become one of reggae music's greatest exponents, and an instantly recognizable figure throughout the world. As a child born to a black mother and a white father, living in the Jamaican capital Kingston, Marley's early life was isolated—shunned by Jamaica's white society, but not fully accepted by its black community. Aged 14 he left home to pursue a career in music, and in the early 1960s he teamed up with Bunny Wailer, a close friend from his days at the Stepney All Age School, and Peter Tosh to form a reggae band. Their first major hit single, "Simmer Down," released in February 1964, went straight to number one in Jamaica's music charts, and heralded a string of hit records. However, many of their live performances were accompanied by crowd disturbances, and after a promising start the Wailers were dropped from radio playlists, and in 1966 the band split up. Within two years they had reformed again, and began recording a wealth of new material, gaining for the first time recognition from outside the Jamaican music scene. In 1972 the band signed to Island Records, and a series of hit records followed, bringing further international acclaim. Marley's burgeoning reputation began to attract attention from established mainstream stars, with Eric Clapton covering his "I Shot the Sheriff" in 1974. The following year, the Wailers themselves made their mainstream breakthrough, with "No Woman, No Cry" entering the UK's top 40. The American market proved harder to break into, and Marley was on the verge of undertaking a major tour across the United States, when he was diagnosed with cancer. A devout follower of the Rastafarian faith, he refused medical help from most doctors and died in hospital in Miami. He is photographed here in the late 1970s.

New York City to promote Ethiopia's liberation, linking it to the fortunes of black folk everywhere. The Federation elevated Haile Selassie as the "Elect of God" and maintained that Africans were the Twelve Tribes of Israel.

The British persecuted and imprisoned Howell and his followers, who in 1940 had established a commune at Pinnacle in the hills of St. Catherine, Jamaica. Released from prison in 1943, Howell led a process through which the tenets of the Rastafari were gradually worked out. Haile Selassie acquired divine status, and the capitalist, imperialist system was identified as Babylon — its rejection symbolized by uncombed, coiled hair known as dreadlocks, symbolizing the mane of the Lion of Judah (one of Haile Selassie's titles), and by the use of ganja (marijuana) and the pipe, introduced to the Caribbean from India. Africans and their descendants were the true Israel, and Ethiopia the promised land, to which the Rasta would eventually return. The Pinnacle was repeatedly raided by the authorities, and Howell was placed in a mental asylum more than once. The Rastafari movement became an international phenomenon, however, influencing the anticolonial struggle and giving rise to a deeply political and spiritual reggae, perhaps best expressed in the artistry (or prophetic office) of Bob Marley.

While the Rastafari borrowed from Judeo-Christian traditions, innovations in the United States engaged with these traditions as well as Islam, forging movements that, while entirely novel in theory and practice, were politically similar to the Rastafari in their anticolonialism and advocacy for the black poor. It was a moment of spectacular developments, with the Great Migration being among the most important. In 1910, some seven million black folk lived in the American South, compared with less than one million throughout the rest of the country. Over one million of them left the South for the North between 1916 to 1930, with half that number, over 400,000, moving during an intense two-year period between 1916 and 1918, coterminous with the United States' involvement in World War I. The northern interest in black labor is explained, of course, by the precipitous decline in foreign immigration from 1.2 million in 1914 to 110,000 in 1918. Fleeing white criminality and the state-supported racism known as Jim Crow, fleeing economic hardship and the ravages of the boll weevil — heavy infestations of which devastated millions of acres of cotton fields in Alabama, Georgia, and Mississippi — black migrants flooded northern cities, exponentially increasing their presence. However, while many jobs taken by blacks were in manufacturing industries, these positions were at the lowest level and called for unskilled and semiskilled labor. Career choices for black women were particularly constricted, as they were confined to largely domestic occupations as laundresses, maids, and cooks. Deplorable living conditions further exacerbated matters; deferred dreams translated into the many living in impoverished, overcrowded, health-debilitating pockets of northern Jim Crow.

A surfeit of organizations emerged to address these challenges, some of which actually began in the South. Many of these organizations either trumpeted claims to a connection with Africa of some fundamental sort, or were centered around a set of religious principles divergent from conventional beliefs and practices, or both. It was an age of unorthodoxy.

Early but important works that cover this period include Arna Bontemps and Jack Conroy's *Anyplace But Here* and Arthur Huff Fauset's *Black Gods of the Metropolis: Negro Religious Cults of the Urban North.*[6] Some examples include Dupont Bell, who founded a movement outside Savannah, Georgia, around 1899, in which he was worshipped as a "self-proclaimed son of God." Although he would be committed to an asylum, he would be followed by such individuals as Father George W. Hurley, born in 1884 in Reynolds, Georgia. In 1923, Hurley founded the Universal Hagar's Spiritual Church, and by 1941, two years before his death, he boasted a membership of 185,000 spread through ninety-five churches—a highly suspect claim. He taught that blacks were the "first people in the world" and the original Hebrews, that they spoke the "original" language of Arabic and were the architects of high civilizations and hieroglyphics, and that they were the most industrious people on earth. Identifying whites as "Gentiles" and the descendants of Cain, "cursed with a pale color because of leprosy," Father Hurley instructed his followers to refer to themselves as "Black" or "Ethiopian," as opposed to the pejorative "Negro," and to eschew interracial marriage. "Contemptuous" of so-called mulattoes, Hurley proscribed pork and alcohol (although he permitted "wine in moderation" for special religious occasions) and flew his own version of the red, black, and green (the colors of Marcus Garvey's Universal Negro Improvement Association flag).

OPPOSITE: Elijah Muhammad (photographed here in 1960), whose original name was Elijah Poole, was one of the major figures in the development of the Nation of Islam. Born on October 7, 1897, to a family of sharecroppers and former slaves in Sandersville, Georgia, Poole witnessed three lynchings before the age of twenty. He married Clara Evans in 1917, moved to Detroit in 1923, and worked in an automobile factory. Sometime about 1930 he became acquainted with Wallace D. Fard, founder of the Nation of Islam, who was impressed with the younger man and renamed him Elijah Muhammad. Fard appointed him his assistant at Temple No. 1, and when the "Minister of Islam" disappeared in 1934, Muhammad took over control of the movement. Internal strife led him to move to Chicago and establish Temple No. 2. Between 1942 and 1946 Muhammad was incarcerated because of his opposition to the Selective Service Act. Following World War II he attracted members to the Nation of Islam by advocating the establishment of a separate nation for African Americans and the belief that blacks are the chosen people of Allah. He frequently referred to white people as "blue-eyed devils." In later years he toned down the separatist rhetoric and emphasized the need for self-help in the black community. During the Civil Rights Movement in the 1960s his most prominent pupil was Malcolm X. However, they developed philosophical differences, and Malcolm X decided to break with Muhammad, especially after discovering his mentor's proclivity for extramarital affairs. The Nation of Islam was heavily implicated in the assassination of Malcolm X in 1965, and its membership declined somewhat thereafter. When Muhammad died on February 25, 1975 in Chicago, his son Warith Deen, or Wallace, took over leadership of the movement. A splinter group with the same name was later formed under Louis Farrakhan.

There were other spiritual contemporaries operating in eastern cities who similarly claimed either divine or special status. They often had ties to the South, including Georgia and the Carolinas, as was the case with Bishop Ida Robinson, who in 1924 founded the Mt. Sinai Holy Church of America in Philadelphia. Then, of course, there was George Baker, a native of Georgia, who originally came to Long Island and Manhattan in 1914, where he was transfigured into Father Divine and established the Father Divine Peace Mission Movement, with a significant following. Bishop Charles Emmanuel "Daddy" Grace," said to be "Negro and Portuguese" in identity, founded the United House of Prayer for All People in Charlotte, North Carolina, in 1925, and likewise acquired a sizable retinue. The leaders of these churches, while approximating or replicating the prerogatives of divinity assumed by Father Hurley, did not necessarily emulate his association with Africa. In this vein,

Hulton Archive / Getty Images

Prophet F. S. Cherry's Church of God in Philadelphia was one of many different black Jewish sects in the North; at least eight could be found in Harlem between 1919 and 1931.

In some contrast to the foregoing were movements launched in North America that drew upon Islamic rather than Christian principles. The Moorish Science Temple of America, possibly founded in Newark, New Jersey, by Noble Drew Ali as early as 1913, offered the startling proposition that African Americans were in fact Moors from Morocco, and as such were part of a larger "Asiatic" community of persons that essentially included everyone except Europeans. The claim of Moorish ancestry, like the claims of the Rastafari, linked the Diaspora back to Africa; but the Asiatic identification suggests a concern that was not limited to Africa. Unlike the Rastafari, Noble Drew Ali never advocated a physical return to Morocco. As Moors, his followers adopted Islam as their religion, but it was unorthodox; Noble Drew Ali penned his own *Holy Koran of the Moorish Science Temple of America: 7*, or *Circle Seven Koran*, drawing upon metaphysical beliefs foreign to conventional Islam. He died under mysterious circumstances in 1929, by which time another neo-Islamic movement was taking root.

The Nation of Islam, founded in Detroit by Wallace D. Fard Muhammad in 1930, certainly employed Noble Drew Ali's notion of an international Asiatic identity, but went much further in its denunciation of Europeans, identifying them as "devils." Indeed, the Nation rejected the principles of sanctioned religion as such, dismissing the idea of an afterlife and the conception of God and Satan as spiritual beings—positing instead that just as whites were devils, blacks were divine, with Fard Muhammad as Allah. The Nation's identification with Africa was not as strong as that of the Moors and the Rastas, however, for although members were given an "X" or an equivalent variable to represent the African name lost through enslavement, the original home of blacks was not Africa but Mecca, from where they had later migrated to "East Asia" or Egypt, and then to other parts of the African continent. The Nation embraced a variant of Islam in conflict with many of the latter's central tenets, including the claim that Elijah Muhammad, Fard Muhammad's successor after the latter's disappearance in 1934, was a messenger of God. With the death of Elijah Muhammad in February 1975, the movement splintered into several factions, with some either embracing or moving towards orthodoxy.

The racialism of the Nation of Islam reversed the assumptions and values of the day. Blackness, long associated by whites with evil, immorality, filth, and worthlessness, became the embodiment of holiness, cleanliness, morality, and self-confidence. The Nation's emphasis on hard work and economic self-reliance was the means by which a disproportionate number of its members achieved middle-class status, and provided a model for black economic development. At the same time, the Nation's early years were very much influenced by global conflict, and by its support of Japan during World War II. An early form of black nationalism, the Nation saw white racism as a phenomenon separate from capitalist venture, condemning the former while embracing the latter; indeed, the Nation was generally opposed to leftist movements, and as such differed in quality from the more radical Rastafari. The Nation of Islam and the Moorish Science Temple of America were also mutual-aid societies. Claude Andrew Clegg III's *An Original Man* is an exhaustive reflection on Elijah Muhammad, while the latter's *Message to the Blackman in America* and his *Theology of Time* provide unmediated access to his thinking. Beynon's "The Voodoo Cult among Negro Migrants in Detroit" furnishes a fascinating glimpse into the Nation of Islam in its earliest years. It was the scholarship of E. U. Essien-Udom and C. Eric Lincoln, however, that set the bar for standards of scholarship on the Nation and organizations like it.[7] Works related but not limited to the Nation are Aminah Beverly McCloud's *African American Islam*, and Richard Brent Turner's *Islam in the African-American Experience*.

The Civil Rights Movement and Religion

The rise of the Civil Rights Movement in the United States was clearly affected by black Christian ministers and laity. The 1956 Supreme Court decision that declared Alabama bus segregation laws unconstitutional signaled the emergence of twenty-seven-year-old Dr. Martin Luther King Jr., who had led the boycott while pastoring Dexter Avenue Baptist Church. In founding the Southern Christian Leadership Conference (SCLC) in 1957, to challenge segregation throughout the South, King exemplified a kind of Africanization of Christianity, as he drew deeply from the well of black experience to fashion the religion into an implement of liberation. One of the most powerful articulations of his faith was his "Letter from Birmingham Jail." There are numerous works on King, and one could begin with David J. Garrow's *Bearing the Cross: Martin Luther King, Jr., and the Southern Christian Leadership Conference.*

As the Civil Rights Movement intensified, the Congress of Racial Equality (CORE) launched its Freedom Rides in 1961 to test interstate antidiscrimination laws. The Student Nonviolent Coordinating Committee (SNCC), newly formed with the encouragement of the National Association for the Advancement of Colored People (NAACP) veteran Ella Baker, also

© Bob Henriques / Magnum Photos

Christianity played a key part in the Civil Rights Movement, and the relationship was embodied by many of the leading figures, including the Reverend Martin Luther King Jr. Born in Atlanta, Georgia, on January 15, 1929, King graduated from Boston University with a Ph.D. in Systemic Theology in 1955, and was already the pastor of the Dexter Avenue Baptist Church in Montgomery, Alabama. During his education, King had discovered the works of Mohandas Gandhi, a key figure in the struggle for Indian independence. King was particularly impressed by Gandhi's commitment to non-violent methods of protest, and sought to follow his example. Within months of King's arrival at the Dexter Avenue Baptist Church, Rosa Parks (1913–2005) was arrested on December 1, 1955, and charged after refusing to give up her seat for a white man on a public bus. King was a leading figure in organizing the Montgomery Bus Boycott. Inspired by her involvement, and aware of the wider cause that needed to be addressed, King was a founder of the Southern Christian Leadership Conference (SCLC) in 1957 and worked tirelessly throughout the 1960s to champion the cause of equality and freedom. On August 28, 1963, King delivered his "I Have a Dream" speech on the steps beneath the Lincoln Memorial, the final act of the March on Washington for jobs and freedom, and in 1964 he received the Nobel Peace Prize for his work. On April 4, 1968, he was assassinated, gunned down on his hotel balcony while visiting the city of Memphis, Tennessee. He is photographed here preaching in 1960.

contributed Freedom Riders, but SNCC and the SCLC both met with stiff opposition in Albany, Georgia, in 1961, followed in 1963 by the brutality of city commissioner of public safety Eugene "Bull" Connor in Birmingham, Alabama. Albany and Birmingham were setbacks, but on August 28, 1963, the March on Washington drew hundreds of thousands, the highlight of which was King's "I Have a Dream" speech. W. E. B. Du Bois had died in Ghana the day before, perhaps a symbolic passing of the torch. For all their differences, King and Du Bois shared a powerful critique of American capitalism and imperialism, emphasizing their concern for the working classes of all races.

The history of the Civil Rights Movement is often written with an emphasis on leaders, especially men, but the movement was borne by the labor of women who cooked and sold chicken dinners, answered the phones, ran the endless errands, cleaned up after the meetings, and were still able to march in the streets as well as help plan strategy. Many of these women were deeply religious. As for leaders, Fannie Lou Hamer joined Ella Baker as one of the most electrifying, male or female, in her capacity as cofounder of the Mississippi Freedom Democratic Party, and was a powerful orator. Anne Moody, activist in SNCC, CORE, and the NAACP; Daisy Bates, leader of the movement in Little Rock, Arkansas; and Jo Ann Robinson, cofounder of the Montgomery Improvement Association, are just a few of the other women prominent in these movements.

Rejecting the tactics and philosophy of King was Malcolm Little, or Malcolm X. In accepting the Nation of Islam's teachings while in prison, Malcolm was in some ways returning to his origins, as his parents were Garveyites. He turned from a life of crime and became the Nation of Islam's most public and articulate spokesman, an ardent advocate of Black Nationalism, and a student of the larger black world. In keeping with the Nation of Islam's principles, Malcolm ridiculed King's vision of an integrated America, calling for racial separation instead. Malcolm viewed nonviolence as counterintuitive and ineffective, a position from which he never wavered. However, Malcolm renounced the racism of the Nation of Islam once he split with that organization and embraced orthodox Islam in early 1964. At that time, he made a pilgrimage to Mecca, after which he returned to Africa to meet with heads of state and students. It was his ambition to coordinate the struggle for freedom in the United States with those elsewhere in Africa and the Diaspora. Cautious for the most part, civil rights leaders began organizing a meeting between King and Malcolm two weeks before the latter's assassination on February 21, 1965. Malcolm's brilliance and oratory had a profound impact and were the modern basis for the Black Power movement. His *Autobiography*, written with Alex Haley, remains a classic.

Given the foregoing discussion of African American religions throughout the Americas and over time, it is reasonable to conclude that religion, resistance, and political struggle have often been inseparable. Religion has been both an ideological articulation and a veritable force, holding communities of the African-descended together during the most adverse of conditions while supplying a focus around which the collective will could cohere, mobilize, and press forward. This multidimensional expression of religion, touching as it did numerous aspects of the personal and corporate life, defied the trajectory of Western culture as an increasingly compartmentalized collection of experiences, and as such conformed much more closely to an African sensibility with respect to the indomitability of the human condition. Whether lamentable or laudatory, it is in any case striking that religious influences with discernible African origins have directly contributed to a wide range of resistance movements in nearly every American land, in every historical period, from the fifteenth century through the dawn of the twenty-first. Such reflection suggests the need for even greater efforts to interrogate cultures and experiences of populations of African descent as sites of linkage and connection.

· ·

NOTES

1. See Stuckey, "Introduction."
2. See Simpson, "Neo-African Religions of Ancestral Cults of the Caribbean and South America."
3. See Thompson, "The Sign of the Four Moments of the Sun."
4. See Thornton, "On the Trail of Voodoo."

5. See Berlin, *Many Thousands Gone.*
6. See Bontemps and Conroy, "Registered with Allah."
7. See Essien-Udom, "The Nationalist Tradition"; Lincoln, *Black Muslims in America.*

BIBLIOGRAPHY

Addoun, Yacine Daddi, and Paul Lovejoy. *The Arabic Manuscript of Muhammad Kaba Saghanughu of Jamaica, c. 1823.* 2002: Available at http://yorku.ca/nhp/shadd/kaba/index.asp.

Adeleke, Tunde. *UnAfrican Americans: Nineteenth-Century Black Nationalists and the Civilizing Mission.* Lexington: University of Kentucky, 1998.

Ali, Noble Drew. *The Holy Koran of the Moorish Science Temple of America: 7.* [1927] 1996. Available at http://www.hermetic.com/bey/7koran.html.

Bascom, William. *Shango in the New World.* Austin, Tex.: African and Afro-American Research Institute, 1972.

Bastide, Roger. *The African Religions of Brazil.* Baltimore, Md.: Johns Hopkins University Press, 1978.

Bastide, Roger. "Survivals of African Civilizations." In *African Civilizations in the New World,* trans. Peter Green. 1967; New York: Harper and Row, 1971.

Bayoumi, Moustafa Mohamed. "Migrating Islam: Religion, Modernity, and Colonialism." Ph.D. diss., Columbia University, 1998.

Berlin, Ira. *Many Thousands Gone: The First Two Centuries of Slavery in North America.* Cambridge, Mass.: Belknap Press of Harvard University Press, 1998.

Beynon, Erdmann Doane. "The Voodoo Cult among Negro Migrants in Detroit." *American Journal of Sociology* 43 (May 1938): 896–97.

Birney, James G. *Mr. Birney's Letter to the Churches: to the Ministers and Elders of the Presbyterian Church in Kentucky on the Sin of Holding Slaves and the Duty of Immediate Emancipation.* Mercer County, Ky.: N.p., 1834.

Blyden, Edward. "Mohammedanism and the Negro Race." *Fraser's Magazine* (November 1875).

Bontemps, Arna, and Jack Conroy. "Registered with Allah." In *They Seek a City,* revised as *Anyplace But Here.* 1945; New York: Hill and Wang, 1966.

Butler, Kim. *Freedoms Given, Freedoms Won: Afro-Brazilians in Post-Abolition São Paulo and Salvador.* New Brunswick, N.J.: Rutgers University Press, 1998.

Cabrera, Lydia. *Anaforuana: Ritual y símbolos de la iniciación en la sociedad Abakuá.* Havana, Cuba: Ediciones C. R., 1975.

Cabrera, Lydia. *El Monte: Igbo–Fina Ewe Orisha, Vititinfinda.* 1954; Miami: Ediciones Universal, 1992.

Cabrera, Lydia. "El Ñañiguismo en el siglo pasado." In *La Sociedad Secreta Abakuá.* 1959; Miami: Ediciones Universal, 2005.

Campbell, Carl. "John Mohammed Bath and the Free Mandingos in Trinidad: The Question of Their Repatriation to Africa, 1831–38." *Journal of African Studies* 2 (1975/1976): 482–84.

Campbell, Horace. "Man in the Hills: Rasta, the Jamaican State, and the Ganja Trade." In *Rasta and Resistance: From Marcus Garvey to Walter Rodney*. Trenton, N.J.: Africa World Press, 1987.

Chevannes, Barry. *Rastafari: Roots and Ideology*. Syracuse, N.Y.: Syracuse University Press, 1994.

Clegg, Claude Andrew, III. "The Knowledge of Self and Others." In *An Original Man: The Life and Times of Elijah Muhammad*. Boston: St. Martin's Press, 1997.

Creel, Margaret Washington. *A "Peculiar People": Slave Religion and Community-Culture among the Gullahs*. New York: New York University Press, 1988.

Creel, Margaret Washington. "Folk Religion in the Slave Quarters." In *A "Peculiar People": Slave Religion and Community-Culture among the Gullahs*. New York: New York University Press, 1988.

Crummell, Alexander. *Africa and America*. 1891; New York: Negro Universities Press, 1969.

Deren, Maya. *Divine Horseman: Voodoo Gods of Haiti*. New York: Chelsea House Publishers, 1970.

Edmonds, Ennis Barrington. *Rastafari: From Outcasts to Culture Bearers*. Oxford: Oxford University Press, 2003.

Essien-Udom, E. U. "The Nationalist Tradition." In *Black Nationalism: A Search for an Identity in America*. 1962; Chicago: University of Chicago Press, 1971.

Fauset, Arthur Huff. *Black Gods of the Metropolis: Negro Religious Cults of the Urban North*. Philadelphia: University of Pennsylvania, 1944.

Fick, Carolyn E. *The Making of Haiti: The Saint Domingue Revolution from Below*. Knoxville: University of Tennessee Press, 1990.

Frazier, E. Franklin. *The Negro Family in the United States*. 1939; Chicago: University of Chicago Press, 1972.

Frazier, E. Franklin. "Significance of the African Background." In *The Negro in the United States*. New York: Macmillan, 1949.

French, Scot. *The Rebellious Slave: Nat Turner in American History*. Boston: Houghton Mifflin, 2004.

Garnet, Henry Highland. "An Address to the Slaves of the United States of America." Reprinted in *A Documentary History of the Negro People in the United States*, ed. Herbert Aptheker. 1843; New York: Citadel Press, 1969.

Garrow, David J. *Bearing the Cross: Martin Luther King, Jr., and the Southern Christian Leadership Conference*. New York: Morrow, 1986.

Gaspar, David Barry. *Bondsmen and Rebels: A Case Study of Master-Slave Relations in Antigua, with Implications for Colonial British America*. Baltimore, Md.: Johns Hopkins University Press, 1985.

Gomez, Michael A. *Exchanging Our Country Marks: The Transformation of African Identities in the Colonial and Antebellum South*. Chapel Hill: University of North Carolina Press, 1998.

Gomez, Michael A. "Muslims in Early America." *Journal of Southern History* 60 (November 1994): 671–710.

Greenberg, Kenneth S. *The Confessions of Nat Turner and Related Documents.* Boston: Bedford Books of St. Martin's Press, 1996.

Greenberg, Kenneth S. *Nat Turner: A Slave Rebellion in History and Memory.* Oxford: Oxford University Press, 2003.

Hall, Gwendolyn Midlo. *Africans in Colonial Louisiana: The Development of Afro-Creole Culture in the Eighteenth Century.* Baton Rouge: Louisiana State University Press, 1992.

Harding, Rachel E. "Networks of Support, Spaces of Resistance: Alternative Orientations of Black Life in Nineteenth-Century Bahia." In *A Refuge in Thunder: Candomblé and Alternative Spaces of Blackness.* Bloomington: Indiana University Press, 2000.

Harding, Vincent. "Religion and Resistance among Antebellum Negroes, 1800–1860." In *The Making of Black America,* ed. August Meier and Elliott Rudwick, vol. 1. New York: Atheneum, 1969.

Harding, Vincent. *There is a River: The Black Struggle for Freedom in America.* New York: Vintage Books, 1983.

Herskovits, Melville. "The Contemporary Scene: Africanisms in Religious Life." In *Myth of the Negro Past.* 1941; Boston: Beacon Press, 1990.

Herskovits, Melville. *Life in a Haitian Valley.* Garden City, N.Y.: Anchor Books, 1971.

Hunter, Tera W. *To 'Joy My Freedom: Southern Black Women's Lives and Labors after the Civil War.* Cambridge, Mass.: Harvard University Press, 1997.

Hurston, Zora Neale. "Hoodoo in America." *Journal of American Folklore* 44 (October–December 1931): 317–418.

Jackson, Luther P. "Religious Development of the Negro in Virginia from 1760 to 1860." *Journal of Negro History* 16 (April 1931): 168–239.

James, C. L. R. *The Black Jacobins: Toussaint L'Ouverture and the San Domingo Revolution.* New York: Dial Press, 1938.

King, Martin Luther, Jr. "Letter from Birmingham Jail." In *Why We Can't Wait.* 1963; New York: New American Library, 1968.

Lincoln, C. Eric. *The Black Muslims in America.* Boston: Beacon Press, 1973.

Lynch, Hollis Ralph. *Edward Wilmot Blyden: Pan-Negro Patriot, 1832–1912.* Oxford: Oxford University Press, 1967.

Lynch, Hollis Ralph. *Selected Letters of Edward Wilmot Blyden.* Millwood, N.Y.: KTO Press, 1978.

Marable, Manning. "The Faith of W. E. B. Du Bois: Sociocultural and Political Dimensions of Black Religion." *Southern Quarterly* 23 (Fall 1984): 15–33.

Marks, Carole. *Farewell—We're Good and Gone: The Great Black Migration.* Bloomington: Indiana University Press, 1989.

Matory, J. Lorand. "The English Professors of Brazil: On the Diasporic Roots of the Yoruba Nation." *Comparative Studies in Society and History* 41, no. 1 (January 1999): 72–103.

May, Cedrick. "Evangelism and Resistance in the Black Transatlantic, 1760–1820 (Jupiter Hammon, Phillis Wheatley, John Marrant)." Ph.D. diss., Pennsylvania State University, 2003.

McCloud, Aminah Beverly. *African American Islam.* London: Routledge, 1995.

Métraux, Alfred. *Voodoo in Haiti*. Translated by Hugo Charteris. 1958; New York: Schocken Books, 1972.

Muhammad, Elijah. *Message to the Blackman in America*. Chicago: Muhammad Mosque of Islam No. 2, 1965.

Muhammad, Elijah, and Abbass Rassoull. *The Theology of Time*. Hampton, Va.: U. B. & US Communications Systems, 1992.

Murrell, Nathaniel Samuel, William David Spencer, and Adrian Anthony McFarlane, eds. *Chanting Down Babylon: The Rastafari Reader*. Philadelphia: Temple University Press, 1998.

Ortiz, Fernando. *Hampa Afro-Cubano: Los Negros Brujos*. Madrid, Spain: Editorial America, 1906.

Pearson, Edward A., ed. *Designs against Charleston: The Trial Record of the Denmark Vesey Slave Conspiracy of 1822*. Chapel Hill: University of North Carolina Press, 1999.

Pollard, Velma. *Dread Talk: The Language of Rastafari*. Kingston, Jamaica: Canoe Press, 1994.

Price-Mars, Jean. "Lemba-Petro: Un culte secret." *Revue de la Société d'histoire et de geographie d'Haiti* 9, no. 28 (1938): 24–25.

Puckett, Newbell N. *Folk Beliefs of the Southern Negro*. Chapel Hill: University of North Carolina Press, 1926.

Raboteau, Albert J. "Death and the Gods." In *Slave Religion: The "Invisible Institution" in the Antebellum South*. Oxford: Oxford University Press, 1978.

Reis, João José. *Slave Rebellion in Brazil: The Muslim Uprising of 1835 in Bahia*. Translated by Arthur Brakel. Baltimore, Md.: Johns Hopkins University Press, 1993.

Simpson, G. E. "Neo-African Religions of Ancestral Cults of the Caribbean and South America." In *Black Religions in the New World*. New York: Columbia University Press, 1978.

Simpson, George Eaton. *Religious Cults of the Caribbean: Trinidad, Jamaica, and Haiti*. Rio Piedras, P.R.: Institute of Caribbean Studies, University of Puerto Rico, 1980.

Smith, Theophus. *Conjuring Culture: Biblical Formations of Black America*. Oxford: Oxford University Press, 1994.

Stuckey, Sterling. *The Ideological Origins of Black Nationalism*. Boston: Beacon Press, 1972.

Stuckey, Sterling. "Introduction: Slavery and the Circle of Culture." In *Slave Culture: Nationalist Theory and the Foundations of Black America*. Oxford: Oxford University Press, 1987.

Thompson, Robert Farris. "The Sign of the Four Moments of the Sun." In *Flash of the Spirit: African and Afro-American Art and Philosophy*. New York: Random House, 1983.

Thompson, Robert Farris, and Joseph Cornet. *The Four Moments of the Sun: Kongo Art in Two Worlds*. Washington, D.C.: National Gallery of Art, 1981.

Thornton, John K. "On the Trail of Voodoo: African Christianity in Africa and the Americas." *The Americas* 44 (January 1988): 261–78.

Turner, Richard Brent. *Islam in the African-American Experience*. Bloomington: Indiana University Press, 1977.

Verger, Pierre. *Notes sur le culture des Orisa et Vodun à Bahia*. Dakar, Senegal: IFAN, 1957.

Walker, David. "Our Wretchedness in Consequence of Ignorance." In *Walker's Appeal, in Four Articles: Together with a Preamble to the Coloured Citizens of the World, but in Particular, and Very Expressly to Those in the United States of America. Written in Boston, in the State of Massachusetts, Sept 28th, 1829.* 1829; New York: Hill & Wang, 1995.

Weld, Theodore. *The Bible against Slavery: An Inquiry into the Patriarchal and Mosaic Systems on the Subject of Human Rights.* 1837; Detroit: Negro History Press, 1970.

Wallace, Barbara Elizabeth. "'Fair daughters of Africa': African American Women in Baltimore, 1790–1860." Ph.D. diss., University of California, 2001.

X, Malcolm, and Alex Haley. "Mecca." In *The Autobiography of Malcolm X.* 1965; New York: Ballantine, 1993.

CHRONOLOGY

1736	Conspiracy in Antigua.
1822	Denmark Vesey conspiracy in Charleston.
1829	Publication of David Walker's *Appeal.*
1830	Founding of Ilê Iyá Nassô, or Engenho Velho (*terreiro* in Brazil).
1831	Nat Turner's revolt in Virginia.
1835	Malê revolt (Brazil).
1865	Morant Bay Rebellion.
1910	Founding of Ilê do Axe Opô Afonjá (*terreiro* in Brazil).
1930	Founding of Nation of Islam.
1935	Italian invasion of Ethiopia.
1963	March on Washington.
1965	Assassination of Malcolm X.
1968	Assassination of Martin Luther King Jr.

GLOSSARY

Abakuá. A clandestine religious organization that originated in the Cross River of southeastern Nigeria and Cameroon and was brought to Cuba by African slaves. It is only open to men, who qualify by being heterosexual and good sons, brothers, fathers, and husbands. The religion has spread throughout the world, but remains strongest in Cuba.

Cabildos. An Afro-Cuban religious society formed in the early 1500s by slaves and based on the Spanish *cofradías* (guilds or fraternities) first organized in Seville in the fourteenth century. In these *cabildos*, slaves would reconstruct their ethnic heritage and combine the Catholic saints of their Spanish masters with their own Yoruba gods.

Candomblé. A collective term to describe the distinctive African-derived religious traditions in Brazilian society, it is also a specific Afro–South American religion. *Candomblé* was originally confined to the slave population of Brazil, but despite a ban by the Catholic Church and being made illegal in some countries, it expanded across the neighboring countries, especially after slavery was ended. The religion itself is spiritualist, involving the worship of a pantheon of gods derived from African faiths, although these are often identified with Catholic saints. It also incorporates crucifixes in its temples and rituals, a further connection with the dominant religious tradition of South America.

"Damnation Oath." A curse in which a petitioner calls down a force that invokes evil.

Gullah. Former black slaves and their descendants who primarily live on the Sea Islands of South Carolina and Georgia.

Hoodoo. African-derived practices that seek to impact the material world through manipulation of the spiritual realm.

Irmandade. Brotherhoods and sisterhoods in Brazil that were mutual-aid societies.

Jêje. A community whose origins lie in Dahomey (now Benin).

Kumina (pukumina, pocomania). An early Jamaican religious tradition that ritualized communication with ancestors. Today Kumina refers to an African-derived ritual of spirit possession practiced by the Pukumina and Pocomania religions.

Lucumí. See Santería.

Malê. African Muslims in Brazil, specifically Bahia.

Mandinka. A West African ethnic group.

Myalism. The employment of spiritual forces and herbs to counteract witchcraft and other evil.

Nation of Islam (NOI). A splinter group of the Muslim faith, its members quietly aspire to black separatism. The Nation of Islam was linked to the 1960s and 1970s Black Power movement and inspired the black nationalist orator Malcolm X.

National Association for the Advancement of Colored People (NAACP). The longest-standing civil rights organization in the United States, established by W. E. B. Du Bois and Oswald Garrison Villard in 1909.

Obeah. The practice of manipulating spiritual forces either to give aid or to inflict harm.

Orisha. Guardian spirits of the Yoruban religion that manifest themselves in the forces of nature.

Pardo. Pardo is a term for a mixed-race Brazilian, one with black and white ancestry.

Prêto. The term for black people in Brazil.

Rastafarianism. A religious and political movement whose origins lie in 1930s Jamaica. It teaches the eventual redemption of blacks, and their return to Africa.

Ring shout. A ritual which features worshippers moving counterclockwise in an ever-quickening circle. Widespread in North America, it was derivative of West Central African and West African practices.

Santería. Also known as Lucumí, or Way of the Saints; a fusion of Catholic and Yoruban beliefs involving animal sacrifice.

Shango. Yoruban guardian spirit or god of thunder.

Terreiros. Large round spaces surrounded by wooden seats and covered with palm-leaf roofs.

Umbanda. An Afro-Brazilian religion, combining spiritism and Catholicism.

Voodoo. African-derived religious observances, practiced today mainly in the Caribbean.

About the Authors

William A. Darity Jr. earned a B.A. (magna cum laude) in economics and political science from Brown University (1974), and a Ph.D. in economics from the Massachusetts Institute of Technology (1978). He is Cary C. Boshamer Professor of Economics, and Adjunct Faculty in Sociology at the University of North Carolina at Chapel Hill, where he is Director of the Institute of African American Research, which promotes research on peoples of the African Diaspora. He also serves as Research Professor of Public Policy Studies, African and African American Studies, and Economics at Duke University.

His most recent books are *Economics, Economists, and Expectations: Micro-Foundations to Macroapplications* (2004), coauthored with Warren Young and Robert Leeson, and a volume coedited with Ashwini Deshpande titled *Boundaries of Clan and Color: Transnational Comparisons of Inter-Group Disparity* (2003), both published by Routledge. He has published or edited ten books and more than 125 articles in professional journals.

Howard Dodson is Chief of the Schomburg Center for Research in Black Culture of the New York Public Library. A specialist in African- American history and a noted lecturer, educator, and consultant, he has taught extensively around the country, at institutions including Emory University, Shaw

University, and Columbia University. He is a former consultant in the Office of the Chairman of the NEH, served as the executive director of the Institute of the Black World, and worked in the Peace Corps. He has also been a consultant for the Congressional Black Caucus, Atlanta University; the Library of Congress; and the U.S. Department of Education.

Michael A. Gomez, Ph.D., is Professor of History and Middle Eastern Studies at New York University. His research projects include African Muslims in the Americas, African repatriation, illegal slave trade to North America, and conversion in the Islamic, Christian, and Judaic traditions. He has been involved with the launching of a new academic organization, the Association for the Study of the Worldwide African Diaspora (ASWAD) and has published extensively. *Exchanging Our Country Marks: the Transformation of African Identities in the Colonial and Antebellum South* was published in 1998 by the University of North Carolina Press, and *Pragmatism in the Age of Jihad: the Pre-colonial State of Bundu* was published in 1992 by Cambridge University Press.

Colin A. Palmer is Managing Editor of the Schomburg Studies on the Black Experience Series and Dodge Professor of History at Princeton University. His interests include African-American Studies, the African Diaspora, Colonial Latin America, and the Caribbean. He is the author of a number of books on slavery.

Linda M. Perkins, Ph.D., is University Associate Professor and Director of Applied Women's Studies at the Claremont Graduate University. She holds an interdisciplinary university appointment in the departments of Applied Women's Studies, Educational Studies, and History. Perkins is a historian of women's and African American higher education. Her primary areas of research are the history of African American women's higher education, the education of African Americans in elite institutions, and the history of talent-identification programs for African American students. She has served as vice president of Division F (History and Historiography) of the American Educational Research Association (AERA) and has also served as a member of the executive council of AERA. She is currently on the editorial boards of the *History of Education Quarterly* and the *Review of African American Education.* Her publications include *Fanny Jackson Coppin and the Institute for Colored Youth, 1837–1902* (Garland, 1987), and "The African American Female Elite: The Early History of African American Women in the Seven Sister Colleges, 1880–1960" in the *Harvard Educational Review* (Winter 1997). Professor Perkins was on the national planning committee for the 50th Anniversary Commemoration of the *Brown v. Board of Education* at New York University and taught a course on *Brown* in the fall of 2004. She organized a national conference on the Impact of the *Brown v. Board of Education* and the 1964 Civil Rights Act on Race and Higher Education Conference at the Claremont Colleges, which convened in February 2005.

Ronald Walters received his B.A. in history and government with honors from Fisk University (1963), and both his M.A. (1966) in African Studies and Ph.D. (1971) in International Studies from American University. Currently at the University of Maryland, College Park, he holds the positions of "Distinguished Leadership Scholar," Director of the African American Leadership Institute in the Academy of Leadership, and Full Professor in the Department of Government and Politics. Walters is the author of over fifty articles and eight books.

His latest books are *White Nationalism, Black Interest: Conservative Public Policy and the Black Community* (Wayne State University Press, 2003), and *Freedom Is Not Enough: Black Voters, Black Candidates, and American Presidential Politics* (Rowman & Littlefield Press, 2005).

In 1984 he was Deputy Campaign Manager for Issues of the Jesse Jackson Campaign for President, and in 1988 was a consultant for convention issues for Jackson. Walters is on the board of directors of the National Coalition of Black Civic Participation, Voices for Working Families, and other organizations.

Chad Williams, Ph.D., is an Assistant Professor of History at Hamilton College. He earned a bachelor's degree in history and African American Studies from UCLA, and a master's degree and Ph.D. in history from Princeton

University. Williams's teaching and research interests include modern U.S. and African American history, World War I, African American intellectual history, and the African Diaspora. In addition to revising his dissertation for book publication, Williams is editing a collection of W. E. B. Du Bois's writings and correspondence on World War I.